CENTURY

A People's History Of Charlotte County

Edited By
James Abraham

All Rights Reserved
Printed in the United States of America
©Copyright 2021 by James Abraham
Book-broker Publishers of Florida
Port Charlotte, FL 33980
ISBN 978-1-945690-66-2

To Dorothy

How can I sing King Alpha's song in a strange land?

Charles Peck

PREFACE

Vernon Peeples was my first friend when I came to Charlotte County and his friendship proved to be the most enduring. Even now it shapes and informs my work.

I met Vernon as an editorial writer for the *Sarasota Herald-Tribune,* back when the county was growing so fast four newspapers competed for readers.

Vernon agreed to meet me at the Punta Gorda Isles Yacht Club, the old one that got smashed up by Hurricane Charley. We did a little sparring, then he started his trademark boring, nonstop recitation of his latest historical find. Except I didn't find it boring. I not only knew what he was talking about, but I also found it fascinating. Soon we began meeting regularly to eat lunch and run our mouths; he'd show me his latest work and I'd pump him for background on the issues I was covering. Vernon was used to a big audience, but I like to listen. Vernon believed the redeemers did the right thing; I called them the white supremacists. So we didn't always see eye to eye. But we always kept the door open.

Vernon was my model as I tried to piece together the history of the county. But he was also my bane, as I considered another conversation we had. He had just finished writing a scorching letter to two community college professors who had written a county history. The book was so bad, Vernon said, he didn't know whether to laugh or get mad. He talked about the professors as if they were schoolboys caught cribbing Encyclopedia Britannica.

CENTURY

So as I worked on this book, the fear of Vernon's censure lingered. Then he sent a sign.

I was struggling to find confirmation on information about Leo Wotitzky, a man who did more good behind the scenes than any minor saint had done publicly. Wotitzky's family was uncooperative. But he was too important a presence to write out of history. Then, would you believe it? I found a transcript of an interview with Wotitzky, conducted by his protégé, Vernon Peeples.

That was an affirmation, a signal that I was on the right course. The point I'm trying to make is that history is life, it's about relationships. And relationships are about why, how, and consequences.

I edited both of Vernon's last books, one of which may never see the light of day. The other, "Punta Gorda: In the Beginning, 1865-1900," has deservedly become the bible of historiography regarding the city and county's early days. As you read my attempt to personify the county, to place it within the human context of its times, my fondest hope is that it's compared favorably to Vernon's landmark study of Punta Gorda's origins.

Another mentor, one whose work graces this book, is Englewood's leading historian, Diana Doane Harris. When I met Diana she was already legendary. A former New York fashion model, she had come to what's now Rotonda on a fashion shoot. Back then, cow-patterned clothing was cool. But the cows on the ranch, which was owned by Alfred and William Vanderbilt, were Santa Gertrudis cattle—they had no spots and the shoot was cancelled.

Stranded for the weekend, Diana contacted Leah Lasbury, heir to a land empire accumulated by her father, James Bartlett, back in the 1920s. She sold Diana a home built out of ship timbers in New Point Comfort. Diana has been immersed in local history ever since.

She was a mainstay in helping organize both the Dearborn Street Book Fair and the *Dearborn Street Literary Magazine*, was a founding member of both the Green Street Church rebuilding committee, helped found the Lemon Bay archives, and is a popular speaker on local lore and culture. Her late husband, Sam Harris, was a former fighter pilot and renowned aerial photographer whose photos still grace the walls and albums of those who appreciate the region's beauty as seen from on high.

My editing and publishing Diana's "Englewood Lives," the go-to book about Englewood history based on her popular *Englewood Sun* columns, brought us together. We've remained friends and I've relied on her work to help present Englewood's portion of our shared history.

This book opens with an anthropomorphic description of Charlotte County, in which I work to establish the character of the county and the forces that shaped it. Because this is a people's history, the focus is primarily on the crescent of settlement that embraces Charlotte Harbor and the Peace River, along with the communities along the tributaries of that river and also the Myakka. That's why meeting Cheryl Frizzell was fortuitous. The subject of her book, A.C. Frizzell, personified the human dynamic as a catalyst for change. Reading her book was like hitting an iceberg; I had to stop what I was doing and contact her.

Cheryl is the granddaughter of the man who once owned more than a third of Charlotte County. The story of how he acquired his wealth, used it, and got rid of it occupies at least 40 years of Charlotte County's existence. And that story is one that turns not on pivots of high decisions in corridors of power, but instead on the fragile pintles of human frailty. Cheryl told the story straight. By doing so she gave posterity an honest appraisal of a man who deserves more analysis. She gave me full access to her work as I reshaped my book to encompass the under-reported magnitude of A. C. Frizzell's effect on Charlotte County. We still live in his shadow.

I also must thank Lynn Harrell, a longtime resident whose work also appears in this book. Lynn is another old friend. We met two decades ago when I joined the directors' board of the Peace River Center for Writers. Back then, the PRCW was an international organization with close to 500 members. Their mission was to assist authors of all skill levels. They provided proofreading and editing services, held

A People's History of Charlotte County

workshops, staged book signings, put out an 8-page monthly newsletter and enjoyed excellent media coverage. As editor-in-chief, Lynn was responsible for a lot of that.

The Sarasota-born writer was hooked on local history almost 50 years ago when she bought a derelict Punta Gorda cottage for $10 and had it relocated. She's been a serious scholar and active preservationist ever since. Lynn has served on numerous non-profit boards, spent ten years on the county's Historical Advisory Committee, organized many events and was one of the first History Park docents. Her knowledge of area history led to work at the Charlotte County Historical Center, where she captioned thousands of photos for the county's online historical collections. She also worked as a collections registrar, curated exhibits, and wrote text for historical site markers. After the Historical Center shut down, Lynn processed collections at the county archives in Englewood before returning to freelancing. An award-winning essayist, she works at home and has four books in progress.

When a student in my writing class is stuck, I ask them to try and write a letter home, a letter to a friend describing the scene or experience they have a hard time constructing. I missed some spots in this book, through laziness, ignorance, or just plain running out of steam, but those omissions in no way diminish the institutions or individuals whose names aren't in this book.

This is my imperfect attempt at a whole, an effort to present enough information that generations yet unborn will understand how we lived during Charlotte County's first 100 years. So please consider this book as my letter home to a future I'll never see. Consider this my letter to a friend about a lot of friends, some I know, some I never knew, and some I won't live long enough to meet.

James Abraham
March 7, 2021

Charles Peck

FOREWORD
HECTOR FLORES
CHARLOTTE COUNTY ADMINISTRATOR

Charlotte County's rich history predates its creation by the State of Florida on April 23, 1921, but this year's Centennial of that date provides everyone with an opportunity to revisit the county's founding and growth and ponder its future.

In these pages, you'll find personal recollections of events past, snapshots in time of momentous occasions and in-the-moment accounts by journalists writing the first drafts of history in a newspaper whose founding pre-dates the county's own.

In the air-conditioned comfort of modern Charlotte County, it's hard to grasp the grit and determination it took for the county's earliest settlers to put down roots in a swampy, mosquito-filled wilderness. Like those who rode the country's Manifest Destiny to the California coast in the 1800s, the people who picked Charlotte County to call home were seeking opportunity. Some came here in the wake of a war that nearly cleaved the country in half. They had manned forts

A People's History of Charlotte County

to the south and east of what would become Charlotte County. Others sought their fortune in land, cattle, and timber.

By 1921, Charlotte County had its first and only city, Punta Gorda, created in 1887 out of the town of Trabue, which was founded by a Kentucky land speculator who convinced a railroad baron to run a line to his Peace River plat. Across the river, residents of a still older settlement first known as Hickory Bluff and later as Charlotte Harbor built the first churches and schools in the area. Smaller enclaves sprouted in every direction amid the 1920s land boom, ambitious plats that painted a picture of paradise waiting to be found by the right people: Tropical Gulf Acres, Grove City, Placida, Solana. Other communities, but still no other cities, such as Englewood, El Jobean, Cleveland, and McCall, came along. Some now exist in name only. But even a decade later when the first Census of Charlotte County was released, only 4,000 people were counted.

Charles Peck

The Great Depression of the 1930s and World War II in the 1940s stunted further growth, except for the pilots being trained at the Punta Gorda Army Air Field. As the 1950s dawned, there were still only 4,300 souls in Charlotte.

The Charlotte County of today started taking shape later that decade as a developer platted a town called Port Charlotte in a cattle pasture. That developer platted additional communities still growing today, like South Gulf Cove. Other developers followed, creating communities like Rotonda, Punta Gorda Isles, Deep Creek and Harbour Heights. From 1950 through 1990, the county's population roughly doubled every decade, barreling past 100,000 to 110,975 in the 1990 Census. Only 30 years later, we're approaching 200,000 people. We're old enough now to count many multigenerational families of Charlotte County natives mixed in with the retirees who responded to developers' heavy marketing in the Northeast and Midwest and family who followed them.

Any historical reckoning of Charlotte County goes much deeper than the statistics, the timelines and the touchstones of the place. Charlotte County's history lies within its people. Its real history is their stories. Having worked for Charlotte County government for one-quarter of its existence, I relish the opportunity in this Centennial year to hear those stories, read those accounts and share mine and my family's.

This book has many of those stories. The coming year will bring opportunities to hear more as the county hosts numerous events and commemorations.

A Centennial website, www.CharlotteCounty100.com, includes more stories and a calendar for you to find celebrations and observations throughout the year.

Happy 100th birthday, Charlotte County. The next 100 will be even better.

TABLE OF CONTENTS

PREFACE V

FOREWORD: HECTOR FLORES, CHARLOTTE COUNTY ADMINISTRATOR VIII

1920s 17

CHARLOTTE: THE COUNTY THAT COULDN'T SAY NO 17

MURDOCK AND EL JOBEAN: THE LAND IN BETWEEN 22

PUNTA GORDA, PEARL OF THE PENINSULA 27

1920S ENGLEWOOD 32
    DIANA HARRIS

THE CLERK THROUGH THE YEARS 35
    ROGER D. EATON, CHARLOTTE COUNTY CLERK OF THE CIRCUIT COURT & COUNTY COMPTROLLER

CHARLOTTE COUNTY TAX COLLECTOR 37
    VICKI L. POTTS, CLC

THE GREEN WAVE: CHARLOTTE COUNTY SHERIFFS 38

THE (GREATER) CHARLOTTE COUNTY CHAMBER OF COMMERCE 42
    TERI ASHLEY

CROSLAND DEVELOPED FISHING INDUSTRY 44
    PAUL L. POLK

FORGOTTEN VICTIMS 46
    LYNN HARRELL

AN OVERVIEW OF THE ORIGINS OF THE MUNICIPAL FISH DOCK AT MAUD STREET 46
    LYNN HARRELL

AFRICAN AMERICAN SETTLEMENT AND CONTRIBUTIONS 48
    MARTHA RUSSELL BIREDA, PH.D.
    SCOT SHIVELY, RET. LT. COL. U.S. AIR FORCE

FIRST BRIDGE WAS OUTDATED BEFORE IT OPENED 49
    FRANK DESGUIN

BURNT STORE ROAD 50
    GRAHAM SEGGER

DESGUIN FAMILY ROOTS HERE GO BACK MORE THAN 100 YEARS 53
    FRANK DESGUIN

A People's History of Charlotte County

1930s 58
TROUBLED WATERS 58
CHARLOTTE COUNTY EXTENSION: OUR TRADITION, OUR MISSION 65
   RALPH E. MITCHELL
MARY NIGHTINGALE 67
   DIANA HARRIS
SALLIE JONES TAKES OVER 69
   FRANK DESGUIN
STUART ANDERSON, AN ENGLEWOOD HERO 70
   DIANA HARRIS
THE DAY THE CHICKENS TOOK A LICKING: STORIES OF A DEPRESSION-ERA CHILDHOOD 72
   BERNIE READING

1940s 76
PERIL AND PROSPERITY 76
PUNTA GORDA ARMY AIR FIELD 93
   FRANK DESGUIN
THE BAILEY BROTHERS 94
   DON MOORE
ENGLEWOOD RESIDENT SHELTERED BY PHILIPPINE GUERRILLAS 98
   JO CORTES

1950s 100
HOME PORT 100
THE HOTEL CHARLOTTE HARBOR CHECKS OUT 111
   GLENN MILLER
CHANGING INDUSTRIES SHAPE ENGLEWOOD 115
   DIANA HARRIS
PUNTA GORDA GARDEN CLUB 117
   MARY YEOMANS
THE PORT CHARLOTTE GARDEN CLUB 119

1960s 122
THE BIG CHANGE 122
SONG FOR RUTH 136
   MICHAEL HAYMANS

CENTURY

THE GIRL IN THE PHOTO 137
    LYNN HARRELL
NEW LIBRARY COMES TO PUNTA GORDA 145
    TONY FARINA
POWELL'S NURSERY AND LANDSCAPING 146
    SANDRA WITZKE
CHARLOTTE COUNTY HISTORICAL CENTER SOCIETY 147
    FRANK DESGUIN
WHEN ENGLEWOOD WAS KIDS' TOWN 148
    DIANA HARRIS

1970s 152

THE NEW PEOPLE 152
WHEN RAILS RULED THE ROAD 159
PORT CHARLOTTE IN THE SEVENTIES 160
    ARLENE KINKAID
BUILDING CHANGE 161
    PETER TAYLOR
A SHORT PERSPECTIVE ON BIG CHANGE 163
    MARYANN MIZE, CCIM 163
    CRAIG DEYOUNG, PRESIDENT, CHARLOTTE STATE BANK & TRUST ... 163
    OF DAIRY QUEENS AND GDC 164
        JEFF FEHR
    A GOOD PLACE TO RAISE A FAMILY 165
        DON GANT
TO BUILD A COMMUNITY 165
    JAMES ANDERSON
THE PEN IS MIGHTIER THAN THE SNOW SHOVEL 166
GROWING UP IN PGI 166
    GAYE JOHNS BROWNIE
THANKSGIVING REMINISCENCES OF AN AGING TARPON'S GLORY DAYS ... 169
PAUL DEGAETA

1980s 171

CULTURE CLUBS 171
LIZ HUTCHINSON-SPERRY AND THE BLOOMING OF LOCAL ARTS ... 178

A People's History of Charlotte County

SEA GRAPE GALLERY 180
   BONNIE BENANDE
HOMEGROWN: THE CHARLOTTE COUNTY CONTEMPORARY ARTS SCENE 181
   DEDO 182
   ROD BECKLUND 182
   PATRICIA TURNER 183
PEACE OUT! THE FOURTH BRIDGE TO SPAN THE RIVER OPENS 184
   AASHTO
KING FISHER FLEET 185
   CAPT. RALPH ALLEN

1990s 187

LEFT HOLDING THE BAG 187
THE FINAL DECREE OF G.D.C 194
   CHIEF JUSTICE A. JAY CRISTOL
$10 DOWN AND $10 A MONTH!: HOW GDC SOLD SOUTHWEST FLORIDA 196
GREG MARTIN
HOAS: LIKE GOVERNMENT, A NECESSARY EVIL 202
GERRI TOWNSEND
PUNTA GORDA, 1990s 204
BILL CURNOW
REBUILDING HISTORY 206
   LYNN HARRELL
THE PUNTA GORDA HISTORIC MURAL SOCIETY – PAINTING THE TOWN WITH HISTORY ... 208
KELLY GAYLORD, PRESIDENT, PUNTA GORDA HISTORIC MURAL SOCIETY
LLI – A PART OF OUR CULTURAL HISTORY 209
BONNIE LEROY
VIRGINIA B. ANDES CLINIC: A MORAL IMPERATIVE 211
MARK ASPERILLA MD FACP THOMAS FERRARA PHD, DAVID M. KLEIN MD FACS

2000s 213

WHEN CHARLEY MET CHARLOTTE 213
HURRICANE CHARLEY 219
KAREN CLARK
PUNTA GORDA RENAISSANCE 222
   NANCY PRAFKE

CENTURY

NEW KID ON THE BLOCK	224
JOHN WRIGHT	
ENGLEWOOD STREET BEATS, SUMMER 2010	227

2010s 229

CLEARED FOR TAKEOFF	229
FREEDOM ISN'T FREE: HISTORY OF THE MILITARY HERITAGE MUSEUM	236
GARY BUTLER	
LGBTQIA+ HISTORY OF CHARLOTTE COUNTY	237
MICHELLE BONE WILLIAMS	
CHARLOTTE COMMUNITY FOUNDATION	239
ASHLEY MAHER, EXECUTIVE DIRECTOR	
SAY HER NAME	241
NAOMI PRINGLE	
THE BALLAD OF TIM BERINI	242
SUE WADE	
THE SNOWBIRDS	247
DAVID ABRAHAM	

2020 246

DREAMS AND DISILLUSIONMENT	246
EPILOGUE	250
ENGLEWOOD	250
PORT CHARLOTTE	251
PUNTA GORDA	251
THANKS	256
PEOPLE, PLACES, AND THINGS INDEX	257

Hotel Charlotte Harbor, 1942 (circa), Florida Memory

1920s

CHARLOTTE: THE COUNTY THAT COULDN'T SAY NO

    The father of President Warren G. Harding once told him that if he were a girl, he'd always be in the family way.[1] That's a terrible thing to say about anyone, but it speaks to a sense of wanting to be liked and a susceptibility to bright promises and big dreams. And such a description can easily be applied to Charlotte County. It's in the DNA, born of a land bordered by rivers debouching on fertile bays and a bountiful harbor, a land well-watered and ready for agriculture. Sustainability in Charlotte County was never an issue when people lived off the land. Those who learned how to exploit the natural bounty grew wealthy beyond belief. That's because Charlotte County is nurturing, Charlotte is forgiving.

---

[1] https://www.usnews.com/news/special-reports/the-worst-presidents/articles/2014/12/17/worst-presidents-warren-harding-1921-1923

CENTURY

Charlotte County GIS

1921
A Congressional resolution by both houses signed by President Warren G. Harding, declaring peace in World War I hostilities with Germany, Austria, and Hungary; The treaties executed one month later

Charlotte, Glades, Hardee and Highlands counties established out of DeSoto County on April 20

Punta Gorda chosen for county seat by public referendum

Name Charlotte chosen by public vote

This zip code map of east and central Charlotte County illustrates the population density pattern, a bow that hugs the two rivers and Charlotte Harbor. Below, the first issue of the Babcock Ranch community newspaper, https://www.babcock-ranchtelegraph.com/

But the county is part of Florida, a land where weather's smiling, sunny face can turn cruel in a heartbeat. Fortunes can and do rise and fall at the drop of a hurricane.

The natural center of such a county is Charlotte Harbor. The populated portion of Charlotte County hugs a crescent of land from the Gulf of Mexico and Cape Haze north by northeast toward Murdock and then south by southwest through Punta Gorda south. Most Charlotte County residents live around Charlotte Harbor the way Plato described the ancient world that grew up around the Mediterranean Sea, like frogs around a pond. So it's understandable that the less-inhabited portions of the county, everything east of I-75 through to the western fringes of the Everglades, get short shrift in both histories and daily commentary.

But a clue to the future that is cognizant of both the mistakes of the past and the promise of the future lies there, beyond I-75 well east of Charlotte Harbor, in Babcock Village, where the cattle range and prairie scrub, mangroves and sloughs are giving way to a new attempt at community building. Babcock Village's plan for sustainability, from home design to solar energy and community amenities, mirrors many of the bright dreams of the county's founders.

Charlotte was born in glory amid the glitter of the 1920s. Many learn of those days as the Roaring Twenties, with bootleg gin, flappers, the mob and speakeasies. All of that was there, but so were seeds of bigotry, race violence, and

A People's History of Charlotte County

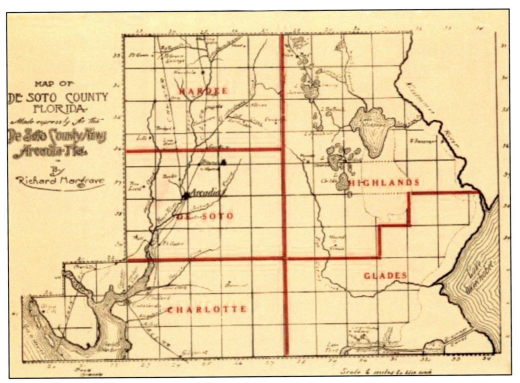

The last map of once-huge DeSoto County, showing the divisions created by the state legislature in 1921. Below, William Goff, an ex-Confederate who is considered Englewood's first white settler.

1921

The Washington Naval Conference begins, leading to arms limitation agreements that would fail to prevent World War II almost 20 years later

Gov. Hardee appoints first rosters of county officers

Englewood grocer Pete Buchan named to Sarasota County Commission

Tampa Bay Hurricane of 1921 strikes, causing property damage along the coastal Southwest

a general loosening of morals and decency. In this liberated, uninhibited age, when the best and worst in men and women seemed to be set free, Charlotte County came to be.

So let's start at the beginning, in April 1921, weeks after the state legislature carved Charlotte County out of a huge mass of stateland that was once the sprawling acres of Hillsborough County. And let's begin on the western fringe of the crescent of settlement that has defined Charlotte County for 100 years. Englewood's very existence defies the mapmakers and the line drawers. While state legislatures create counties, communities like Englewood spring up organically, of their own accord, along bodies of water and routes of trade. Hence the development of a community like Englewood, that straddles the Charlotte-Sarasota county line and defines a piscatorial culture embraced as far south as Lee County.

What's bred in the bone often stays in the soul, to mangle a phrase, and the key to Englewood's noncomformity may be that its first recorded citizen was a rebel.

1921
National quota system on the amount of incoming immigrants established by the United States Congress in the Emergency Quota Act, curbing legal immigration

Newly appointed County Commissioner William M. Whitten advances his own money to complete construction of first bridge across Charlotte Harbor

Bridge opened July 4 with a free fish fry at Trabue Park, renamed after Albert Gilchrist for the occasion

Diana Harris Collection

Anderson farm in the early 1900s with Joseph "Jody" Daniel Anderson in front of four of his sons. L to R: Stuart, Charlie, Phillip, and Clyde. Below, Pete Buchan.

William Goff, according to Englewood journalist and historian Josephine Cortes, was a former Confederate soldier who settled in the area in 1878.[2] His family would come to be one of the most prolific in southwest Florida, with more than 1,000 Goffs accounted for at a 1978 reunion organized by Cortes.

Another prominent early family was the Andersons, who were the first to settle on the northern edge of Englewood, on what is now SR 776 near Manasota Beach Road.[3] But the man who helped bring many of those disparate settlers together to create a common core called Englewood was Pete Buchan, a catalyst and leader. Diana Harris, author of the definitive folk history of the area, "Englewood Lives," credits the merchant with helping to coalesce the community in the years before WWI. In 1916 Buchan built a small trading post at the foot of Dearborn Street.

---

[2] Cortes, Josephine, *The Goffs of Southwest Florida*, 1978
[3] Harris, Diana, *Englewood Lives*, 2013

A People's History of Charlotte County

Street scene along Dearborn Street, a collection of shops and restaurants.

He was uniquely positioned on the main road and at a dock for coastal vessels bringing goods and mail. The roads then were so bad that many people preferred traveling and sending goods by sailboats or steamers rather than land transportation. In no time the street became the center of commerce and the heart of Englewood. Buchan, a civic-minded merchant, saw the benefits of coastal navigation and so led a work group to open up Blind Pass. He set up a Post Office in his store, served as a school board member, and was also the first Englewood representative of the first Sarasota county commission.[4] Buchan served for 21 years and was instrumental in having a paved road connecting Englewood with Sarasota.

Today Buchan's home and store are preserved as monuments. Dearborn Street has met the challenges of change by transforming itself into a gaudy, funky collection of studios, antique stores, restaurants painted in garish colors and other touristy items.[5] Buchan's homesite is now a resort, although the actual building was moved to a new site at the foot of Dearborn Street. The resort owner, reminiscent of Buchan, also runs a modern version of Buchan's enterprise, a convenience store directly across from the homesite.

Englewood was a field of dreams for another group of settlers, lured by dreams of lemon groves that would create a cash crop and make the settlers wealthy. A sharp turn in the weather killed the lemon trees, but left the name of Lemon Bay to mark the death of a dream. Instead of lemon groves, the bay became a major fishing

1921

Dixie, Sarasota, and Union counties established

Reader's Digest founded, first issue published by Dewitt and Lila Wallace

Margaret "Madge" Densten appointed postmaster at Southland

Tomb of the Unknown Soldier dedicated in Washington D.C., part of an international movement in which the unidentified remains of a soldier are consecrated to represent each nation's war dead following World War I

---

[4] https://eipoa.org/englewood-history
[5] Harris, Diana, *Englewood Lives*, 2013

1922

WDAE in Tampa becomes Florida's first radio station

Punta Gorda buys first fire truck, a British-built Seagrave

Cleve Cleveland first Punta Gorda fire chief

Charles Wright, a black man, burned at the stake by a white mob during the Perry Race

The Lincoln Memorial, dedicated in Washington, D.C.

"April Showers" by Al Jolson is top song of the year

ground and a route into the Gulf of Mexico through which Englewood navigated its future as a fishing town.

Englewood first families such as the Goffs and the Futches, along with investors and businesspeople such as the Lampps and the Chadwicks all gravitated toward the growing commercial center of Dearborn Street and the rich fishing and hunting around Lemon Bay and Grove City, another failed citrus venture, to build almost a community of the mind, a sense of place that meanders along Charlotte County's western shore. Through the stewardship of men like Buchan and others readers will come to know, Englewood would grow as the fortunes of the fledgling county waxed and waned.

Charlotte County History Services

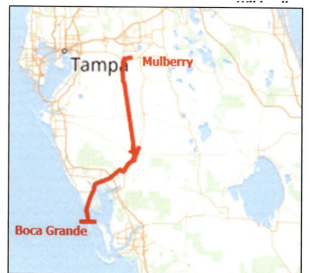

The Charlotte Harbor and Northern Depot in Murdock, circa 1920s. Below, the railroad's route from central Florida to the Gulf of Mexico.

MURDOCK AND EL JOBEAN: THE LAND IN BETWEEN

Between Englewood and Punta Gorda lay a vast wilderness, a true frontier of pines, palmetto, pasture-land and swamps which we know today as El Jobean and Port Charlotte. Some folks still call it a wilderness.

The story of the land in between features a quixotic dreamer and a true land pirate who combined to write a tale that would be repeated with amazing fidelity half a century after the dreamer died and the schemer slipped out of town.

To tell their story properly, readers have to go back in time, before county incorporation. The land pirate was a fast talker named John M. Murdock, whose moniker graces the business and government hub of Port Charlotte.

Murdock was a wheeler dealer who, like Punta Gorda founder Isaac Trabue, understood the importance of the railroad to the community he named. Murdock

A People's History of Charlotte County

Library of Congress

1923

An idealized vision of the city beautiful, the Columbian Exposition of 1893 in Chicago sparked interest in southwest Florida.

convinced the Charlotte Harbor and Northern railroad, which ran through the upper portion of Charlotte County before making a sharp turn southwest to Boca Grande, to name their local station after him. That literally put Murdock on the map.[6]

The Desoto County commissioners (Charlotte had not been created yet), couldn't say no when the smooth-talking Murdock convinced them to create for him a special drainage district that coincidentally covered his property.[7] That authorized him to dredge the swamplands in an effort to create a community of canals and vistas similar to Venice, Florida, a planned community built by the Brotherhood of Locomotive Engineers. His plan was an iteration of the "city beautiful" movement of municipal planning, the first wave of which spanned the 1880s through the pre-Depression years, that emphasized canals, leafy public spaces, and stately avenues with plenty of foliage.[8]

But Murdock sold what he didn't own and promised what he couldn't deliver as he built his community at the intersection of what became the Tamiami Trail, or US 41; and SR 776, El Jobean Road. After a series of setbacks, Murdock ran away with his secretary. He left behind a wife and kids—and settlers who found out that their land titles were invalid.[9]

Great Florida Land Boom begins

Harry Chapin buys Buchan store and pavilion at Englewood, builds Royal Casino at end of pier for dancing, gambling, and illegal liquor

Nathan Mayo elected Commissioner of Agriculture; becomes Florida's longest serving public servant (37 years - died in office in 1960)

State Livestock Board created, begins mandatory cattle dipping for ticks

Henry Luce publishes first issue of Time Magazine

---

[6] Charlotte County History Services
[7] Charlotte County History Services
[8] Naomi Blumberg and Ida Yalzadeh, "City Beautiful Movement" *Encyclopædia Britannica*, January 04, 2019, https://www.britannica.com/topic/City-Beautiful-movement
[9] Charlotte County History Services

1923

Florida Legislature bans leasing of convicts for private labor in turpentine camps

Stephens Brothers turpentine camp at Southland suspends operations and sells its acreage to Joel Bean

Rosewood, Florida, a predominantly African American town destroyed by white mobs in race riot

Talking movies invented

Bessie Smith's "Down Hearted Blues" top song of the year

Early 20th century postcard depicting workers prepping pine trees to be tapped.

The dreamer was Joel Bean, who in 1923 capitalized on the Florida land boom by creating a community called New Boston on the shores of the Myakka River. It would feature Mediterranean architecture and canals—a variant on the city beautiful vision. The novel part of the plan was that the communities would resemble a series of hexagons, each of which would be lined with boulevards that led to common areas.[10]

He hawked the development in his native Boston and other points north by conjuring up a fake duke, from whose estates the development had been carved. He changed the name to an anagram of his name, El Jobean, that he hoped would sound exotic to potential homeowners. But maybe one reason his lots never made him rich was because of the land's legacy as a hell on earth.

Much of El Jobean was once Southland, a thriving turpentine operation where convicts, many of whom were black, were worked like beasts. Recently county government dedicated a marker to The Southland Trail Cemetery near the site of the Weeks-Gurganious turpentine camp. It served as the camp's burial ground and as a cemetery for blacks until 1966.[11]

Turpentine camps were so dangerous that few white men would work there. But, as Rev. Ellison Haddock once said, "back then black people were everywhere there was work."[12]

Englewood pioneer L.A. Ainger grew up in Vineland, about where the Tiffany Square strip mall is located on SR 776. He recalled the horrors of the turpentine camp near his school.

---

[10] Harris, Diana, *Englewood Lives*. 2013
[11] Charlotte County History Services
[12] Interview, Rev. Ellison Haddock, 2020

A People's History of Charlotte County

"We lived nearby and we would see the mule-drawn wagons go by taking the black convicts to work at the still...they leased 'em from the jails.... One day there was a 55-gallon wooden barrel of hot rosin busted and scalded several black workers, killing 'em. It was awful! There were several convict camps around here... the convicts were paid $1 a day, same as the guards, but the convicts had to give half of theirs to the guards."[13]

"It was a horrible place," remarked attorney Leo Wotizky as he described a childhood trip to Southland. "The camp leased prisoners, all black. They were treated like slaves. Several were killed by beatings or died in forest fires fed by pine resin dripping from the trees. It was uncivilized."[14]

As one scholar wrote:

During the 1920s and 1930s, approximately 15,000 to 20,000 African American (and some white) workers, both men and women, lived in company towns operated by phosphate companies, and lumber, turpentine, and other naval stores operators. Located deep in the vast pine forests of northern and central Florida, the turpentine and lumber industries subjected many of these workers to forced labor or peonage. The State of Florida was considered one of the worst peonage offenders and indeed one special agent of the U.S. Department of Justice as early as 1906 likened the state to one giant peonage camp.[15]

This was no isolated problem, rather it reflected a coarseness and rapaciousness in society, fueled and implemented primarily by white men against women, minorities, Catholics, Jews, and foreigners.

In Florida and elsewhere this tide of hate masquerading as "Americanism" manifested itself with the blessing of Governor Albert Sidney Catts. The governor, a defrocked Baptist minister from Alabama, had been rejected as too radical by the Democrats, so he tapped into the populist vote and was elected as an independent. Beholden to neither party, he set out to create what one writer called an Age of Barbarity.

Women considered "loose" were dragged off into the woods and whipped, a Catholic priest in Tampa was castrated by whites, race riots scored Ocooee after black people tried to vote. Rosewood, an all-black community, was razed, leading 60 years later to the first reparations paid by a state government to victims of white racist violence.

What was taking place in the 1920s had always been happening. The difference is that the violence and exploitation had once been confined to portions of Florida where tourists and outsiders seldom ventured. But the murder of a young white man who was sent to the turpentine camps as part of a convict work-gang system led to national headlines. That wasn't good, as state promoters and speculators were just starting to cash in on the Florida land boom. The state

1924

Lots at New Boston not selling well so Joel Bean renames the town El JobeAn, an anagram of his name, to give it a romantic sound.

He builds a hotel for prospective customers and obtains permission to rename the post office.

Years later the name shortened by the Postmaster General to El Jobean

First Olympic Winter Games held in Chamonix, France.

---

[13] *Charlotte Sun*, July 26, 2019
[14] *Florida Weekly*, July 29, 2010
[15] Miller, Vivien M.L., *Hard Labor and Hard Time: Florida's "Sunshine Prison" and Chain Gangs*, University Press of Florida, 2012

1925

Barron Collier buys the old Hotel Punta Gorda, enlarges it, adds modern plumbing, and renames it Hotel Charlotte Harbor

Town of Cleveland incorporates; Dr. Vernon Jordan, dentist, elected mayor

Englewood incorporates

Road to Fort Myers paved

Barron Collier starts bus service over Tamiami Trail, including a station at Punta Gorda. route later sold to Trailways

Punta Gorda Rotary and Kiwanis clubs organize

Cheryl Frizzell

A.C. Frizzell assessing storm damage after the 1926 hurricane.

legislature reacted and outlawed such practices in 1923. One of the men who faced convict labor charges was by-then former Governor Catts.[16]

But if the past didn't doom El Jobean, a hurricane and a failing land market did the trick. The community of tomorrow would prove susceptible to the same twin plagues that wiped out much of the land boom, Mother Nature and a stock market crash.[17]

Joel Bean never went home again. Instead he tried a few land partnerships with A. C. Frizzell, who would become the baron of central Charlotte County. He holed up in his planned community where he died a pauper. His funeral was paid for by Frizzell, who also bought up the rest of his abandoned holdings at tax sales.[18]

Frizzell, an ambitious railroad telegrapher and stationmaster, had come to Murdock with his wife, Patti, in 1918. Although they weren't parsimonious, they knew what to do with money. Patti, twenty years A.C.'s senior, appeared to be the more level-headed of the two, while A.C.'s thrusting ways meant the couple always had a seat at the table.

After buying up Murdock's mass of property, Frizzell began expanding into timber, turpentine, and eventually cattle.

"We just naturally wanted land that adjoined ours," explained Frizzell.[19]

---

[16] Jeffrey A. Drobney, "Where Palm and Pine Are Blowing: Convict Labor in the North Florida Turpentine Industry, 1877-1923." *The Florida Historical Quarterly* 72, no. 4 (1994)

[17] Diana Harris, *Englewood Lives,* 2013, pp. 53-54

[18] Cheryl Frizzell, pp. 132-133

[19] Cheryl Frizzell, p. 68

A People's History of Charlotte County

Punta Gorda Historic Mural Society

In 1929 the first permanent Catholic Church was built in Punta Gorda. The Twenties was a decade of intolerance, and Catholics suffered lynchings and other indignities across the state and nation. But, perhaps because of its status as a port and rail terminal, Punta Gorda had a more cosmopolitan attitude toward ethnicity and religions than comparative parts of the state and south. At least in the 1920s, green was the only color that mattered among white people and the almighty dollar was a religion unto itself. Below, Punta Gorda's first fire truck.

Charlotte County History Services

PUNTA GORDA, PEARL OF THE PENINSULA

Punta Gorda had a head start on the rest of what became Charlotte County, an advantage it has yet to relinquish. It remains the only city in Charlotte County.

A reporter once asked former Mayor Marilyn Smith-Mooney why the city and county would both have fire and rescue service—why duplicate effort?

"There's something about seeing your city's name on a fire truck," she said, an overture to a discussion on civic pride.

Punta Gorda did and does have pride. The community was one of the first examples in Florida of true self-rule, as a group of citizens ripped the city away

1926

DeSoto Manufacturing sells its electricity plant in Punta Gorda to Florida Power and Light Corp. The King Street plant is listed on the National Register of Historic Places

Baltimore Orioles hold spring training at Punta Gorda

Albert Gilchrist dies May 16, Florida Legislature names a new county in his honor. Among his bequests - a perpetual trust to provide free ice cream for children at Halloween

CENTURY

1927
Grand reopening of the Punta Gorda hotel as the Hotel Charlotte Harbor

The municipal railroad dock and rail line at King Street demolished and a new municipal dock built at Maud Street

The Ice Factory railroad spur re-laid to the dock

Charlotte High School opens with W.E. Riley, principal

Chadwick Brothers build first bridge to Palm Ridge

Harrell Family Collection

The hotel-railroad nexus illustrated here as well-dressed tourists disembark.

from its founder, a litigious lawyer named Isaac Trabue. Punta Gorda is unique because it didn't just grow, it was laid out and platted.

Ironically, Trabue may have lost the city because he stiffed his surveyor, a man named Kelly Harvey who helped mobilize the movement that incorporated the city, thus stealing it out from under its founder's nose.[20]

One of the first things Trabue did was encourage the railroad to lay track to Trabue in July of 1886. Just as Allegiant Airlines sought to build a destination resort in Charlotte County, so did the owners of the railroad build the city's signature edifice, the Hotel Punta Gorda. The resort did indeed put Punta Gorda on the map, fostering tourism industry that's been a mainstay of Punta Gorda into the 21st century.

Suddenly goods, services, and people could be transported from anywhere in the United States reached by a rail line to Punta Gorda. Conversely, fish, pineapples, and other fruits of the sea and soil could be rapidly sent throughout the country, thus making Punta Gorda an economic and agricultural cockpit.

Even the Peace River became an industrial and economic engine. When phosphate was discovered in the lower watershed of the river near what is now Deep Creek, a whole town, Liverpool, sprang up. Towns like Cleveland flourished because of the river traffic. Maintenance and storage shops, and an entire chandler's industry developed along the Peace River, much of it centered near Punta Gorda. George Brown, probably the city's most famous black man, made his money through this period with his Cleveland Marine Steamways Company.

So poised as a railroad hub and blessed with a navigable river that opened into a bountiful harbor, Punta Gorda's wealth of geography offered not only natural wealth, but also the kind of lucre that clinked and jingled.

---

[20] Peeples, Vernon, *Punta Gorda: In the Beginning*, 1865-1900

A People's History of Charlotte County

But by the 1920s things had changed. Ft. Myers had replaced Punta Gorda as the end of the railroad line, and commerce soon followed the rails south.

The bridge across the Peace River proved to be defective at a time when a major new cross-state road was barrelling toward Punta Gorda.

And after the phosphate beds played out in the Peace River, Liverpool died and Cleveland began its descent.

The grand hotel was now old and faded, as travel and tourism suffered during World War I and its aftermath, the Spanish Flu. But residents weren't ready to just roll over and play dead. So Punta Gorda set out to reinvent itself as the county seat.

William Whitten, a county commissioner and planter, anted up the money to complete the first bridge across the Peace River. Henry W. Smith, a Punta Gorda businessman, sank a fortune into developing Smith's Arcade, the county's first enclosed shopping mall.

George Brown, owner of the biggest shipyard in the county, gave the city a great deal on a site for its new courthouse, which soon competed with its new high school and new city hall as brick and mortar evidences of city pride. This was not the "Zip-Zip, Zenith," type of cheerleading and glad-handing from Sinclair Lewis' "Babbit." Civic engagement meant walking the walk and putting the money where one's mouth was.

After paying for the final portion of the bridge across the Peace River, Whitten visited Tallahassee in 1922 to petition

Top, William M. Whitten, who used his own money to complete the first Peace River Bridge (Charlotte County History Services).

Above, Punta Gorda's pride, its new courthouse. (Harrell Family Collection).

Below, A disgusted Hotel Punta Gorda guest complains that "This Hotel has not been painted in years." (Harrell Family Collection).

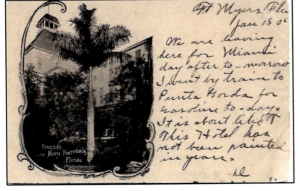

1928

Worst hurricane in Florida history ruptures Lake Okeechobee dike and kills more than 2,000 people, hundreds more unaccounted for; Charlotte County residents mount assistance program of money and supplies.

Tamiami Trail opens

Charlotte County Court House completed

CENTURY

1929

Atlantic Coast Line Rail Road builds a new Punta Gorda depot near site of old Florida Southern Railway station

Stock market crashes, Florida Land Boom collapses

Banks close, savings accounts wiped out or depreciated, national Great Depression begins.

City of Cleveland Charter rescinded

State Library of Florida, Florida Map Collection

By 1926, the date of this map, the Tamiami Trail was well on its way. Commissioner William Whitten and others in the county saw the value of routing the road through Punta Gorda and the coastal communities rather than through the center of the state. Note the cross-hatched portion of Road No. 5 (which would become US41) between Venice and McCall. As the Depression worsened, planners walked back on the promises to send the road through Englewood and instead built a short spur southeast through what is now North Port and Port Charlotte. Below left, the most ardent cheerleader for both Road No. 5 and a bridge across the Peace River was the Punta Gorda Herald. Also note the "expose" on domestic pricing.

state lawmakers for money to cover maintenance of what would become Tamiami Trail or US41. As the *Punta Gorda Herald* announced on its front page Oct. 27, 1922, his mission was successful.

The loudest voice and biggest cheerleader for the county generally and Punta Gorda specifically was the *Punta Gorda Herald,* a paper that actually is older than the county. As one reporter wrote, "The *Punta Gorda Herald* literally watched the city of Punta Gorda grow up, starting with the arrival of the Florida Southern Railway."[21]

In 1901 the original owner, Robert Kirby Seward, sold the newspaper to crusading editor Adrian Pettus Jordan.

---

[21] *Charlotte Sun-Herald,* January 2, 2000

Charlotte Sun-Herald

Editor Adrian P. Jordan, far left, checks a copy of the **Punta Gorda Herald**. *From left are Ivan Pettus, Lillian Undine Jordan and Beatrice Bershaw.*

1930

Florida Census: 1,468,211

Charlotte County population, 4,013

Sacred Heart Roman Catholic Church dedicated at Punta Gorda

Englewood charter rescinded

Through a succession of owners, it expanded to a weekly model to cover a larger portion of Charlotte County as Port Charlotte grew. In 1989 Derek Dunn-Rankin purchased the last incarnation, the *Daily Herald News*, as he expanded a media empire from Venice south through Punta Gorda and west to Arcadia.[22]

The revenant of the original *Herald* can still be found once a week in the daily *Sun-Herald* as a tabloid titled the *Punta Gorda Herald*.

But probably the greatest winder and source of pride to county residents, particularly those in Punta Gorda, was the re-emergence of an old presence, the new Hotel Charlotte Harbor. Built around the shell of the old Hotel Punta Gorda, the new hotel was crafted and marketed by a new power in southwest Florida, Barron Collier. Upon buying the hotel, Collier had railroad lines shifted and landscaping added. He also began advocating for a bigger, better bridge over the Peace River. Like William Whitten before him, Collier used his own money to complete the last stretch of what's now the Tamiami Trail. In return, state officials named Collier County after him.[23]

---

[22] *Charlotte Sun-Herald*, January 2, 2000
[23] https://www.gulfshorelife.com/2018/06/25/how-barron-collier-got-his-county/

Diana Harris

At the height of the Florida Land Boom Walter H. Green's wonderful 21 passenger Studebaker bus brought prospective real estate buyers from Sarasota to Englewood daily. The photo was taken on Englewood's beach. The bus was named "Miss Englewood." Photo late 1920s.

1920s ENGLEWOOD

Diana Harris

The beginning of the 1920s found the Englewood area still a quiet, small, rather isolated, spread out community. Many residents still farmed but more commercial fishing was taking place.

Buchan's Landing, the town's supply store and Post Office, was still the only sizable commercial enterprise in town. One noticeable change had taken place, there were fewer sailboats bringing in supplies to Buchan's dock as a vehicular road coming into town had finally been finished.

But there was unbelievable excitement afoot. It was the beginning of the Florida Land Boom and Englewood, like other towns, was swept up in the frenzy.

Times were good across the country. WW I had ended. People had jobs, extra money, leisure time to take vacations. Many wanted to see for themselves the exotic, tropical "Florida Lifestyle" that was being talked about. Imaginations were piqued by rumors huge amounts of money could be made on any parcel of Florida land you were able to purchase and resell.

Seemed like the whole outside world wanted a piece of sunshiny Florida. The selling of the state was underway. People were buying, trading or selling land as fast as they could. Huge amounts of land were even being sold by mail, sight unseen. All our surrounding locales were caught up in the maddening land craze. Old timers remembered when real estate salesmen were elbow to elbow on Englewood's Dearborn Street.

Many of the early Englewood area families had originally farmed and owned sizable tracts of land. They were thrilled to sell excess parcels for the sky-high prices being offered. In just a few months of 1925, real estate transactions, locally, amounted to $1.3 million and it was predicted that was just the beginning of an era where everyone was going to get wealthy.

A People's History of Charlotte County

Charlotte County History Services

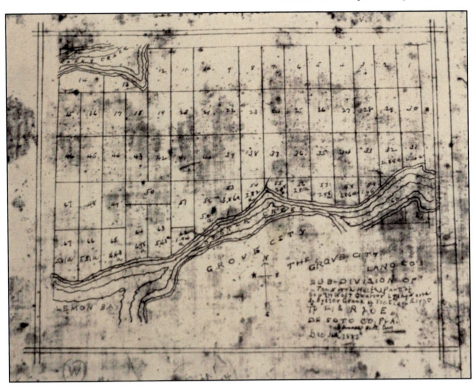
Original plat map of Grove City drawn up by John Cross

Harrell Family Collection

1928 Englewood Elementary School building.

Some growth had taken place in the Englewood area since the three Nichols Brothers filed the original plat for the town in 1896, but nothing like what was now being predicted.

The small farming/fishing village of Englewood was about to undergo a sophisticated transformation. Proposed plans included a Memorial University; a City Hall and a Chamber of Commerce building; an upscale residential development catering to New York Broadway celebrities and Hollywood movie stars to be called Hygeia; a country club, and hotels, one with a casino directly on the beach.

The Sarasota newspaper predicted the Casino Hotel on Manasota Key "will give Englewood one of the finest casinos in the entire nation along with a large pool with a full set of spring boards, swings and other amusement devices."

Subdivisions of hundreds of homes were drawn up. The arcade building on West Dearborn Street would be built and a business block of eight stores. There was even talk about a deep-water port being dredged at the south end of Lemon Bay.

CENTURY

Of course, all of this was only on paper. But there was a short-lived burst of growth in the 1920s for Englewood and some important things happened. The population was still only a couple of hundred people but growing almost daily with the land boom under way.

In 1922 a new sizable school was built on West Dearborn Street which quickly outgrew itself because the town was expanding so rapidly. In 1928, a second school, a Spanish-style, architecturally designed, truly modern elementary school opened in Englewood.

In 1925 Englewood become an incorporated town and even elected a mayor. It was estimated that year 50 to 288 cars were passing through Englewood daily on the road that had finally been built coming

Bernie Reading

The pavilion at Chadwick Beach, which later became a grocery store during the Great Depression.

from Venice and working its way down to Punta Gorda. 1925 saw Englewood's first bank open.

In 1926 the first house of worship building was constructed, a Methodist church, now known as the Green Street Church Museum.

By 1926 the newly formed Lemon Bay Woman's Club had finished their new building. The clubhouse itself and the activities of the club would play an enormous role in the development of the community. The club presented the first beginnings of a town library. In earlier times, the varied programs they provided were about the only entertainment in town and for years their clubhouse would remain the only community building large enough to be used for civic and social events.

By 1927 the first mainland-to-keys bridges crossing Lemon Bay were in use. The toll bridges were privately built by the wealthy Chadwick family for $48,000, a huge sum of money for those days, to service sales of their proposed Chadwick Beach Subdivision.

Although their beach development was never built, it created an enormous sensation when at least 108 sets of human remains were uncovered.

A worker and his horse team, leveling the ground, started turning up skulls and bones. It was thought at first to be signs of some dastardly crime. The April 9, 1926 *Punta Gorda Herald's* headline read,

"Ghosts of Past Stalk through Chadwick Beach When Scraper Bares Marks of Ghastly Crime." The Smithsonian Institute later said it was a huge Native American burial ground dating from 1600 to 1800.

In 1928, five years after it had been started, the Tamiami Trail became reality. Englewood was ecstatic. The good times were still rolling. Everyone was very optimistic about the economic advantages The Trail was going to bring all along its route. It traveled via the new road, which we now call Old Englewood Road, turned on West Dearborn Street and exited out River Road. People started speculating that when The Trail was finished the traffic count in Englewood would number in the thousands every day. It was rumored the railroad was soon to follow through town taking a course along the route Indiana Avenue takes today.

But suddenly the wild ride ended. The hurricanes came in 1926 and '27, the land boom ended in 1928 and the stock market crashed in 1929. The endless flow of tourists and land buyers abruptly stopped. The good times came to a screeching halt.

All of Englewood's grandiose plans went up in smoke. Mr. Green's "Miss Englewood" stopped running. The Hygeia development was never built and dreams of northern millionaires and famous movie stars populating Englewood never materialized. No one had money to dine and dance at the Royal Casino and it became a fish house. The railroad never arrived. And to make things even worse the friendly, well liked banker absconded with all the funds from the new bank. Englewood had to unincorporate, reportedly, because the town couldn't raise the $50 yearly fee.

THE CLERK THROUGH THE YEARS

Roger D. Eaton, Charlotte County Clerk of the Circuit Court & County Comptroller

While the Charlotte County Clerk's Office celebrates 100 years, the original Clerk of Court offices celebrate 200 years. Our journey as the Clerk of the Circuit Court & County Comptroller began in 1821. The creation of the Clerk of Court began with Governor Andrew Jackson when the first two Florida counties, Escambia and St. Johns, were created. The Governor recognized the importance of accurate record keeping for the State of Florida.

From 1821 through 1921, Clerk of Court offices were created throughout Florida. Important issues such as the length of a Clerk's term, their form of compensation, and where they would actually keep their records were never addressed in any great detail. In 1838, Florida's Constitution formally established the Clerk of the Circuit Court's position, stating only that "The Clerk of the Supreme Court, and the Clerks of the Courts of Chancery, shall be elected by General assembly; and the Clerks of the Circuit Courts, shall be elected by the qualified electors, in such mode as may be prescribed by law."

While the Clerk's position was becoming clearer, Florida's struggle for statehood hung in the balance. During this time, Florida was dealing with an economic depression while war raged during the Second Seminole War.

Finally, in 1845, the United States admitted Florida to the Union, adding the twenty-seventh star to the U.S. flag. The Florida legislature met in Tallahassee during the summer of 1845, and passed the Act to Organize the Circuit Courts. A Clerk's term was set for a two-year period.

With Florida's statehood came a half century dominated by two bloody wars, attempts at Reconstruction and Redemption, as well as a series of natural disasters, including the Great Freeze of 1895. During this difficult time, the Clerks throughout Florida learned to make do with what was available to them at the time. All Florida clerks struggled for years to find workable space to do their jobs.

The Florida Constitution was revised in 1868 to increase a Clerk's term from two to four years, which remains true today. However, Clerks at this time were appointed by the Governor rather than being elected by a county's citizens. During the summer of 1885, a constitutional convention met again to consider wide-ranging changes to the Florida Constitution. During this time, there was a strong push for more elected offices rather than Governor appointments. After two months of debate, a compromise allowed for the popular election of Circuit Judges, County Commissioners, County Judges, Justices of the Peace, and Clerks of Court throughout Florida.

The Florida Legislature created Charlotte County in 1921 by dividing DeSoto County into five counties: Charlotte, Hardee, Highlands, Glades, and DeSoto. During Charlotte County's first 100 years, it has only had nine Clerks of Court:

Florida Memory

1. R. Chester Blount (1922-1926)
2. William T. Oliver (1927-1932)
3. Thomas C. Crosland (1933-1935)
4. Edward H. Scott (1935-1950)
5. Helen Brawner (also known as Helen Wotitzky) (1950-1957)
6. John T. Lawhorne (1957-1977)
7. Buddy C. Alexander (1977-1985)
8. Barbara Scott (1985-2016)
9. Roger D. Eaton (2016-present)

Constitutional officers were once housed in Charlotte's courthouse, which opened in 1928 as a source of pride to residents of the county seat.

By the 1970s, Florida Clerks performed 926 constitutional and statutory tasks. This number has since increased to well over 1000 functions and duties. In addition to its constitutional and statutory tasks, Florida Clerks must also comply with all court rules and administrative orders at the local level, and with all orders of the Florida Supreme Court. The number of tasks, duties, and responsibilities of Florida's Clerks continue to grow with each passing year.

As Charlotte County's current Clerk of Court, I will always focus on delivering exceptional services to our citizens through digital transformation, office modernization, and increased efficiencies. As we begin the next 100 years, we look forward to the ever-changing duties we'll face, and will embrace the new challenges which lie ahead. Charlotte County is my home, and its citizens are my neighbors.

CHARLOTTE COUNTY TAX COLLECTOR

Vicki L. Potts, CLC

With the establishment of Charlotte County in 1921 came the responsibility of collecting taxes. Florida's 1868 Constitution made first mention of the position of a Tax Collector, then referred to as a Collector of Revenue. Collectors in this period were appointed by the governor to serve two-year terms. Under the 1865 Constitution, gubernatorial appointments were curtailed to provide for the election of Tax Collectors for a four-year term in each county. This practice continues today under the State's current Constitution. There have been five Tax Collectors since 1921.

1921-1933 **Albert F. Dewey** was born in Granby, Connecticut in 1857. He arrived in Punta Gorda in 1892. Mr. Dewey was active in the drive to carve Charlotte County from a portion of DeSoto County and when that occurred in 1921, was appointed Charlotte County's first Tax Collector.

1933-1952 **Edward B. Yeager** was born in Kentucky in 1889 and came to Punta Gorda as a young man. Mr. Yeager was elected Tax Collector of Charlotte County in 1933 and held the position until his passing.

1952-1972 **Areta Alderman Yeager** came to Punta Gorda from Fort Myers in 1923 as a bride. Mrs. Yeager filled the unexpired term of her husband, E. B. Yeager, as Tax Collector in April 1952 as appointed by Governor Fuller Warren at that time.

1972-1996 **L. Victor Desquin** arrived in Punta Gorda on September 9, 1936 at the age of ten. In the 1960s he got a job with Tax Collector Mrs. E. B. Yeager during the day and worked at the family theater at night. Victor Desguin had been working in the Tax Collector office for 6 years when he got the momentous call. Mrs. Yeager called Mr. Desguin into her office four days before she retired and told him to hurry and apply for her job. Mr. Desquin met with the local nominating committee. The committee sent Mr. Desquin's name to Governor Askew and was appointed to complete the last 6 months of the term. In 1972 Victor Desguin was elected to the position of Tax Collector. Mr. Desquin held office for the Charlotte County Tax Collector Office from 1972 – 1996 until he retired.

1997- Present Vickie L. Potts relocated from Ohio to Englewood with her family in the early 1960s. She attended Lemon Bay School and Charlotte High School. In 1980, she married her husband Mike, and together they raised their children in Charlotte County. Mrs. Potts began her career in the Tax Collectors office in 1974. She had the privilege of working under Tax Collector Victor Desquin and is thankful for his mentorship and tutelage. In 1996, she was elected as the Charlotte County Tax Collector and is honored to have been re-elected each consecutive term.

CENTURY

THE GREEN WAVE: CHARLOTTE COUNTY SHERIFFS

No other constitutional office has seen more turnover than the sheriff's office. The graphic below, excerpted from the Charlotte County Sheriff's Office website, offers surprising and frank reasons for the tradition of turmoil at the top in the highly politicized office. One encouraging sign is that from the 90s on, with a brief exception, stability at the top has become the hallmark of the Sheriff's Office rather than the exception.

1921 - 1941
J. H. Lipscomb
Democrat

Charlotte County's first sheriff was James H. Lipscomb, a school teacher, former town marshal and long-time member of the local Masonic Lodge. Governor Hardee appointed J. H. Lipscomb the first Charlotte County Sheriff on May 4, 1921.

1941 - 1957
Arthur F. Quednau
Democrat

Arthur F. "Fred" Quednau, a Punta Gorda native, defeated Sheriff J. H. Lipscomb in the 1940 election. Sheriff Quednau had a force of two deputies -Travis Parnell and Ira Atkinson. Besides being sheriff, Quednau owned a charter boat business and a diner. Many knew him as "Captain Fred." Sheriff Quednau's daughter, Tosie Hindman went on to be the Supervisor of Elections for Charlotte County.

1957 - 1965
Travis Parnell
Democrat

Travis Parnell, Sheriff Fred Quednau's chief deputy and former jailer, ran against Quednau's other deputy, Ira Atkinson in 1957 when Sheriff Quednau decided not to seek re-election. Parnell won by 304 votes, a near landslide in a race in which 2,390 people voted. Parnell was a butcher before he and his wife became the county jailers. The couple lived in an apartment in the courthouse. He locked up the prisoners, and his wife cooked the meals. Sheriff Parnell was defeated in the 1964 election.

1965 - 1966
Richard A. Stickley
Republican

Richard Stickley was a former South Bend, Indiana cop who retired to El Jobean. In 1964, he ran for sheriff against Sheriff Travis Parnell. The vote from an influx of northerners allowed Stickley to become the first Republican to be elected sheriff in Charlotte County. However, only 18 months after he took office, in July 1966, a Charlotte County Grand Jury "indicted" Stickley on 10 criminal charges. Many of the charges were either dropped or dismissed prior to the trial. Stickley was acquitted of the remaining charges during the trial. By the time he was cleared, however, his term as sheriff had expired.

A People's History of Charlotte County

1966

John P. Shannon
Democrat
John P. Shannon, a former Chicago motorcycle cop, was working as the Chief Deputy for Sheriff Richard Stickley when Stickley was indicted and removed from office by the governor in 1966. According to the Charlotte Herald newspaper, Shannon received a telegram from Gov. Hayden Burns that said: "This is to authorize you to take over the responsibilities of Sheriff Richard Stickley who I suspend today until I have time to consider this matter." A month later, Burns replaced Shannon by appointing David Deegan as sheriff.

1966 - 1967

David Deegan
Democrat
In 1966 Governor Hayden Burns appointed David Deegan, a local real estate salesman, as sheriff when Sheriff Richard Stickley was indicted on criminal charges by a Grand Jury. Deegan succeeded Sheriff John P. Shannon, who served as sheriff for about a month after Stickley was removed from office. Deegan had served as Governor Burns' Charlotte County campaign manager during the 1960 gubernatorial election, and as the Mayor of Punta Gorda. Deegan served a little more than a year before he was removed from office by the next governor, Claude Kirk, a Republican. Governor Kirk then appointed Jack Bent, a fellow Republican, to complete Stickley's term of office.

1967 - 1977

John P. 'Jack' Bent
Republican
Governor Claude Kirk, a Republican, appointed Jack Bent, a fellow Republican, to complete Sheriff Richard Stickley's term of office as Sheriff in 1967. Bent was living in Sarasota at the time. But he was familiar with Charlotte County, having served as a state forestry arson investigator, highway patrolman, and Lee County deputy. During Sheriff Bent's 10 years in office, the county population grew from about 20,000 to about 80,000. The number of Sheriff's Office employees also grew, from 18 to 114. Sheriff Bent moved the Sheriff's Office from the County Courthouse to its first stand-alone private headquarters on Airport Road.

1977 - 1981

Alan L. LeBeau
Democrat
Alan L. LeBeau was a deputy under Sheriff Jack Bent. In 1976, LeBeau ran against Sheriff Bent and defeated him by some 700 votes. Sheriff Lebeau was the youngest Sheriff elected in Charlotte County at 26 years of age. During Sheriff LeBeau's term in office he took steps to modernize the county's ambulance service which came under the Sheriff's Office. The Sheriff's Office got its first computers and had a 911 emergency call system installed during this time. Sheriff LeBeau was responsible for the Sheriff's Office starting an aviation division by obtaining its first helicopter. LeBeau was defeated in his 1980 bid for re-election by Glen E. Sapp.

1981 - 1985

Glen E. Sapp
Republican
Glen E. Sapp came into office in 1981 fresh from an 11-week FBI course on professional law enforcement methods. He had formerly worked for the Starke Police Department, Bradford County Sheriff's Office, Florida Highway Patrol, and the State Attorney in the 8th Judicial Circuit before coming to Charlotte County. In 1985, a grand jury indicted Sapp on charges of grand theft involving the sale of an airplane to a corporation that leased it back to the sheriff's office. Sapp was convicted in 1986, but the conviction was overturned on appeal and he was returned to his position as Sheriff that same year.

CENTURY

1985
J.M. 'Buddy' Phillips
Democrat

In 1985 when Sheriff Glen E. Sapp was indicted on criminal charges and suspended from office, Governor Bob Graham needed to find someone who could immediately fill the vacancy. He turned to someone who had experience at being a sheriff - J.M. "Buddy" Phillips. Phillips had been a military policeman in the Army before joining the Suwannee County Florida Sheriff's Office in 1963. In 1968 he was elected Sheriff of Suwannee County, serving one four-year term.

1985 - 1986
John J. McDougall
Republican

John J. McDougall spent seven years as a Franciscan monk before getting into law enforcement. He first worked in Norfolk County Massachusetts before joining the Lee County Sheriff's Office in 1974. By 1985, McDougall was a captain serving as the agency's public information officer. In that year, Charlotte County Sheriff Glen E. Sapp was indicted on criminal charges and suspended by Governor Bob Graham. The governor's office accepted applications to fill the position more permanently. McDougall submitted his application and was selected. Sheriff McDougall served Charlotte County for almost 14 months. Sheriff Sapp returned to office in July 1986. John McDougall returned to his job at the Lee County Sheriff's Office.

1986 - 1989
Glen E. Sapp

1989 - 2001
Richard H. Worch Jr.
Republican

Richard H. Worch Jr. began his career with the Charlotte County Sheriff's Office as a road patrol deputy under Sheriff Alan L. LeBeau. He was instrumental in Glen Sapp's election campaign in 1980 against Sheriff LeBeau. After Sapp was elected Sheriff, Richard Worch was promoted to a lieutenant's position at the Sheriff's Office. Shortly after Sheriff Sapp returned to office in 1986, Worch took a high-ranking position with the Monroe County Sheriff's Office. In 1988, Worch ran against Sheriff Sapp and defeated him. Sheriff Worch instituted a "community policing" philosophy at the Sheriff's Office. He also began the "district" concept by initially dividing the county into three patrol districts. After 12 years in office, Sheriff Worch was defeated in the 2000 election by Democrat William E. Clement.

2001 - 2003
William E. Clement
Democrat

William E. "Bill" Clement was a second-generation native Floridian. He was born in Arcadia and lived most of his life in southwest Florida. Sheriff Clement had served in various positions from road patrol to chief investigator. In 2003, Sheriff Clement was removed from office by Governor Jeb Bush when he was charged with a felony stemming from allegations of election law violations. The governor appointed J.M. Phillips to serve as the "interim" sheriff again. Then Bush appointed Lee County Sheriff's Office Captain William F. Cameron to complete Clements's term of office. Clement was convicted in early 2004. Later that year, his conviction was overturned on appeal. The State appealed the decision, but it was upheld by a high court in early 2005.

2003
J.M. 'Buddy' Phillips

A People's History of Charlotte County

2003 - 2005

Bill Cameron
Republican
Bill Cameron began his law enforcement career at the Fort Myers Police Department in 1982 where he worked on road patrol, in narcotics and as a training officer. In 1987, he joined the Lee County Sheriff's Office. While there he worked his way up to the rank of captain. Hurricane Charley literally blew through the Sheriff's Office on August 13, 2004, ripping one-third of the roof from the administration building, starting in the corner with Sheriff Cameron's office. Much of Charlotte County was as devastated as his own office. Sheriff Cameron lead the Sheriff's Office through the process of recovery. Keeping his word to Governor Bush, Cameron did not seek election at the end of his appointed term. John Davenport who served as Cameron's chief deputy was elected sheriff in November 2004. When he took office in January 2005, he kept Cameron on as his chief deputy. It was the first time in Florida history that a former sheriff remained at the agency as the chief deputy.

2005 - 2009

John Davenport
Republican
In November 2004, John Davenport was elected to be Sheriff of the agency where he had started his law enforcement career almost 27 years earlier. Sheriff Davenport began his law enforcement career in 1978 when he became a corrections officer at the Sheriff's Office. Within a few years he had worked his way up in rank to being the Jail Commander. Sheriff Davenport retired in January 2009 at the end of his term after almost 31 years in law enforcement in Charlotte County. He noted in an email to his employees that he had begun his career without any fanfare and he wanted to end his career the same way.

2009 - 2012

Bill Cameron
Republican
In November 2008, Cameron was elected as Charlotte County's Sheriff, making him one of the few people who have ever been both appointed and elected to the office of Sheriff. Sheriff Cameron decided not to seek re-election in 2012 and endorsed one of his Captains, Bill Prummell to succeed him. Prummell won election in August 2012 to become Charlotte County's next Sheriff.

2012 - present

Sheriff Bill Prummell is a 26-year veteran in law enforcement, who began his career with the Charlotte County Sheriff's Office in 1992. He worked his way through the ranks and throughout most areas of the Agency. He was elected as Sheriff on August 14, 2012 and assumed the Office of Sheriff on January 8, 2013. He ran for re-election in 2016 winning both the primary and general elections.
Sheriff Prummell holds a Bachelor of Arts Degree from St. Leo University in Criminology with a minor in Psychology; a Master's Degree in Business Administration from IMPAC University; and a Master's Degree in Criminal Justice from American Public University. In addition, he is a graduate of the Florida Sheriff's Institute, the National Sheriff's Institute, the 239th session of the FBI National Academy in Quantico, Virginia, The Law Enforcement Executive Development Seminar out of the University of Virginia, and Florida's Senior Leadership Program in Tallahassee, Florida.

THE (GREATER) CHARLOTTE COUNTY CHAMBER OF COMMERCE

Teri Ashley

Charlotte County and the Charlotte County Chamber of Commerce have grown together for almost 100 years—96 years, to be exact.

The word "greater" may have been dropped from the name of the Greater Charlotte County Chamber of Commerce in 1982, but not the greatness. Putting the 96-year Charlotte County partnership into perspective, the business organization and the county as a whole have diligently ensured the economic vitality of our community. This book is an excellent remembrance of the hurdles, milestones, setbacks, and glorious successes.

The precursor to today's leading business membership organization began in 1925 as the Board of Trade in Punta Gorda. The Board of Trade was later renamed the Punta Gorda Chamber of Commerce, and in 1966 merged with the Port Charlotte chamber to become the Greater Charlotte County Chamber of Commerce. And here we are in 2021, the Charlotte County Chamber of Commerce.

Actually, let's back up another 322 years to 1599, in Marseille, France, for an extended history lesson. That is when and where the first "Chambre de Commerce" was formed by a group of involved business leaders. The word "chamber" was used to signify both the physical offices where meetings and work were conducted and the business association itself.

Chambers were pretty much what they remain today, local organizations of businesses with goals to further the interests of businesses. Business owners and operators form and operate these local organizations to advocate on behalf of their business communities.

The Port Charlotte location of the Charlotte County Chamber of Commerce was initially housed in a tiki hut, A-frame-style building at the Promenades shopping center site in Port Charlotte. After our merger with the Charlotte chamber, it seemed like an excellent plan to move the building across Tamiami Trail to a vacant lot next to the

At the height of the great depression, in 1936, the Chamber launched a series of advertisements such as the one above to bring tourism and commerce to Charlotte county. Below, the ill-fated tiki hut.

Charlotte County Chamber of Commerce

LaPlaya Shopping Center. Once the move was underway, the building would not fit under the electrical wires. The relocation plan was abandoned mid-move!

Thanks to Dr. Fred P. Swing, the chamber was provided office space in LaPlaya Shopping Center for several years. Later, First Federal of Charlotte County provided space at the corner of Midway Blvd. and Tamiami Trail, then the chamber moved to the Carousel Realty Building.

In the summer of 1982, the operational office of the Charlotte County Chamber of Commerce was opened at its present location, 2702 Tamiami Trail in Port Charlotte. The building has since been renovated and expanded to include additional offices and a conference room.

For many years, the Punta Gorda location of the Charlotte County Chamber of Commerce was in another long-gone building near the corner of Retta Esplanade and northbound Tamiami Trail. When the building was eventually condemned and demolished, the chamber office was moved to the historic City Hall building in 1992.

Following Hurricane Charley and the city's purchase and relocation of the Freeman House to city property on Retta Esplanade, the Charlotte County Chamber of Commerce has leased the building, which is on the National Register of Historic Places, for its operations.

The Chamber has remained a partner at the county's side.

The effects of Florida's many catastrophic unnamed, unannounced hurricanes—and those more familiar such as Donna, Alma, Charley, Irma, and Eta—have been experienced together. The Chamber worked through those crises to best serve our business community with guidance and resources.

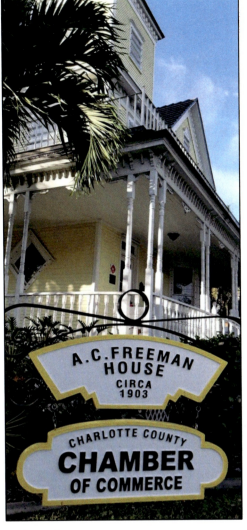

Together.

President Calvin Coolidge was in office when the initial Board of Trade was created, followed by 16 presidents. During our years together the Tamiami Trail was built, the stock market cycled from climbs to crashes, and Florida enjoyed booms and suffered collapses. Wars have been fought, global markets have evolved, and technology is created in an almost constant state of unbelievable.

And just when we were to step back for a moment, and rest on our laurels, if you will, to celebrate 96 years of partnership in a 100 year centennial milestone, 2020 presented the Novel Coronavirus Covid-19 Global Pandemic.

As you might expect, Charlotte County and the Charlotte County Chamber of Commerce did not skip a beat. In fact, they added a few new beats. We have been here together, we are here together, and we will be here together. Congratulations, Charlotte County.

CROSLAND DEVELOPED FISHING INDUSTRY

Paul L. Polk

Originally from Marlboro County, South Carolina, Thomas Cecil (T.C.) Crosland came to Florida in 1899 working for L.T. Blocksom and W.H. Adams' Florida Fish and Produce Company in Jacksonville. In 1905 he moved to Punta Gorda and upon the death of Mr. Blocksom acquired the financial interest of Blocksom's heirs and in 1912 formed the West Coast Fish Company.

In 1916 Crosland reported to the Punta Gorda Herald that one of his fishing crews caught 76,000 pounds of fish in one haul. Another boat caught more than 21,000 pounds of mackerel the same day. That day the West Coast Fish Company shipped five iced boxcar loads of 20,000 pounds. During the great Florida land boom in July of 1925 the Chadwick Brothers sold their fish business to Crosland's West Coast Fish Company.

On November 14, 1906, in Punta Gorda he married Emily Adelia Whitten, a native of South Bend, Indiana. They had seven children - Mary Agnes, Emily Elizabeth, Laura Mildred (Dee), Thomas Monson, Cecelia, William Whitten, and Robert Elder.

West Coast Fish Company maintained fish camps and icing

"Crosland Hall" built c. 1883 by John Lewis, purchased in 1907 by William Whitten as a wedding gift for his daughter, Emily, upon her marriage to Thomas Cecil Crosland. The Crosland family lived here for generations; Robert and William Crosland, sons of Emily and TC, remodeled the house in 1960, replacing the upper and lower verandas with the majestic columns seen here. William Crosland was born in the parlor of this house in 1922. Crosland Hall was heavily damaged by Hurricane Charley in 2004 and the 1880s appearance was restored during reconstruction of the facade.
Charlotte County History Services

PGH 1-15-20

stations from Charlotte Harbor to the Ten Thousand Islands. Run boats from Punta Gorda would travel "down the bay" two to three times a week delivering ice, groceries, mail and other supplies to the fishing crews. In exchange they would bring back mullet, trout, pompano and mackerel to Punta Gorda to be shipped north by train.

On one such trip to Smallwood's trading post in Chokoloskee, a West Coast fishing crew aboard the Chase encountered a Seminole Indian who had come across three orphaned bear cubs. A trade ensued and the bear cubs were brought back to Punta Gorda; unfortunately only two survived. Mr. Crosland promptly

Crosland's bears made the society page of the Punta Gorda Herald.

A People's History of Charlotte County

Charlotte County History Services

The West Coast Fish Company.

built a pen for the two bear clubs and they took up permanent residence behind his home on Retta Esplanade.

Stories of their capers soon became common in downtown Punta Gorda. As the bears got bigger it became more difficult to keep them in their pen. During one breakout the bears found their way through the back door of a neighbor's home. To their delight they found several jars of freshly made guava jelly that were set out on the dining room table to cool. They were quickly identified as the culprits by the jelly stained paw prints on the white table cloth.

An article in a December 1919 issue of the *Punta Gorda Herald* solved the mystery of what happened to the bears. "Two of Punta Gorda's noted citizens, Bruin and his brother, pet bears belonging to T.C. Crosland left Tuesday for Palm Beach, Mr. Crosland having sold them to the Atlantic Coast Fish Co. They were quite an attraction to newcomers here and many of the older citizens were much interested in them, making frequent trips to their lair to watch their peculiar and amazing antics."

The West Coast Fish Company continued operation until May of 1939 when a fire struck, destroying all the fish houses located along the Maud Street docks. The remaining assets of the West Coast Fish Company were purchased by the Punta Gorda Fish Company. After the fire Mr. Crosland turned to other business ventures, including a trucking company and a restaurant. He also owned and cared for a 25-acre citrus grove located on Washington Loop for many years.

A dedicated public servant, he served many years on the Punta Gorda City Council and in 1932 was elected Charlotte County Clerk of Courts. He was also a member of the board of directors for the Punta Gorda State Bank. A longtime member and deacon of the First Baptist Church of Punta Gorda, in his honor Crosland chapel and Sunday school were dedicated January 28, 1962.

As a fifth-generation resident of Charlotte County, I truly feel blessed to live in the same community where my family first settled over 100 years ago. Growing up in a much different Charlotte County than we see today I had the choice like so many of my friends after high school and college to move on to pursue dreams and ambitions in other places like Atlanta or Tampa. For me that was never a consideration, this was my home where my roots had been laid generations before. My wife and I knew we wanted to raise our son here so he could experience that sense of history and belonging we had felt. From creeks and bays of Charlotte Harbor to the flatwoods and telegraph cypress, Charlotte County is unique and special in so many ways.

FORGOTTEN VICTIMS

Lynn Harrell

Historical research is like going down a rabbit hole. You don't know how deep it is, or what lurks at the bottom. I was recently asked to summarize the lineage of the two docks that preceded Fishermen's Village, a subject I know pretty well. But while skimming through local books, confirming specifics, I got snagged. Buried in a story about the 1915 King Street wharf fire was a tidbit I'd never noticed. In 1939, there was a major fire at the Maud Street fish dock wherein "a resident couple and young child" had died. I added that to my summary and sent it off. Then I went back down the rabbit hole.

I re-checked standard resources -- nothing. I tried more obscure sources – more nothing. A digital archive of old PG Heralds has no 1939 issues. There's no trio of same-day deaths in Indian Spring. But a Find-A-Grave search of the Charlotte Harbor Cemetery revealed three members of the Willis family who all died on May 19, 1939; John Henry, Rosalie B., and Edwin. Other than birth years and estimated ages, there were no details.

Had I found the Maud Street fire victims? It seemed so. I reached out to Scot Shively, a colleague with access to multiple databases. Within a few hours he sent me an AP article from a 1939 Panama City Pilot, datelined Punta Gorda, May 19. Rosalie's name is misspelled and the ages are a little off from the cemetery file. But the formerly anonymous victims are now confirmed.

John Henry Willis, wife Rosalie, and toddler son, Edwin, are long gone. But they're no longer forgotten. May they rest in eternal peace.

AN OVERVIEW OF THE ORIGINS OF THE MUNICIPAL FISH DOCK AT MAUD STREET

Lynn Harrell

It is fairly well known that Fishermen's Village Resort & Marina was constructed on the site of the former Municipal Fish Dock, which was built in 1928, although the resort's origins can be traced further back. The first dock at the foot of Maud Street was actually a cattle chute, built in 1902 for the DeSoto Cattle Wharf Association to replace a dilapidated dock across the bay at Knight Bros. general store in Charlotte Harbor. Principal partners of the association included Ziba King and Willoughby Whidden. The contractor was C.L. Fries; the narrow chute was 3,100 feet long and just wide enough to herd cattle single file to a waiting ship. Capt. James McKay carried the first shipment aboard his schooner, 327 head bound for Cardenas, Cuba. Cattlemen driving their herds down Marion Avenue became a common sight. But the water depth at Maud Street wasn't always adequate, so two years later the chute was extended another 90 feet into deeper water.

A People's History of Charlotte County

Charlotte County History Services

The Seaboard Coast Line railroad spur that ran from Tamiami Trail to the Punta Gorda city docks on Maude Street. The tracks were removed in early 1972. Photo by George Lane

After the rail lines on the Long Dock were removed by Henry Plant in 1897, the hub of commercial activity, including the fishing industry, was moved to the railroad wharf at King Street which ran alongside the Hotel Punta Gorda. In June 1915 a fire on the wharf destroyed five buildings, part of the wharf and five railroad cars. Companies housed in the burned out buildings included the ACL office, Terry Packing Co., S.E. Johnson, H.L. Blakeley, the Chadwick Brothers, Everglades Fish Company, Arthur & Lewis, and the West Coast Fish Company. Luckily, the Standard Oil tanks near the wharf did not explode. Other surviving structures were Charles Dean's boat house, the Punta Gorda Ice Co. dock, the J.C. Lewis fish house and the Punta Gorda Fish Co. office. The wharf was rebuilt, but several uninsured companies went out of business.

When Barron Collier bought the hotel in 1925 and began renovations, the unsightly wharf and its activities were not conducive to the elegant resort atmosphere he envisioned. Collier proposed to the City that the rails and fisheries be relocated to deeper water, as the wharf had a water depth of only five feet. Collier also proposed that a second bridge across the bay be built in place of the wharf. The first bridge that ran from Nesbit Street on the south to Live Oak Point on the north had just opened in 1921, but had proved to have structural issues. He offered financial assistance to fund the new bridge. The City agreed. Construction of the Barron Collier Bridge began in 1928 and by March 1929 commercial fisheries and wholesalers occupied the new municipal pier and fish houses that had been built at the site of the old cattle chute at Maud Street.

In 1939, the Maud Street docks also suffered a major fire. This time lives were lost; a couple with a young child who were living on the second floor of a warehouse died in the blaze. The municipal pier was repaired and facilities rebuilt. A new industry was added after WWII when commercial shrimpers joined the fishing fleet, and one other post-war addition arrived – Arnold "Slim" Keys, a local auto mechanic, bought a surplus airboat, refurbished it, and kept it tied up at the municipal dock.

By the mid-1960s, the Maud Street docks were past their prime, commercial fishing was waning and only a few companies remained – the Punta Gorda Fish Company, Gulf Shore Seafood, Gulf Oil Company, and Matt Weeks Marine Service. The oldest of these, the Punta Gorda Fish Company, was the last to close. It was founded in 1897 by Eugene Knight and Harry Dreggors after the Long Dock was abandoned. Other principals of the company over the years were S.D. McCullough, William "Billy" Knight, Harry Goulding and William Guthrie. William H. Monson had become president of the corporation in 1947 and his son, Walter Homer Monson, succeeded him in 1968. It ceased operations in 1977, when the 90-day cancellation clause in its municipal dock lease was invoked by the City, clearing the way for a 45-year lease agreement between the City and Earl Nightingale, a well-known radio commentator, and the subsequent construction of Fishermen's Village.

Citations:
Vernon Peeples, "Punta Gorda and the Charlotte Harbor Area"
Byron Rhode, "Punta Gorda Remembered"
Williams & Cleveland, "Our Fascinating Past," Volumes 1 & 2
O'Phelan & Shively, "Punta Gorda," (Images of America)

AFRICAN AMERICAN SETTLEMENT AND CONTRIBUTIONS

Martha Russell Bireda, Ph.D.
Scot Shively, Ret. Lt. Col. U.S. Air Force

Florida Memory

1902 photograph of Benjamin Baker with students from what was then called the colored school.

By the time Charlotte County was established, a small "colored high circle" or society flourished among the African Americans in Punta Gorda, whose entertainment included yachting to Boca Grande. African American businesses such as the Ingram Hotel, O.B. Armstrong Grocery/Restaurant, and Starlight Barbershop were located in the central business district in Punta Gorda. An employment agency owned by Will J. Brown was located on Marion Avenue.

George Brown was one of the most important businessmen and employers in the early history of Charlotte County. In 1916, he opened the Cleveland Marine Steamways, the largest Steamways in Southwest Florida. Mr. Brown was a major landowner in the Punta Gorda area. The Old Charlotte County Courthouse was built in 1928 on lots purchased from Brown. Mr. Brown left a legacy of charitable giving and fair treatment for all.

The U.S. Census Bureau Populations estimates from July 1, 2019, indicate that the African American population of Punta Gorda was 2.4 percent. Of the pioneer African American families listed in the 1900 census, only the descendants of A.B. Coleman and James Andrews continue to reside in the area (most returning retirees).

The high value placed on education by the early African American pioneers accounts for this factor. By 1900, 70 percent of the settlers, the children of enslaved parents, could read, and 60 percent could read and write. Adults attended school with children and parents paid Mrs. Giles, who taught at the community Seventh Day Adventist School, 15 cents per week to attend until a public colored school was established. The African American settlers sacrificed to provide their children with a high school and in many cases, a college education. Because of Jim Crow laws, the educated descendants of the settlers did not return to the area and joined others in the Great Migration. The legacy of African American contributions to the civic life of the community continues.

Jaha Cummings, Councilman of Historic District I is the great grand-nephew of Dan Smith and the grandson of community activist and visionary of the Blanchard House Museum Bernice Andrews Russell.

A 1920s postcard of the first bridge between Punta Gorda and Charlotte Harbor, a horse and buggy crossing for the automotive century.

FIRST BRIDGE WAS OUTDATED BEFORE IT OPENED

Frank Desguin

Construction of the first bridge across the Peace River connecting Punta Gorda to Charlotte Harbor began in 1916. One motive of the backers was to entice planners of a new highway from Tampa to Miami (Tamiami Trail) to not follow the initial inland route, which avoided the lower Peace and Caloosahatchee Rivers' wide expanses. Bonds were issued locally for $200,000 to finance the bridge with no state or federal help.

By the time work began though, the original plan to construct it of wood had been abandoned. Germany's involvement in World War I severely restricted the supply of creosote needed for waterproofing, so a reinforced concrete structure was envisioned. The war continued to plague construction. Work actually ceased after completion of just the midpoint hand cranked swing span due to significant increases in the price of cement and steel.

Work did not resume until 1920 and then only due to the persistence of local businessman, engineer, and County Commissioner William Whitten.

After the DeSoto County commission diverted money to construction of a new courthouse in Arcadia (what became Charlotte County was still part of DeSoto County back then), Whitten advanced considerable personal funds and supervised construction. The bridge was then completed in less than two years, with a dedication party on July 4, 1921. More than 6,000 people attended the opening celebration. About a mile long, the structure ran from Sandy Point on the Charlotte Harbor side, where Live Oak Point Park is today, to Nesbit Street where the Laishley Park fishing pier is today.

Six years of intermittent construction was not the bridge's only problem. Designed in 1915 during the horse and buggy era, the bridge had a span of only 14.5 feet; it was barely wide enough for two automobiles to pass. A more serious problem was the use of beach sand and bay water for the concrete. Residual salt in the mixture soon caused reinforcing rods to deteriorate. Large sections of concrete fell away. Those structural issues and the increased car traffic following the completion of the Tamiami Trail in 1928 led to calls for a new bridge.

Punta Gorda History Center

The Allapatchee Lodge. It was built as a hunting and fishing retreat where Burnt Store Villas and the seventh hole of the Twin Isles Country Club are now positioned.

BURNT STORE ROAD

Graham Segger

Burnt Store Road is an enigma for many residents of Charlotte County. It traverses most of the southern half of the county but its stories have often been overshadowed by those of its more northerly neighbors. This important thoroughfare, which links Punta Gorda with Pine Island and Cape Coral, has seen the rise and fall of many enterprises and communities over the last 100 years. Following are a few of those stories.

On April 23, 1921, when the Legislature of Florida passed Act 118 to establish Charlotte County, the main industries in the Burnt Store Road area were turpentine distilling and a sawmill for processing pine lumber at Acline with cattle ranching farther south. There were orange groves cultivated along much of Alligator Creek and more groves were later planted along the east side of Burnt Store Road.

Later in the 1920s Louis Calder and a group of investors purchased 550 acres on the north bank of Alligator Creek and created the Allapatchee Lodge. It was built as a hunting and fishing retreat where Burnt Store Villas and the seventh hole of the Twin Isles Country Club are now positioned. The original Punta Gorda Airport was also located in this area at the northwest corner of Highway 41 and Burnt Store Road until the 1940s.

Early Burnt Store Road settlers Louise (Driggers) Lowe, Max Jones and Carl & Jerry Powell have provided vivid oral histories of what Burnt Store Road was like up until the introduction of land enclosure in the late 1940s and drainage ditches in the 1960s. Their accounts all tell similar tales of a hard but rewarding life lived on a land blessed with bountiful hunting, fishing and cattle grazing terrain. Each of them bemoaned the impact of the mosquito control and drainage ditches, the introduction of Brazilian Pepper and Melaleuca trees as well as residential development on the local environment and wildlife. Many of the lakes found along Burnt Store Road were dug to provide aggregate for building the Tamiami Trail, which was completed in 1928.

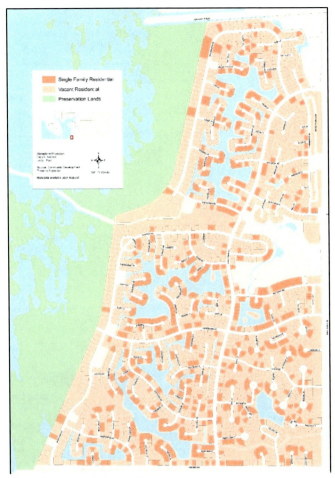

Charlotte County Community Services Division

Subdivision of Burnt Store Lakes.

Several large gladioli and chrysanthemum growing enterprises were also developed along Burnt Store Road. The largest of these in the 1950s and 1960s were the Hobbs & Cowan operations at the southern end of the county near Turtle Crossing (Charlotte County ends at Vincent Road on the north side of Burnt Store Marina). Harvey Hobbs even built a two-runway airstrip on his property and shipped his flowers all over the country. The Hobbs farm is now the location of the Burnt Store Lakes subdivision. Burnt Store Meadows farther north was also the site of flower growing farms.

Pirate Harbor, located just north of Burnt Store Lakes at Zemel Road, is one of the most eclectic communities in Charlotte County. It consists of eight canals dredged in from Charlotte Harbor bordered by nine streets: Jolly Roger, Yacht Club Blvd., Captain Kidd, Pirate Harbor, Buccaneer, Treasure Island, Henry Morgan, Blackbeard and Jean La Fitte. The 260-acre site was developed in the late 1950s by Erich and Lydia Quast who in 1959 were selling lots with 100 feet of canal waterfront for $2,246 (less for cash).

The newest community to grace Burnt Store Road, located just north of Pirate Harbor, is the Heritage Landing Golf & Country Club. This location has had a fascinating history, including at least four development attempts. Back in the 1940s an oil exploration team struck not black gold, but rather a 97°F mineral hot spring on this site. The spring was capped until 1967 when a development group was

CENTURY

Community Names
- River Haven Mobile Home Park
- Park Hill Mobile Home Park
- Gulf View RV Resort
- Eagle Point Mobile Home Park
- Seminole Lakes
- Burnt Store Meadows (PGI Sec. 18)
- South Punta Gorda Heights-West
- Heritage Landing Golf & CC
- Burnt Store Colony
- Pirate Harbor
- Burnt Store Village (PGI Sec. 16)
- Harborside Boulevard
- Burnt Store Lakes (PGI Sec. 21)

operating the hot springs as a local attraction and trying to sell home sites around the property. This development went bankrupt in 1968.

Current owner Lennar appears to be making great strides with the current incarnation of this development with 187 homes completed or in progress – but do they have any new plans for the hot spring?

The Burnt Store Lakes, Burnt Store Village, Burnt Store Meadows, Burnt Store Isles and Burnt Store Marina communities were all developed by Punta Gorda Isles, Inc. beginning in the 1960s and 1970s.

Much of the west side of Burnt Store Road is protected as part of the Charlotte Harbor Preserve State Park and the Charlotte Harbor Environmental Center. There is, however, a significant amount of available land on the east side which suggests that there are likely to be many more residential communities developed over the next 100 years. The accompanying chart provides a list of the current Charlotte County Burnt Store Road communities.

Burnt Store Isles (PGI Sec. 15) at the north end of Burnt Store Road has about 1,400 homes. Burnt Store Marina (PGI Sec. 22) just south of Charlotte County is 99% built out with about 2,000 homes.

The trading house which came to be known as the Burnt Store was established in 1845 as the first commercial enterprise of the settlement era on the mainland section of Charlotte Harbor. It was located just below the current Charlotte—Lee county line.

For more information about the southern half of Charlotte County, the pre-1921 history of the area, and citations for the material included in this chapter, see the author's book titled *Where Do We Live?* It is available at local bookstores and online at www.wheredowelive.com.

Above, frolicking at the springs; below, a c. 1967 aerial of the springs. Harrell Family Collection

DESGUIN FAMILY ROOTS HERE GO BACK MORE THAN 100 YEARS

Frank Desguin

Did you know a picture is not only worth a thousand words, but can literally cause folks to move? Frank Rigell was born in September 1901 on the family farm near Slocomb, Alabama, a small town southwest of Dothan, just across the Florida state line. The youngest of seven, when he was about 2 years old, his Dad moved the family to town and opened a dry goods store, J. C. Rigell and Company. Frank grew up helping out at the store and in his late teens, pitched for a semi-pro team out of Sheffield in northwest Alabama near Muscle Shoals.

It wasn't uncommon in those days for just about every town to have a community supported ball team. It also wasn't uncommon for young men to earn a few extra dollars working during the season in Florida's citrus groves. When some of Frank's friends did just that, one of them sent him a picture post card with palm trees silhouetted against a magnificent Florida sunset. When his friends returned, Frank asked about the postcard, inquiring if what it depicted is real. When assured that it was, right then and there he decided Florida is where he wanted to be.

When asked if the postcard that really brought him to Florida might have been one of those showing a bathing beauty about to get her rear end bitten by an alligator, he just chuckled and said, "No, it was the sunset." With Florida on his mind, Frank, who didn't finish high school, enrolled in Dothan's business college, earning a diploma. He then took out an ad in Jacksonville's newspaper, The Florida Times-Union, seeking employment. After a brief stint at a lumber yard in Cairo, Georgia, his dream was fulfilled when, at 22 years old, he took a job in Haines City. From there, he was transferred as payroll clerk to a crate factory in Nocatee, just up the road from Punta Gorda.

Was this the postcard that launched a local dynasty? Above, Rosa Fred and Frank Rigell; Desguin collection.

When the timber was cut out, he went to Woodmere, a sawmill community between Englewood and Venice that no longer exists.

CENTURY

Punta Gorda Historic Mural Society

A section from the mural commemorating Rigell Lumber located on Taylor Road in Punta Gorda. During World War II, Rigell's two daughters, Peggy (later Mrs. Victor Desguin) and Jean, worked at the lumber yard while Frank was off to war.

He must have impressed his bosses because he was about to take a job in Lake Garfield, near Bartow, when asked to manage one of the company's lumber yards. Although nervous at the prospect, he took the offer, arriving in Punta Gorda during 1925 to run West Coast Lumber and Supply's (West Coast) yard on Taylor Road, close by the railroad tracks where Quality Self Storage is today.

Now, while in Nocatee, a pretty young school teacher, whose brothers-in-law also worked at the crate factory, had caught Frank's eye. Rosa Fred Reynolds, ("Freddie" to her friends) family had come to Nocatee in 1904, when she was just one year old, and was in the citrus business. They were from Newton, Alabama, a small town just northwest of Dothan, not 20 miles from Slocomb. He must have caught her eye too because they married in 1926, one year after she graduated from Florida State College for Women in Tallahassee. Freddie taught in Punta Gorda's elementary schools until her retirement in the early 1960s. They had two daughters, Peggy and Jean. Peggy would marry Vic Desguin in 1951.

During the Great Depression, West Coast was about to close its Punta Gorda yard when Frank persuaded them to let him purchase it. Thus, it became Rigell Lumber and Supply. The business was kept

A People's History of Charlotte County

Charlotte County History Services

Several of the men and women in this photo would guide the county's destiny well into the 90s,. At the 1940 buffet party for William T. Adair's 80th birthday party, (Adair was president of the World Syndicate Company and shareholder in the Punta Gorda Finance Company and also managed the Allapatchee Lodge in the 1930s), are, from left to right: Roscoe S. Maxwell, Helen Adair (hostess), Phil Adair, W.T. Adair (seated), Madie Mobley, G. William Quednau, Richard Adair, Mrs. R.S. (Mary) Maxwell, Elizabeth Nagy, John M. Cobden, Esther Jordan, Thelma King, Mrs. J.M. Cobden, Fred B. King, Dr. Vernon J. Jordan, Helen Wotitzky, Frank Wotitzky, Mrs. Frank Rigell, Leo Wotitzky, Frank Rigell, Sue Farr, and Louis V. Desguin.

alive by not only serving Punta Gorda and nearby areas, but by developing a clientele on islands in Pine Island Sound, particularly Sanibel and Captiva, locations the larger yards in Fort Myers were apparently not interested in. Rigell Lumber and Supply operated until the late 1950s when Frank sold the business to A. C. Frizzell, shortly after Frizzell sold the ranchland that would become Port Charlotte. He was asked back to liquidate the yard when Mr. Frizzell died a few years later.

Frank's later years were spent pursuing his two passions, golf and baseball. He also was an early president of the Punta Gorda Kiwanis Club and served on Punta Gorda's City Council in the early 1960s. Freddie passed away in 1966 and Frank remarried five years later, taking longtime family friend Lou Persons as his bride. He passed away in March 1999 and is interred at Charlotte Memorial Gardens, alongside Freddie.

CENTURY

Desguin Collection

The New Theater on Marion Avenue where Ace Hardware's parking lot is located.

Gertie and Louis Desguin

Louis Victor Desguin was born during the summer of 1898 in Cleveland, New York, on the north shore of Oneida Lake. Growing up in a French speaking household, he attempted to enlist as an interpreter when the United States entered World War I, but at 18, was too young. Instead he went to work in a munitions factory where he met a young lady from nearby Taberg, Gertrude Mullen. They married in 1918 and by 1926, when their son Louis Victor, Jr. (Vic) was born, the family was in Oneida, New York where Louis worked as a silverware die cutter for the Oneida Community.

When the Great Depression hit, Louis lost his job with Oneida and for the next several years made a living at different occupations, including a theatre manager in Canastota. Meanwhile, his brother-in-law, Fred, had established a chain of theatres in south central Florida from Mulberry to Sebring. Louis enjoyed his time in the theatre business so one day mentioned to Fred he'd be interested in a theatre his family could operate. In August 1936, Fred phoned and said he'd found one in Punta Gorda, Florida. Louis' response, "Where in the h--- is Punta Gorda, Florida?"

Needless to say, although employed with IBM at the time, Louis loaded up the family and with Vic's cousin Freddie in tow, headed to Florida. During a breakfast stop in the Carolinas, a bowl of grits was brought to the table and the kids asked for cream and sugar to put on their "cream of wheat," providing the waitress with her day's amusement.

Arriving in town September 9, 1936, Vic and Freddie were immediately placed under two-week quarantine before attending school. Dad claims it wasn't "just because we were Yankees," but I don't know about that. When finally allowed to enter school, they were a real hit in their knickers, coats, and ties.

The New Theatre, in the 200 block of West Marion Avenue where the Ace Hardware parking lot is today, operated until the early 1960s, with Gertie running the box office and the boys selling popcorn in the early days. One of the things folks remember about the Desguins is how they brought moving pictures to Punta Gorda's African-American community.

One can say Louis was just an entrepreneur, but it had never been done before and in a highly segregated time, when public buildings had separate drinking fountains, waiting rooms, and restrooms, noted "white" and "colored," if there even was one for black folks, it could have been risky.

A panel from Movie Memories, *a mural located at the Charlotte Harbor Event and Conference Center. At far right, a young Desguin is portrayed rushing the latest film to the black theater on Milus Street in Punta Gorda.*

Nonetheless, Louis rented a large wood frame building at the southwest corner of Milus Street and East Charlotte Avenue, installed wooden bleacher seats, and purchased a 35 mm projector. The cartoon and movie would start about 30 minutes after the feature began on Marion Avenue with Vic and Freddie shuttling reels and popcorn on their bikes. A mural on an outside wall in the Event Center parking lot depicts the theatre operation. I can recall boxing up popcorn and accompanying my granddad in the late 1950s.

After living in several rentals, they settled in a home at the southwest corner of West Olympia and Sullivan Street, now a vacant lot. During their years in Punta Gorda, Louis also served as president of the Kiwanis Club, as a city councilman during the early 1940s, and as mayor in 1944.

Vic married Peggy Rigell in 1951 and together they had five sons and a daughter. When Vic and Peggy moved across the river to a home on the bay in Charlotte Harbor, their folks were apprehensive since they'd be so far out of town.

In 1958, the family purchased the Charlotte Harbor Drive-In Theatre, on US41 where the Town and Country Shopping Center is now located. It closed in 1968.

Gertie and Louis passed away in 1976 and 1977 respectively. Peggy also passed away in 1977 and Vic married Charlotte Oglesby a few years later, adopting her son.

I once asked Dad, since he didn't move here until he was 10, why he considered Punta Gorda his hometown and this is what he said, "That first summer after we'd moved to Punta Gorda, I couldn't wait to get back to Oneida for a visit with my friends. We got there all excited and began telling everyone about Florida. Florida, they exclaimed! We thought you had just moved across town."

When the Desguins got back to Punta Gorda though, within a week, all their buddies were by the house to visit saying how much everyone had been missed. Vic looked at Gertie and said, "I don't care if I ever go back to New York."

Peggy and Vic Desguin

1930s

Top of page, Gov. Doyle Carlton, Barron Collier, Seminole visitors, and anyone able to squeeze into the picture gather for the ribbon-cutting of the second bridge over the Peace River to Punta Gorda. Above, A.C. Frizzell's company store, the Mercantile. The site later featured a DeSoto Groves fruit stand, which was demolished in the early 2000s to make way for an optometrist's office.

Charlotte County History Services, lower left photo Cheryl Frizzell.

TROUBLED WATERS

The people closest to the soil were the first to feel the Great Depression. Books such as John Steinbeck's "Grapes of Wrath" and images of beaten-down farm women illustrate how hard the blow fell on those least prepared. People in Charlotte County, many of whom were agriculturalists, suffered.

"They were hard times," recalled Chris Goff Maerski. "But they were good times too." She was born in 1925, too late for the incorporation parties but just in time to grow up during the worst economic tragedy to befall the United States, the Great Depression. She was born in Charlotte Harbor but spent her formative years in Murdock, where her family owed all they had to the company store.

Matter of fact, several of her siblings all worked at the store, which was owned by A.C. Frizzell, the same man who owned everything they could see for as far as they could see.

Goff Family

Christine Goff Maerski's big brother, Belford, on far left riding for A.C. Frizzell. With him are Corrie Guess, Rob Walker, Pat Johnson, and Charlie Slaughter.

By 1947 he owned 100,000 acres of county land and leased 100,000 more.[24] The Thirties was a decade of slow and steady accretion of wealth, as his thrift in the good times left him and his wife, Patti, with the money to grow. But he was not stingy. He had business enterprises throughout central Florida, and provided employment in tough times to friends and relatives. He also was one of the largest employers of black people. But even that contained contradictions. Frizzell made his first big foray into land speculation by leasing acres of land where turpentine tapping could be profitable. He then leased tapping rights to turpentine manufacturers, who'd set up taps in the woods to draw resin from trees.

His exploitation of human capital was also reflected in his ability to take what nature gave him and profit from the exchange. When the turpentine trees ran dry, Frizzell went into the lumber business, buying a portable sawmill and chewing through the woods with his crew. Then he realized there was a market in the pine tar that was captured in the trunks of the trees he and his crew had cut down. He dug up the stumps, had his men burn them down to release the tar, and thus made another nice bit of money off the land. Then, taking advantage of a government incentive program for land development, he turned the deforested land into cattle pastures.[25]

He exploited the land and as more farmers, landowners and others fell into bankruptcy, Frizzell was there to pick up the pieces in a manner similar to his acquisition of Joel Bean's failed development. As Cheryl Frizzell writes in "A.C. Frizzell: His Family, Life and Times":

1931

Florida Census: 1,468,211

Charlotte County population, 4,013

Barron Collier bridge completed across Charlotte Harbor to replace the narrow first bridge. Again, the event celebrated with a giant fish fry, including moonshine, whiskey, and beer ignored by police for the occasion.

1932

Macedonia Baptist Church organized in Punta Gorda The Rev Andrew J. Warren, the first pastor.

---

[24] Cheryl Frizzell, p. 7
[25] Cheryl Frizzell, p. 74-75

CENTURY

1933

John Foster Bass Jr. establishes a marine laboratory at New Point Comfort First full-time facility of its type in Florida

Charlotte County buys Chadwick Bridge and Beach, renames latter the Punta Gorda Beach

1934

Works Progress Administration builds new sea wall for Gilchrist Park

Charlotte County votes for homestead exemption of property taxes, and repeal of Prohibition

While doors were closing throughout the world, yet another door of opportunity was opening for Granddaddy and Granny. They had wisely invested their money in land, and Granny, because she did not trust banks, had stashed their cash in her mattress, according to family lore, rather than in one of the three banks in Punta Gorda that had sadly closed in 1929. It was during the Depression years, while the rest of the world was hungry, that Granddaddy and Granny built an empire. They built it by buying land for delinquent taxes that had not been paid for two years. On the outside steps of the new courthouse in Punta Gorda, Granddaddy bought thousands of acres for 20 to 30 cents each, including most of Joel Bean's 4,000 acres of land in El Jobean..[26]

Frizzell's success illustrated the invisible hand rule promulgated by economist Adam Smith—basically as a man grows wealthy, so does his community. No, few who worked for Frizzell grew wealthy. But they had roofs over their head—provided by Frizzell. They had medical care, also provided by Frizzell. They used scrip provided by Frizzell to buy food and goods at the Mercantile, a company store owned by Frizzell. But in the real world of the Great Depression, when wealth came down to a full belly and a roof that didn't leak, Frizzell made a lot of men and women rich.

Among them was the family of Chris Goff Maerski. She was the youngest of 10 children, (Marie, James, Elmer, Woodrow, Belford, Frank, Lonnie, Perry, and Charles were her siblings) eight boys and two girls. She remembers fondly Frizzell's wife, everyone called her Miss Patti, giving her family used clothing and blankets.

"They helped a lot of people during that time because everybody was in need of work and there just wasn't too many jobs around at the time," she recalled. Of the Frizzells, "The boys worked on the ranch and my sister worked in the store—it was a lucky thing for them to have a job."

Maerski's dad rented his farm from Frizzell in what was a semifeudal arrangement, more like sharecropping, and also rode the range when needed.

"Dad did a little farming and we didn't own the place but it was a seven-room

Goff Family

Top, James "Steely" Goff, Chris Goff Maerski's dad. Below, James Goff, his wife, Ellen Goff, and the first four of their children; James, Belford, Woodrow, and Elmer.

---

[26] Cheryl Frizzell, p. 84

house and barn, about 40 acres of land," she said. The family supplemented their diet by hunting and ninety years later, her mouth still waters when she recalls her favorite fowl.

"If it wasn't for hunting we would have gone hungry," she said. "All of my brothers loved to hunt—they loved quail and that quail was very tasty. Ahh, I can still taste it. My mom would fry them just like chicken and that was a real treat for us. You would find that on our table instead of turkey for Thanksgiving."

Charlotte County actually stocked the woods with quail back then, the game birds were so popular.[27]

Fishing was also popular, she said, recalling one particularly exciting occasion.

"There was always freshwater fish around Murdock in creeks and occasionally we'd get saltwater fish. One experience I had that I'll always remember—in 1940 Charlotte County had a big freeze—the whole county was under ice—the bay froze and of course it froze the fish. There were people picking fish up in Punta Gorda. If they couldn't eat them they sold them to the Punta Gorda fish house. That was an experience when the bay froze…it was a sight to see."

Upper right, Chris Goff Maerski about to enter high school. Above, Marie Goff, Christine Goff and Charlie Goff gather to reminisce.

January 1940 still ranks as the coldest month ever in Florida.[28] But winter always brought one thrill for Maerski as a young girl - hog-killing time.

"Daddy kept hogs and when the weather got cold, he'd slaughter one or two of them," she said. "The neighbors would come around and we'd all have fun."

Better yet was cane pressing time. Maerski's father also grew sugarcane and once a year he'd host a pressing. In those Depression years, any excuse for a cheap party was fine, so the neighbors would come, bonfires would be lit and, at least for one night, fun times would be had by all.

"We kids would climb up on top of the piles of crushed stalks and then slide down them," she said. "That was so much fun."

1935
Charlotte County starts mosquito control program

Harbor front from bridge to Nesbit Street reclaimed, filled in, used to create more parking for tin can tourists

1936
Tin Can Tourists convene national meeting in Punta Gorda as Royal Chief James Smith proclaims that Tin Can Tourists of the World is the premiere mobile home association

Punta Gorda officials look to recoup the investment made in filling waterfront area for the peripatetic community.

---

[27] Punta Gorda Herald 1-16-41
[28] http://flcitrusmutual.com/render.aspx?p=/industry-issues/weather/freeze_timeline.aspx

CENTURY

1937
Sallie Jones, one of the original 21 teachers assigned to Charlotte High School, appointed the first female superintendent of schools in the State of Florida, served 16 years as superintendent. Created the first school lunchrooms and set the standard that all teachers had to be professionally certified, retired in 1953 after 31 years as an educator

New municipal water plant built in Punta Gorda

1940s family album: Above, Ellen, Marie, and Chris Goff. Top right, Charles Goff making music and lower right, Chris having fun. (Goff family)

Food was in short supply, Maerski recalled, but there was always plenty of love and fun. At night her mom would teach the boys to dance while a brother would play the guitar. They'd do sing-alongs and get together with other neighbors for square dancing. They laughed in the face of what, years later, still ranks as one of the greatest economic catastrophes to scar the United States.

At the midpoint of the hungry decade, a federal survey painted this picture of the county in 1936.

> *Although Charlotte County still has a large undeveloped backcountry, the growing importance of agriculture is indicated by the fact that the number of farms in the county increased from 93 in 1930 to 145 in 1935, while the average size of farms increased during the same period from 83.1 acres to 546.8 acres. This period was one during which the value of farm lands and buildings in most counties of the State was materially deflated, yet their value in Charlotte County increased from $874,070 to $1,114,475.... Stock raising was the principal industry of old DeSoto County and is growing in importance in Charlotte County, where 71,123 acres were in pasture in 1935 as compared with 3,065 acres in 1930. During those years the number of cattle in the county increased from 873 to 4,205...* [29]

The period described in the report coincides with Frizzell's ongoing acquisition of land and his transformation of timbered-out acreage into cattle land. Frizzzell had gotten a government grant for developing agricultural lands, which was an added incentive for him to create pasturage.[30]

---

[29] "Brief History of Charlotte County", *Florida Works Progress Administration's Historical Records Survey*, 1936
[30] Cheryl Frizzell

A People's History of Charlotte County

https://www.vintagetrailercamp.com/gallery/Trailer-Parks-and-Camps/pctp247a

In 1990 Punta Gorda demolished the Municipal Tourist Camp to make way for riverfront development as part of a master plan to remake the city and spark tourism. City crews moved many of the survivors to Buttonwood Village, south of the waterfront near Aqui Esta Boulevard. But in the Thirties and beyond, the city welcomed the tin can tourists. This postcard illustrates the rough and homey camp with the popular community center in the upper right. Below, the national Tin Can Tourist convention was front page news in 1936. PGH 1-23-36

1938

Zora Neale Hurston began working for the Florida division of the Work Projects Administration (WPA).
At the time, Hurston had already published *Jonah's Gourd Vine* and *Mules and Men*

1939

Municipal fish dock burns, three lives lost, only Punta Gorda Fish Company reopens

State Highway Patrol launched

Germany invades Poland, France and England declare war on Germany, World War begins.

It also speaks to the work of N.H. "Doc" McQueen, the area's first state agricultural extension agent, who helped agriculturalists find new ways to use what they had and improve stock.

By the mid-Thirties the county was looking for any source of revenue. One sure draw, then as now, was the climate. The Punta Gorda Chamber and city government set out to capitalize on the new bridge, which in itself was built to drive traffic to town. Their goal? Just as Punta Gorda had been the southernmost terminus of the North American rail system, why not make Punta Gorda the end of the line for the burgeoning legions of tin can tourists?

Hard times and wanderlust had helped create a new phenomenom, the traveling tourist who brought with him his own home. Suddenly vacation spots like Punta Gorda were within the means of anyone with a car and a contrivance that could be legally dragged behind as a temporary home.

CENTURY

1940

Population is 3,663, a −8.7 percent drop off since 1930

Banana River Naval Air Station opened; later would become Cape Canaveral Space Center

The Selective Training and Service Act of 1940, the first peacetime draft in American history, became law

Franklin D. Roosevelt becomes the United States' first third-term president

"I'll Never Smile Again" by Tommy Dorsey was the number one song in the nation

Punta Gorda was first billed as a resort for the wealthy. Now, anyone with a car and something that could pass inspection could bring their home with them to winter in Florida.

The tin can tourists were a new breed and antecedents of today's snowbirds. By 1934 they were such a lucrative and essential part of a city economy wracked by the Great Depression, that the city moved, for the third straight year, to add improvements to the facility. The city also took over operation of the community center located on the grounds of the trailer camp.[31] The center soon became a popular hang-out place. Paul Frizzell, heir to the A. C., Frizzell fortune, met his future wife at a dance there.[32] As other communities lost their way, Punta Gorda went with the traffic flow and recreated itself.

Above, the Lemon Bay Woman's Club building (Wikipedia). Below, L.A. Ainger and his wife at the site of their store and home (Charlotte County History Services).

At the other end of the populated crescent of Charlotte County, Englewood's position on the cusp of two counties did it no favors. Both Charlotte and Sarasota governments had their own issues as the Depression worsened, leaving the community to fend for itself. One of the groups that filled the vacuum was the Lemon Bay Woman's Club. As one historian writes:

During the Great Depression the Lemon Bay Woman's Club's continued support of civic and social functions became all the more important. There was a concerted effort on the part of the community to maintain as much of the quality of life of the past decade as was possible. The clubhouse, being the only public building, became the center for the civic and social lives of the residents of Englewood.[33]

But even as Englewood waned, a future community leader's star was waxing. L.A. Ainger's parents had set up a small store on the main road in Englewood. It would serve as a meeting place and gathering point for local residents, giving the younger Ainger an appreciation for politics and people that would serve Englewood well in the years to come.

---

[31] PGH 8-24-34
[32] Frizzell, p. 146
[33] https://www.eahmuseum.org/history-corner

CHARLOTTE COUNTY EXTENSION: OUR TRADITION, OUR MISSION

Ralph E. Mitchell

N.H. "Doc" McQueen

In 1935 Mr. N.H. "Doc" McQueen started his first day of work on the second floor of the Punta Gorda Courthouse as the first University of Florida Extension Agent in Charlotte County. He was the only non-elected county official there for 31 years until his retirement in 1966. Other than a short stint working in Gainesville with the University of Florida's 4-H Division from 1941 to 1942, McQueen's time in the field as an extension agent was spent in Charlotte County.

Extension agents bring research information from the university and its research stations to the public. Delivery of this knowledge is conducted by one-on-one consultations, group programming, hands-on demonstrations, field trials, site visits, tours, and written materials.

Of the many activities that Mr. McQueen was responsible for, 4-H provided an opportunity for him to work with youth. He would drive a bus of 4-H-ers up to Camp McRoy (now Camp Ocala) in the Ocala National Forest each summer for a week of camping. This was the only 4-H Camp available until the development of Camp Cloverleaf. McQueen led the efforts that established 4-H Camp Cloverleaf in the early 1950s on Lake Placid. Charlotte County 4-H members still camp at Camp Cloverleaf.

CENTURY

> **UF/IFAS CHARLOTTE COUNTY EXTENSION SERVICE PROGRAMS**
>
> **4-H:** Offers life skills from public speaking to citizenship within projects such as animal science, family and consumer science and workforce preparation as standard educational experiences. Youth from five to eighteen, as well as adult leaders, enjoy learning new skills by doing them.
>
> **Sea Grant:** Conducts research, education and outreach to use and conserve coastal and marine resources for a sustainable economy and environment. Programs facilitated by Sea Grant in Charlotte County include commercial and recreational fisheries, the popular Master Naturalist Program, boating and waterways issues, and marine ecology education within both adult and youth audiences. Recent programs with exceptional impact have included work on mangrove restoration, redfish monitoring, crab trap clean-ups and scallop monitoring.
>
> **Horticulture:** Another word for gardening. In fact, horticulture can mean home gardening, urban forestry, Florida Yards and Neighborhoods, the Master Gardener program, safe pesticide use, and Commercial Horticultural topics. Our Horticulture Department conducts popular programs such as the Master Gardener Program. Educational group programs for homeowners include plant selection, common sense pest management and care of Florida Friendly yards. Within the well-known Florida Yards and Neighborhoods Program, water conservation is high on our agenda with outreach efforts such as the rain barrel program. Commercial horticultural interests are also addressed with regular green industries-best management practices training, pesticide applicator training and recertification, plant pest and disease diagnostic services and soil testing.

McQueen's work with agriculture was extensive. Working closely with the Florida Cattlemen's Association, he was recognized as an innovator in this sector of agriculture. In 1974 he was awarded the recognition of "Pioneer in the Florida Cattle Industry." His work benefited the local cattle industry by introducing new grasses and demonstrating various improved pasture management techniques as well as promoting new cattle varieties for crossbreeding. The closest veterinarian was in Desoto County, so McQueen was also involved in animal health programs that routinely had him vaccinating hogs and other livestock.

Being the only agricultural extension agent for some time meant that he had to wear many different hats. In addition to livestock management, McQueen also worked with the local citrus industry and facilitated its expansion in the county. The vegetable industry was also important to the local economy of Charlotte County. McQueen worked with large vegetable growers that had packing houses near the railroad depot in Punta Gorda.

Additionally, he assisted the tropical fruit jelly and juice processors in the area and advised local guava growers, who had extensive plantings that once dotted Charlotte County. These guava growers produced fruit processed by three large jelly and juice plants in the area.

During his tenure as the agriculture agent, McQueen also worked with the large gladiolus, cut flower, and chrysanthemum industries in Charlotte County. He collaborated with former U. S. Vice President Henry Wallace, an innovative agriculturalist, in acquiring research in gladiolus pollination and hybridization benefiting the Gladiolus Growers Association. McQueen's efforts with large nurseries growing ornamental plants for shipping throughout the country were also a success story.

McQueen's legacy laid a foundation for the future Cooperative Extension Service that our community benefits from today. Some 75 years later, the Charlotte County Extension Service continues to play an important role in the education of Charlotte County citizens by providing University of Florida Institute of Food and Agricultural Science fact-based information concerning agriculture, horticulture, 4-H youth development and sea grant programming.

A People's History of Charlotte County

MARY NIGHTINGALE
Diana Harris

Mary Nightingale. Photo taken in the late 1930s near the McCall building used for church services for the black community. It was located in back of where Pelican Pete's once stood on SR776. Below, her husband, Abe, the original horse whisperer. (all photos Diana Harris)

I became friends with Mary Nightingale when she was 80 years old. I wish I had met her sooner to have had the chance to have known her better. She was a tall, handsome woman, with an unlined face, a quick wit, and a wonderful outlook on life.

Mary was a very intelligent, very remarkable lady who had never let the unequal decades of segregation get her down. "Those were unfair times. Segregation was wrong and it was stupid," Mary told me, "But we had to get through it."

She had had to work hard all of her life and she was proud of it. At the age of six, her parents passed away. She was sent to Plant City, Florida to live with her older brother and his family.

By the time she was sixteen, Mary recalled, "I was going to work in the daytime picking strawberries, then I would go to the boss man's house and cook and clean up their house - did the same thing every day of the week - except we didn't pick strawberries on Sunday. Then when I would go home I would cook the late meal, which we always called supper, for my brother's family, and then I would go to bed.

"I guess I was pretty lonely—all the people I had to talk to were my brother's children as I cooked supper.

"I was never a bad girl. What I mean is, go out at night, go to dances or smoke and all kinds of things. I had a very good reputation. That's why, I guess, some people told Abe about me, my future husband. I think he was looking for the kind of wife that people had told him I would be. He had never seen me.

"I guess it was love at first sight for him when he did meet me. I don't honestly remember telling him I would marry him, but two weeks after we met, we were married. I was sixteen, he was twenty-three, and it was 1931."

It turned out to be a real love match for Mary and Abe. "When we had been married fifty years," Mary said, "Abe told me he wanted to get married again.

"After we married, we lived in Arcadia before we came to McCall. Abe worked in the groves. He knew about citrus trees. In 1932 we paid $1.25 a week on a 1928 car until we paid for it. Then in 1933 or '34 we traded up to a 1931. I seem to remember gas wasn't but 20 cents a gallon in those days.

"And then, my husband was out of a job in Arcadia. You know, back in those times it was awful hard to get a job, especially for a black man. But Abe was a real citrus expert. He heard about the grove they were putting in at McCall. We came to McCall in 1935. We stayed out there in the grove in a trailer when we first came here.

"You know where the big curve is on SR776 after you have passed the Pik & Run (now SuperDay) going toward Port Charlotte? Then, there wasn't any curve or even a road. That curve was where the first grove was. Then later it went down towards Placida on what is now SR771. I don't know for sure, but I think the whole grove finally went up to 200 acres or more. It was a real big grove.

"In the later part of 1935 there was a real storm. Blew away our tent top we had over the trailer, and all my clothes were scattered all over the grove. We had a fireplace set up under that tent top to cook on, and after the storm I was standing in water almost up to my knees when I was cooking. That's how much water there was after the storm.

"That's when we moved over to McCall - there used to be a little house on Sailors Way that used to be the post office."

Charlotte County History Services

Above, one of the endless series of phosphate hoppers that wound through McCall from central Florida to Boca Grande. Below, the route of the Charlotte Harbor and northern railroad through Charlotte County.

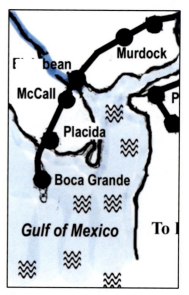

McCall was a small but active community which had originally sprung up because of the CH &N Railroad having built a two-story railroad depot there. Its location is best described as the intersection of SR776 and SR771.

When the Nightingales moved to McCall in 1935 there were about 50 people living there. Most residents, both black and white, worked for the railroad. Some of the black men worked as cowhands for Mr. A. C. Frizzell.

"Sometimes in those days the freight trains would come through McCall twice a day," she recalled. "And I was here when there were passenger trains and you didn't have to pay but a dime to ride over to Boca Grande. Of course, there wasn't any road going over there then, you had to go on the ferry or the train. I remember when the passenger trains came through McCall going to Boca Grande they would pull all the curtains on the train before they got here so the passengers wouldn't have to see the black people living beside the tracks.

"We went to Boca Grande a lot because we had church there. The white folks had a church here in McCall but we didn't. You know the white people and the colored people didn't mix then so we had our own church. It was just a little shed with a top over it. You know my husband was a minister—the House of God Church. But he wasn't one of those high-hat ones. He tried to help everyone; it didn't make any difference if you were white or black if you needed help. Anything he could do to tell you the right thing, or do the right thing for you, he was ready.

"Blacks and whites weren't real friendly, but I guess you could say they accepted each other.

"Back in those times you didn't walk up and talk to white people very much 'cause, oh boy, that could have been terrible.

"We were the only blacks living on the white side of the tracks. Once we had a problem about that. Some white men threatened to run us out, even kill us, but a friend of ours, a white gentleman, George Whidden, told them if anything happened to the Nightingales they would answer to him; he would turn 'em in to the police. That was in the 1940s.

"I decided I would raise some cows. I drove up to Tampa to buy 'em, $2 apiece, a day or two old. They had to be kept warm, so I put 'em—one at a time—in the trunk of the car. I would leave it open just enough to give the calf air. I would sell 'em in Arcadia at the auction for maybe $60 when they were yearlings.

Diana Harris

A.C. Frizzell ended up giving Nightingale this purebred champion Brahman bull. His name was Emperor Manso the 24th.

"I did all the work with the cows, but I never could kill anything. Abe would slaughter them. Sometimes, I would take the whole beef to the Ainger Store in Englewood. This was before meat inspection days. I would line the truck bed with green palmetto fronds before I put the beef in to keep it clean.

"At one time I had fifty to sixty cows. We had open ranges then. Everybody branded their cattle, mine was A.N., then just turned them loose to let them graze wherever they wanted. 'Course, my cows I had hand-fed since they were babies with bottles, so at 5 p.m. every afternoon they would all come home.

"I did have a couple of problems. Once I bought twenty Santa Gertrudis calves. Mr. Keene, the foreman of the Vanderbilt Ranch, rounded them up and took 'em back there on the ranch. He knew they weren't his. I got 'em back.

"Another time I bought a very special bull—not pure Brahman, a cross. He was very expensive. A.C. Frizzell, the big rancher, had a lot of purebred Brahman cattle around here. I guess he didn't want my bull getting to his cows, so he castrated him. Mr. Frizzell finally knew he had done something wrong, that he had gone too far. He ended up giving me one of his prize champion Brahman bulls plus $200.

"When the open-range policy went out, then I leased pasture land for my cattle. After my husband passed away, I finally sold my cattle. But I sure did love my cows."

SALLIE JONES TAKES OVER

Frank Desguin

Around 1900, Charles Jones was city marshal of Bartow, Florida, when malaria took his life at age 38. His widow, Josie, then moved to Punta Gorda with their four children to be near her brother, prominent rancher W. Luther Koon. Her only daughter, Sallie, was 5 when the family arrived.

The first school Sallie attended, at 215 Goldstein St., still stands and is now the Old School House apartments. When that building became overcrowded, a new school was built in 1911 on Taylor Street between West Charlotte Avenue and King Street (US41 north), where she completed her secondary education. That school burned in the mid 1950s, and the triangular site is now the location of medical offices. During her senior year, a roadshow came to town and as a promotion, a popularity contest for young ladies was held. Although voting was reportedly close, Sallie Jones was declared winner.

Charlotte County Public Schools

Sallie Jones Elementary School; Sallie Jones.

After graduating, "Miss Sallie," as she came to be known, attended Florida's six-week training course and was certified to teach primary grades. She began her teaching career to the south on Chokoloskee Island, moving north to Pine Island before returning home to teach in the primary grades at her alma mater.

Always intent on obtaining a college degree, Miss Sallie began attending Florida Southern College in Lakeland during the summers. Upon graduation, around 1929, she began teaching at the high school level. Some say, during her time at Florida Southern, she met and became engaged to a fellow student who was tragically killed in an automobile accident, so Miss Sallie never married.

A popular and well-respected educator, Sallie Jones became Charlotte County's elected school superintendent in 1938, the first woman in Florida history to hold that distinction. Her office was in the historic courthouse on Taylor Street and she had one administrative employee, a secretary.

Miss Sallie instituted a policy that all teachers be professionally qualified in their field of instruction and introduced the first lunchroom programs. She retired the end of 1953 and the county's new elementary school, completed for the 1957-58 school year across from Charlotte High, was named in her honor. Sallie Jones Elementary, expanded over the years, was replaced with a new two-story building in 2003.

Miss Sallie passed away in October 1960 after a long illness and is interred at Indian Springs Cemetery. There is also a small monument located on a vacant West Helen Avenue lot dedicated to her memory.

STUART ANDERSON, AN ENGLEWOOD HERO
Diana Harris

There was unbelievable excitement afoot in the little town of Englewood in the early 1920s. Seemed like the whole outside world wanted a piece of sunshiny Florida. The selling of the state was underway. People were buying, trading or selling land as fast as they could. In just a few months of 1925, real estate transactions, locally, amounted to $1.3 million and it was predicted that was just the beginning of an era

A People's History of Charlotte County

Diana Harris Collection

Stuart Anderson's Lemon Bay Fisheries was located at the end of Wentworth Avenue and stayed in business until the late 1960s.

where everyone was going to get wealthy. But suddenly the frenzy of the early 1920s came to a screeching halt. The real estate land boom ended in 1928, the stock market crashed in 1929 and Englewood, along with many other towns in Florida, was left, literally, penniless. So were all those "Paper Millionaires," a popular term that was coined after the crash.

In 1925 Englewood voted to incorporate itself. But suddenly it became obvious the requirements, such as providing municipal services to the town, could not be provided. The cash flow into town had ceased abruptly. It was said at the time the only real money coming into town each month was a total of $59, which came from three retirees who received pensions. Another vote was taken to dissolve the incorporation and in 1929 it became final. The Depression hit Englewood with all its force, things looked more than dismal. All the grandiose plans that had been generated by the land boom had gone up in smoke. The town was faced, along with other problems, with the basic, harsh reality of feeding itself.

At this point in time, Stuart Anderson emerges into the foreground of Englewood history. In this day and age he probably would be compared to a caped crusader.

Stuart had previously worked on his family's farm and was at one time a deputy sheriff. Dr. Oscar Anderson, Stuart's brother, said by the late 1920s Stuart had gone into the seafood business.

"He was of sound judgement and a clear thinker with his feet on the ground," was how Dr. Anderson described him, just the kind of a leader Englewood needed at that moment.

Anderson brought the local fishermen together. He presented them with an idea of using the old barter system to get some business activity going in town.

Since he was highly respected and liked they listened to him and were very receptive of his idea. He suggested they round up all usable vehicles in town that were sitting unused anyway because no one could afford gas. They would load them with ice and pack them full of their fish catches. The fishermen would haul the fish up through the state to North Florida, the idea being to sell their fish along the way for cash, if at all possible, but if not for cash, barter for anything they thought was useful.

The fishermen liked the idea, they put it into motion quickly and were thrilled with its immediate success. They hauled their fish as far as away as Georgia and would return with small livestock, meats, vegetables, eggs, syrup. They proceeded to help feed the town.

Stuart Anderson was hailed as a hero for his savvy idea. Many people later would say he saved the town. If not for Anderson's dedication many would have fled the area leaving the town half deserted.

Eventually Stuart built his business, the Lemon Bay Fisheries, into one of the largest and most productive fisheries on the west coast of Florida. At the height of business it produced more than one million pounds of fish yearly.

All photos Bernie Reading

THE DAY THE CHICKENS TOOK A LICKING: STORIES OF A DEPRESSION-ERA CHILDHOOD

Bernie Reading

Mom and dad with the boat and truck at our Englewood Beach campsite around 1939.

My dad was a carpenter during the Great Depression of the 1930s. In those days work was very scarce no matter how good you were. So we spent a lot of time traveling to other parts of Florida and the South just to survive. Our home base was Englewood and my dad loved to fish, so when there were no jobs available he fished, Mom gardened and raised chickens, and I filled in the food supply by harvesting clams and oysters. We managed to live pretty well until Dad would get a letter from some friend in the construction business offering a few months of work. Then we would pack up and hit the road.

We had developed, through trial and error, a fairly efficient traveling rig. We had an eighteen-foot wood boat with a small half cabin up forward with a one-cylinder Kermath engine. The boat was on a trailer that Dad had built. We loaded all our house-keeping gear in the boat, covered it over with a tarp and tied it all down. Mom refused to leave her chickens behind so they were put into a poultry carrying crate and roped down on top. I know that this arrangement may seem a bit strange. But in those days we were concerned with just doing whatever worked and this did.

We would leave at dawn and drive all day, stopping only briefly for lunch and gas. The chickens didn't appear to mind this mode of transportation and they would lay eggs in the straw in the bottom of the crate which we would collect up at the end of the day.

One day in 1937 Dad had just finished up on a construction job near Orlando. We had set up camp with some friends who visited us every winter from up north, Al Maurice and his wife Matt. Al loved to

A People's History of Charlotte County

My dad, my friend Jerry Smith and me with the big hat.

fish almost as much as my dad and they made good use of our boat in some of the large freshwater lakes in that area. Al's wife Matt wasn't interested in fishing but she and my mother were buddies and they both were very fond of the chickens.

After a few days, my folks and their friends decided to head back to Englewood and settle down there for the rest of the winter. I rode in the car with Al and his wife.

In late afternoon we made the turn off US41 and on to a narrow bumpy road that is now SR776.

We passed through some scattered frame buildings that marked El Jobean and just before we got to the bridge over the Myakka River, which at that time was a rickety wooden structure, we saw the boat and trailer separate from my dad's pick-up truck. It slowly coasted off the road, hesitated on the edge of the steep ditch, rolled upside down and came to rest with the wheels still slowly turning in the air.

"Ohmigod, the boat!" Al shouted.

"Oh god, the chickens!" Matt screamed.

I had seen so many unusual things in my life up to that point that I was rather calm about the whole thing. I do remember thinking that we would be in for a lot of work getting the mess put back together.

I felt sorry about the chickens because I was not allowed to have any pets at that age so I usually had no one to talk to but the chickens. I thought of them as pets. I would go stand by the chicken pen after I came home from school and talk to some of my favorites. This disturbed my dad, one day I heard him say to my mother, "Ellen, tell that boy to quit talking to those chickens, anybody hears him doing that they'll think he's a little off." Mom never said anything, so I just assumed that it probably wasn't that bad.

Anyway, the cage was broken up and we lost one chicken and five eggs in the mishap. Dad managed to find a friendly soul with a large truck and some log chains. Some onlookers offered to help us and we soon got the trailer back on the road and chained to the truck so we could work our way on to Englewood.

* * *

Englewood back in the 1930s was like living in another world. My family traveled a lot to follow construction, my dad's line of employment, but we always had Englewood as our home port.

The first few years here we lived in a tourist and camping area over on the beach called Chadwick Trailer Park. The Chadwick family developed the area as a tourist attraction during the Twenties and Thirties. They built the first bridge across Lemon Bay in the Twenties and it was a toll bridge until the county made a deal and took it over.

CENTURY

The Chadwicks built a two-story beach pavilion for the use of campers and tourists. The pavilion was located where the Captain's Club is now. It provided showers and changing rooms on the ground floor. On the second floor they offered groceries, a place to hold dances, refreshments, weekly bingo sessions in season, and even a small lending library with magazines to trade.

Like most people on the beach we did not have a telephone. It was my job to walk over to the post office and check for mail in case some friend would write to my dad with a job opening in some other part of the state. The post office was located in the Englewood Hardware building on Dearborn Street. That building is still there.

It was a long walk, but I was raised to believe that everyone in the family had their jobs to do and that happened to be one of mine. When going over the old wooden bridge across Lemon Bay I would take my time and enjoy the view. Even at high tide a person could see all the way to the bottom. The water was as clear as glass, and I would lean over the rail and watch the schools of mullet and other fish swim under the bridge.

Sometimes I would hitch a ride, but cars were very few, especially in the summer. I can recall walking that whole distance and being passed by only two or three cars; and some of them were going the wrong way.

At some point in the 1930s all of what was called Chadwick Beach was sold to a gentleman by the name of Lou Woods. Lou had traveled with the Royal American Carnival, America's biggest, for many years and owned the big food concessions on the midway. Lou and his wife, Anna were very careful with money and had become quite wealthy.

Back in those days a lot of carnival people came down for the winter and stayed until time to go back on the carnival circuit in the spring. One of the first times we came to Englewood after moving down from Tampa it was winter. The trailer park was almost full of carnival folks. I got out of the car and no more than 20 feet away was a huge man exercising with weights that looked like they weighed a ton. Just a few feet away from him was the fattest woman I had ever seen. She was laughing and talking with another woman who was wearing a bathing suit. Every visible inch of her body was covered with tattoos.

I stood and gaped in complete amazement until my mother took me by the shoulders and turned me around.

Nine years old - life really was a beach. Lou Woods with a friend.

"Bernard, it is impolite to stare, don't do that," she said firmly. I followed her reluctantly and started helping my folks set up camp.

During the winter I got to know quite a few of the carnies. They were kind, friendly folks and interesting to talk to. At one point I told my mother that I would like to travel and work with the carnival. She said, "Bernard, you have a long time to think about that, and you may decide later on to do something else." My mother was very diplomatic.

A People's History of Charlotte County

* * *

I started riding a bicycle when I was a little over 10 years old and I liked being able to get around on my own. I took some very long rides just for the fun of it. I rode to Placida and back many times just to satisfy my urge to ride. I would start out from wherever we were living in Englewood and ride up the Old Englewood Road to Route 41 and back. I also rode to El Jobean to fish off the old wooden bridge.

But this story is about a very long ride I made to see a dentist. I had a lot of tooth problems as a kid; and this time I had a tooth that needed to be filled. It was giving me a lot of trouble. My dad was working out of town so I had no ride to the nearest dentist, a Doctor Porter who had an office in Punta Gorda.

13 years old.

I had a friend whose father made runs to Punta Gorda to sell clams he harvested in Lemon Bay. I got my friend to ask his father if I could ride down on his next trip because I needed to go to a dentist. His father said O.K., he was going down on a Tuesday and I could ride along. He said he would drop me off at the dentist and pick me up on the way back to Englewood.

My mother liked this idea. She had talked to someone who had work done by this dentist and she figured what I needed done wouldn't run any more than four or five dollars. She wadded up five one-dollar bills in a bandana and made me stuff it way down in my pocket. Then I started the ride to my friend's house. When I got there I saw some legs sticking out from under their little old truck and as I got closer I heard some very spirited cursing. As I watched, my friend's father crawled out from under the truck and wiped the grease off his hands.

"I'm sorry about the ride, son," he said. "I don't know when I will get this damn truck fixed, but it's not going anywhere today."

I turned my bike around and walked it back out to the road. I stood there trying to figure out what to do. That tooth was giving me a fit. All I could think was that relief from this pain was about 25 miles away in Punta Gorda.

I decided to go for it, jumped on my bike and took off down the road. It was a little after 8 o'clock and I figured I could make it by noon. The only stop I made was to get a drink of water at the old Murdock gas and grocery store.

I got to Punta Gorda about an hour after that. I found the dentist's office. He was busy so I sat down and waited, glad for the rest. When that patient left he asked me to come and sit down in the dentist's chair. He found the problem and filled the tooth.

"Did your mother bring you in son?" he asked. "Is she going to pick you up?"

I said no, I had ridden there on my bike.

"Where did you come from?"

I told him and he raised his eyebrows with surprise.

I pulled those five one-dollar bills out of my bandana and asked him how much I owed him. He stared at me and said, "Son, how old are you?"

I told him I was 12 going on 13. I offered him the money and he pushed it back to me.

"You take that money back home. After what you did to get here I think you deserve a free one."

I thanked him, went out, got my bike and rode back home. I got there in the late afternoon. I gave Mom back the money and told her he didn't charge me because I had told him my mother was a nurse.

One day, when I was a lot older, I finally told my mother about that long ride.

Historic Punta Gorda Army Air Field/Punta Gorda Historic Mural Society

1940s

PERIL AND PROSPERITY

After years of struggle, Charlotte County and the rest of the nation faced a shooting war. The misery of the conflict, erupting first in the far East and then ignited by irredentism and revenge in Europe, would set off a boom in Charlotte County. The clouds of war carried with them a silver lining. The impact of World War II was felt in ways that were new, dangerous, different, exciting, and profitable to county residents.

As Europe and Asia appeared headed to war, President Franklin Roosevelt and Congress took the prescient step of creating a nationwide aviation program.

The CPTP planned to train 20,000 civilian pilots a year because this would create a pool of potential military pilots that he believed the country would need soon.[34]

Air bases for training were in short supply, which soon led the Army (the air forces then was part of the Army) to search for sites. Arcadia once billed itself as the "Aviation City of Florida" because of two Army Air Corps bases established there during World War I.[35] Those bases, plus a third, to be located in Punta Gorda, would comprise the Army's

Joyce Hindman, a nephew of A.C. Frizzell and a future mayor of Punta Gorda, was first to the colors.

---

[34] https://www.nationalmuseum.af.mil/Visit/Museum-Exhibits/Fact-Sheets/Search/CPTP/
[35] *The Arcadian*, Nov 8, 2018

training programs in the area. English pilots were trained in Arcadia; Army Air Corps cadets trained at the Punta Gorda airfield, which would become the Punta Gorda Airport.

The greatest wartime threat to the city occurred when a bad change in wind direction wafted a cloud of poison gas over Punta Gorda. It turned out that a gas attack drill, in which all the affected personnel on the air base had gas masks, went awry when the wind shifted. Army officials promised that it would not happen again.[36]

According to Aviation Archaeological Investigation & Research, 135 accidents were reported in Punta Gorda associated with the flying training and airfield operations. The lives of six pilots were lost in training-related accidents.[37]

Beyond the hazards of high-speed aviation training, the greatest danger faced by the cadets themselves, along with staff and crews, was the 1944 Cuba–Florida hurricane. The year of 1944 was a treacherous one for storms, having already spawned the Great Atlantic Hurricane a month earlier. As the Cuba-Florida Hurricane bore down on Charlotte County, cadets were sheltered at the Hotel Charlotte Harbor.

Almost 80 years later, Aaron "Jim" Marshall still remembers the fury of the storm.

"My dad and Mr. Burdett (a neighbor) were standing in the doorway looking out, and I guess they could see what was happening out there, and I was holding my dad's hand, and I just heard him say, 'Well, there goes the church,'" Marshall said. That was doubly bad because Marshall's dad was the pastor.

"A moment later he said, 'I can see the piano.'"

Marshall and his family lived in a Florida-style wood frame house.

"There was a house next door to us that I believe was a cement block house, so when the hurricane was coming my dad took us next door," he said. "The couple that lived there retired from up north, Mr. and Mrs. Burdett was their name, and we went next door to their house because they were concerned that the house we were in may not stand. It did."

Jim Marshall

Jim Marshall. Below, impact of the 1944 Cuba-Florida hurricane.

Wikipedia

1941

Japanese attack Pearl Harbor, U.S. declares war against Japan and Germany

Military draft of men begins, Joyce Hindman, later mayor of Punta Gorda, is first inducted from Florida

During his State of the Union address, President of the United States Franklin D. Roosevelt presents his Four Freedoms, as fundamental global human rights.

The keel of the USS Missouri is laid at the New York Navy Yard in Brooklyn.

Meat and gasoline rationed to conserve for war effort

---

[36] Shively, Scot, Punta Gorda Army Air Field (PG AAF) Fact Sheet and Timeline
[37] https://www.charlottecountyfl.gov/core/fileparse.php/397/urlt/PGAAF-Interactive-Web.pdf

CENTURY

Jim Marshall

Fred Babcock assembles 63,000 acres for Babcock-Webb Wildlife Management Area in east Charlotte County

In a BBC radio broadcast from London, Victor de Laveleye asks all Belgians to use the letter "V" as a rallying sign, being the first letter of victoire (victory) in French and of vrijheid (freedom) in Dutch. This is the beginning of the "V campaign" which sees "V" graffities on the walls of Belgium and later all of Europe and introduces the use of the "V sign" for victory and freedom. Winston Churchill adopts the sign soon afterwards.

Parishioners of Souls Harbor Church of God in 1946 outside their rebuilt church.

But the church was lost. Marshall said his father, however, was not only a minister but also a skilled carpenter. He and a team of parishioners soon rebuilt Souls Harbor Church of God.

"It probably took them close to a year to build it because it was all done by hand," Marshall said. "There was a lumber yard in Punta Gorda that I recall furnished the material to build it."

Marshall came to Charlotte County from Manatee County, where he was born, when he was six months old.

His father was sent to Punta Gorda by his Pentecostal denomination.

"I started school in Punta Gorda, first grade, and went there first, second and third grade," Marshall recalled. "My third-grade teacher would occasionally give me a quarter and send me down the street to the Lawhorne's Grocery store to buy her a little packet of cream cheese and that's what she'd have for lunch. But it was kind of funny. I looked forward to that because I got out of school for a few minutes."

Aratha Jones also remembers the Cuba-Florida hurricane of 1944. She and Marshall became friends back then and are both still active members of their church. Recently they had lead roles in celebrating Souls Harbor's centennial. They grew up in what was known as the Five Corners section of Punta Gorda, roughly between the Smokehouse Restaurant along Cooper Street to Marion Avenue west and Charlotte High School on McKenzie St.

Jones still remembers the thrill of meeting the student pilots during the war.

"I remember my mom getting up early on Sunday morning and cooking a big dinner," she recalled, "and the soldiers who came to church would come to dinner and visit with the family."

Jones, who was born in 1937, came of age during the war. Her family, like many that suffered through the Great Depression, saw unparalled prosperity during the war years—and accomplished this by doing their part for the war effort. For example, fishermen were exempt from service because they harvested food. And did they ever. County fishermen, mostly from Englewood, shipped out more than 2 million pounds of seafood annually during the war years.[38]

Diana Harris, in "Englewood Lives," writes of fishermen acquiring luxury yachts made moot by war and cruising in style while catching their quota. The boats soon proved impractical but they were pretty.[39]

In Punta Gorda, Aratha Jones' dad and his relatives decided to get in on the boom. The men undoubtedly worked hard, but Jones remembers the fun times she and other kids had.

"They'd string the nets up to dry, right down there where Fishermen's Village is now," she recalled. "We'd have so much fun running back and forth around the nets chasing each other."

Jones' dad did most of his fishing near Punta Gorda at the mouth of the Peace River, where the water is so shallow a tall man can walk across on a good day.

"We'd love to fall out of the boat," she said with a smile. "There wasn't any danger because the water was so shallow and all of us could swim. My father was born on Charlotte Harbor in 1891. My family has quite a history in the Punta Gorda area. They were all commercial fishermen."

Her father and his relatives primarily fished for mullet, Jones said. Her grandfather, Jim Jones, lived where Punta Gorda Isles begins now, just past Fishermen's Village in Punta Gorda. Back then several fish companies processed the daily catch from fishermen who roamed the harbor waters.

"Grandpa Jones had six sons that all fished for him at the Punta Gorda Fish Company," Jones said. "At the time fishing was quite prosperous; if you caught a big school of fish you could buy a house with what you made."

Diana Harris/Englewood Lives

Englewood fisherman landing mullet.

1942

Doolittle raids Tokyo

Manila captured by Japanese forces. They also take Cavite naval base, and the American and Filipino troops continue the retreat into Bataan

Charlotte County schools, courthouse used as registration points for food rationing. Teachers assigned to help process the applications

Men 45 to 64 now eligible for draft

Punta Gorda Woman's Club burns building mortgage

Battle of the Coral Sea in Japanese-American stalemate

---

[38] Harris, Diana, *Englewood Lives,* 2013
[39] Harris, Diana, *Englewood Lives*, 2013

CENTURY

Battle of Midway ends in American victory

Guadalcanal Campaign begins in the Pacific.

The cruise liner SS Normandie catches fire and capsizes in New York Harbor. Although the cause was probably a welder's torch, various conspiracies imagined in the media.

Floyd Alford, Jr., who managed the Hotel Charlotte Harbor since 1934, announced his resignation.

Benjamin J. Baker, a prominent teacher for the black community, dies. Baker Elementary School named in his honor.

Charlotte County History Services

The east side of Punta Gorda, with the Five Points neighborhood at center.

That's what happened. When Jones was still in single digits, her father struck it rich with a mammoth catch. He bought a house and had it moved to Cooper Street, about midway between Charlotte High School and Marion Avenue, in Five Points.

"That's where I spent my growing up, between the Five Points, Souls Harbor Church of God, and the high school," Jones said. "When I was growing up the presence of the Christian faith was really an asset. The school system and everything sort of worked together. Our school activities were sort of based around the church's activities. Now that isn't the case anymore. When I was growing up it was possible to participate in school and church and most of our teachers were involved in local church."

Jones remembers a simpler Punta Gorda, when whites and blacks on the east side of the city lived close enough to know one another. Cooper Street was a predominantly white community, while black people lived on the western fringe of Five Points and beyond, centered on what was then Cochran and is now Martin Luther King Jr. Blvd.

"The Baker Academy was really close to where we lived and they had a basketball court and all of us children played together and skated on the basketball court."

She remembered fondly the woman who helped deliver her, Pauline; and Mary, the woman who helped Jones' mom cook and clean. Both were black women from across Cooper Street. During most of the county's history, there were few jobs for black women other than as domestics or laundresses. The local school for black people, the Baker Academy, had courses in domestic science that left girls with little aspirations other than to work for a white family in the area.

A People's History of Charlotte County

Charlotte County History Services

This undated photo shows the few remaining commercial fishing buildings left as the city razed the docks for what would become Fishermen's Village, a condo/high-end shops mall with fine dining. To the left, as Aratha Jones remembers, there are still several packing and shipping facilities waiting for the wrecking ball. The oil tanks and ship's stores shops that once were clustered on the right of the dock is now a marina, and condos overlook the area where nets were once dried.

Charlotte County public education for black children ended at sixth grade, unless parents were willing to have their children bused to Fort Myers for junior and senior high school.[40]

"Mary came and cooked and helped my mother—she was like part of my family," Jones said. "She lived a little further back in the area that was between Cooper Street and Punta Gorda and my ma would send us to Mary's house to pick up food that Mary was cooking for us or to pick up laundry. It was a good life, everybody knew everybody. I would walk from the school there on Charlotte and 41 and walk up Virginia Avenue as a child. I'd wave at Pauline, the midwife who delivered me; everybody knew I was White Jones' daughter."

The water was the source of the family wealth and Jones came to love being out on the harbor.

"I remember going fishing with my father in the summertime," Jones said. "They would throw the net in then they would make a big circle with the nets—they were gill nets. It was really fun to be out on the water—sometimes we would swim while he worked. We'd jump off into the water and then the water was just rich with sea life. We'd find starfish, we would find seahorses, crabs, because the water was shallow where they caught the fish. You could walk waist-high in it."

1943

The Soviet Union announces that 22 German divisions have been encircled at Stalingrad, with 175,000 killed and 137,650 captured.

Guadalcanal Campaign ends in American victory

Americans and Australians recapture Buna, New Guinea

County Commission offers acreage for a U.S. Army Air Corps training field near Punta Gorda

The USAAF 14th Air Force formed in China, under General Claire-Chennault, former head of the "Flying Tigers"

---

[40] Gunn, Barbara, *Call Us Colored, 1978*

CENTURY

Mussolini is arrested and relieved of his offices after a meeting with Italian King Victor Emmanuel III, who chooses Marshal Pietro Badoglio to form a new government.

Allied Expeditionary Force for the invasion of Europe is officially formed. Planning for D-Day begins full force.

The Wainwright shipyard in Panama City builds over 100 Liberty Ships for the U.S. war effort.

50 bombers mount the first all American air raid against Germany: Wilhelmshaven is the target.

This was during World War II, when fishing was an essential industry and consumption was high, driven in part by government contracts. Jones' father and other intrepid fishermen had a chance to do very well.

"I don't know who they sold it to but they sold a lot of fish," she recalled.

Tourists and folks seeking fine dining would probably be amazed to see what Fishermen's Village looked like back when it was indeed a veritable village of fishermen.

"Where Fishermen's Village is today—as you're going down the middle of the shops, on the righthand side would have been the fish house where they brought in the boatloads of fish and loaded them into the icehouse. On the lefthand side there was a big gas tank and things for the boats. That's where Grandpa bought the gas and supplies.

"There was a lot of vacant land there too, that's where they'd spread their nets out and put tar on them to keep them from rotting. All of that water on the righthand side of Fishermen's Village was just full of wooden frames that the fishermen would spread their nets on. We'd go down there and Mom and Daddy would work on the nets and we children would just run and play. Punta Gorda was just a great place for children."

Jones admits that she was spoiled as a girl, primarily because of family birth order.

"I had four brothers, all of them were older, then three younger sisters," she recalled. "My mom always said my daddy wanted a girl so bad; then I came along. So my daddy and my brothers all babied me. It was like I had five fathers."

This was during the early '40s, as America was sucked into World War II. So when the war came she had special reason to fear for two of her "dads," who were called to the colors.

"They were in the Pacific," said Jones, who would eventually marry a Navy man. "Navy runs in the family—we love the water. My third brother was in Vietnam and my youngest brother was wounded in the Korean War. I'm very proud of our service to America."

Jones' brothers, Snooker and Buddy, on leave from the Pacific, along with her grandfather.

A People's History of Charlotte County

After the war, Jones' flexible father switched gears and went into the construction supply business.

"There was a period when I was in my teens when construction developed in Charlotte County," she said. "So Daddy brought two dump trucks and he and my brother drove them."

The men took advantage of the postwar construction boom, which started locally before flaring to full flame with the arrival of first General Development Corporation in Port Charlotte and later the Punta Gorda Isles Corporation south of the Peace River.

"He did that for a while," she said, "but he loved the water and he loved fishing so he went back to that."

In 1954 Jones married. A year later she left for a twenty-year tour of duty around the world with her husband, a jet engine mechanic. But they'd return one day to claim their small corner of the Charlotte County sky.

Chris Goff Maerski's family also waited and worried for sons overseas during

Goff Family

Lonnie Goff, Ellen Goff, Marie Goff, and Christine Goff welcome home brother and son Belford.

the war years.

"My parents had five sons go to war," she said. "They all came home without a scratch. I can remember my parents, they were so worried."

In 1942, during the Guadalcanal Campaign in the Pacific, five brothers named Sullivan drowned when their ship was sunk by the Japanese. A movie later commemorated their sacrifice.

1944

Cuba-Florida hurricane

Hotel Charlotte Harbor undergoes third transformation, now billed as Charlotte Harbor Spa

Major Gregory "Pappy" Boyington, the USMC fighter ace, shot down

The SS United Victory, the first Victory ship, launched

The Battle of the Bulge begins as German forces attempt a breakthrough in the Ardennes region The main object of Hitler's plan - the retaking of Antwerp

1944

West Loch disaster: Six LSTs are accidentally destroyed and 163 men killed, in Pearl Harbor

Hotel Charlotte Harbor at Punta Gorda sold. Refurbished as Charlotte Harbor Spa

D-Day: 155,000 Allied troops shipped from England land on the beaches of Normandy in northern France,

Jack Pearson, a local fisherman, organizes the Englewood Cooperative Fisheries Ltd. Five months later, a hurricane destroyed the cooperative.

"When my parents heard about the Sullivans, that was heartbreaking to them. I remember going to see that movie and we'd just sit there and cry and cry."

Maerski was in high school then and spent a lot of time at the movies.

"I remember one time, I don't remember the name of the movie but back then they always had a newsreel at the beginning of a movie—not everybody got a newspaper back then. At this one movie, this lady saw this military guy in the newsreel and she just swore that it was her son, who was overseas at the time. The owner of the theater was so kind that he re-ran the newsreel to see it over again. I was very young at the time and I don't think it was him, but those things happen."

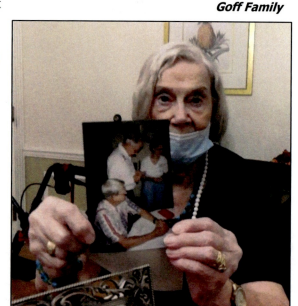
Goff Family

At 97, Christine Goff Maerski still recalls the shared sacrifice of her family and others during the war years.

Maerski remembers a community pulled together by the common threat.

"We were closer—the situation the country was in, the churches were over-packed on Sundays, they just stuck together...it just made better people out of us."

* * *

One of the greatest stories of service is that of one family, the Baileys of Punta Gorda. As journalist Don Moore recounts in his book, "War Tales," the Baileys sent six soldiers and sailors off to fight, including a Tuskegee airman who fought Nazis over the skies of North Africa and Europe. That airman's story includes an interesting brush with greatness that changed his life.

Charles Bailey's family was an ambitious one. His father and mother were recalled as hardworking churchgoing people. The father was a jack-of-all-trades who was always employed and Mom worked as a domestic. They believed in education; through saving and sacrifice they were able to send their children to school beyond the sixth grade. Until the 1950s, Charlotte County did not provide public education for black children beyond the sixth-grade level.

Don Moore

Charles Bailey

Bailey was able to attend Bethune-Cookman College in Daytona Beach. The school's founder, Mary McCleod Bethune, was a confidante of the first lady, Eleanor Roosevelt. Family lore has it that Mrs. Roosevelt helped introduce Bailey to the woman who would become his wife.

A People's History of Charlotte County

Don Moore/War Tales

Charles Bailey, with foot on wheel of airplane, and an unidentified airman. Bailey named his plane after his dad. He named his first airplane after his mom.

Cheryl Frizzell
Paul Frizzell in Italy

But she also suggested that he apply to be one of the Tuskegee airmen. The rest was history.[41] Bailey was one of seven brothers who fought for the United States during World War II and later Korea. At the time of their exploits racism precluded any public mention or acclaim for their service. Thanks to Moore, their story was resurrected and has since become a recognized part of Charlotte County's history.

Meanwhile, back at the ranch, A.C. Frizzell had his own fears about a loved one in harm's way. Paul, his heir, insisted on doing his part. He served in Italy and had a bad war, suffering two physical wounds and a host of less obvious injuries.

He would never be the same man he had been before the war, with catastrophic consequences for the future of the Frizzell dynasty.[42]

1945
Battle of the Bulge ends

Franklin D. Roosevelt, America's only four-term President, dies in office.

Germany surrenders unconditionally

Atomic bomb dropped on Hiroshima and Nagasaki, Japan, ending the war in the Pacific

World War II ends with Charlotte County seeing fifteen of its young men killed in the line of duty

Good Shepherd Church in Punta Gorda reopens

Jackie Robinson signs a contract with the Montreal Royals baseball team.

---

[41] Harding Bailey, Jr. Interview, February 2019
[42] Cheryl Frizzell, p. 133-136

Ulysses Samuel Cleveland was born in 1919 and moved to Punta Gorda with his family when he was two. As a boy he loved taking photographs and recording the sights and sounds of his adopted hometown. The war years gave Cleveland direction and a sense of purpose. For once, the notoriously bad Army system of assigning men to what they did best worked. The creative Cleveland became part of a deception unit that managed to fool Hitler's Nazis into thinking the D-Day invasion would strike a port far from the actual attack site.

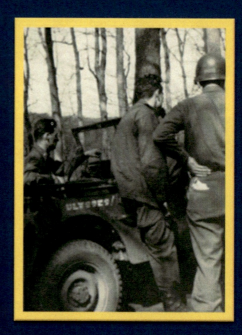

Cleveland was decommissioned as a major, then returned to Punta Gorda and became the assistant postmaster. Cleveland was involved in numerous organizations. As a member of the American Legion Post at Punta Gorda, Cleveland produced its monthly newsletter and helped manage weekly bingo games. Cleveland found enjoyment installing and operating sound systems at various events including the annual Florida International Air Show. He was also a historian for the Punta Gorda Kiwanis Club, treasurer for the Punta Gorda Historical Society, charter member for the Punta Gorda and Charlotte County Historic Preservation Boards and a member of the First United Methodist Church of Punta Gorda. Cleveland co-authored two volumes of local history books with Lindsey Williams called "Our Fascinating Past." Cleveland also edited and published "Punta Gorda Remembered," by Byron Rhode.

"It just seemed like whenever there was anything of historical significance, he was always there and was always straightforward and factual," said Charlotte County Commissioner Adam Cummings, who lived near Cleveland.

Vernon and Edna Jane in Miami, 1946; below, in Gilchrist Park, 1951.

In the middle of World War II love blossomed between a bookish pack rat and the belle of the ball, a girl so gorgeous and outgoing that her senior class invited her to its banquet despite her having moved almost 200 miles away.

In 1945 Vernon Peeples was on his way to a Charlotte High football game. He recalled flipping a silver coin in the air as he walked, happy to be enjoying a fine day in Punta Gorda. Suddenly an imperious man opened his door and ordered Peeples to come to him.

Back then kids obeyed adults—any adult—so Peeples complied.

What happened in that house changed his life forever. He met a girl, a very special girl, named Edna Jane. She was one of two daughters of a widowed minister who had just been assigned to Punta Gorda. It seems that Edna Jane, already cross about the move, had been complaining about having to take Latin. Her father called Peeples in and asked if the dead language was on the curriculum.

By then, Peeples knew he had met his wife. For 65 years, through tender looks, long letters, and eventually a marriage that lasted until the end of their days, they built a life together that enriched the county as a whole. But back then many, including the respective parents, dismissed the young people's affection as evanescent puppy love.

And the parents were formidable. Vasco Peeples and Lois Peeples have written their own places in history and, as often the case, probably loomed even larger in their home. Edna Jane's father actually accepted a pastorship in Miami, in part to get his daughter away from Vernon, whose own father once tried to bribe him into dating someone else.

Vernon's mom, Lois Peeples, defied her father and got a business degree during the 1920s, when women weren't supposed to do such things.[43] During the war she ran the family store while Vasco served in the army. She was twice president

1946

President Harry S. Truman begins visiting Key West for rest and relaxation The house he stayed in becomes known as the "Little White House" and is used by subsequent presidents

Everglades National Park established

Weeki Wachee Springs amusement park opens

Pete Parks moves surplus Army housing from Venice Air Base to Englewood for post office and private homes.

Indian Prime Minister Jawaharlal Nehru appeals to the United States and the Soviet Union to end nuclear testing.

---

[43] Conversation with author, circa 2012

The Basketball Association of America, known as the National Basketball Association (NBA) since 1949 after its merger with the rival National Basketball League, founded

The Philippines given independence by the United States, ending 425 years of dominance by the west

UNICEF (the United Nations Children's Emergency Fund) is founded

Frank Capra's *It's a Wonderful Life,* featuring James Stewart, Donna Reed, and Lionel Barrymore is released in New York

Ancestry.com

The Charlotte County Chamber of Commerce placed this tribute to Vasco Peeples in the 1985 visitors guide.

of the Punta Gorda Woman's Club, president of the Business and Professional Women's Club, and president of the Charlotte County Democratic Women's Club.[44]

Vasco Peeples, Vernon's father, was also a force to be reckoned with. The family had moved to Punta Gorda during the worst days of the Great Depression, in 1933, to run an IGA store. They lived above the store, located in the building at SB41 and Marion that most recently housed an ice cream shop. He invested well and after service during WWII in the Army Corps of Engineers, went on to become a Charlotte County commissioner, (from 1948-1956),[45] a big landowner, realtor, and a heavyweight in the community. He had a national presence as head of a campgrounds lobbying organization.

But love is love. One morning Vernon got up early, slipped out of the house, and caught a bus to Miami to see Edna Jane.

"If you do that again don't ever come back," Vernon recalled his father saying when he came home.

"That was the day I became a man," Vernon recalled.

During Vernon's last year of high school, class officers voted to invite the popular Edna Jane back to the class banquet. Everything was going fine until the principal exercised executive discretion and forbade her from attending. It was a matter of protocol, he said.

Back then, it was customary for seniors to pony up for a class gift, the magnificence of which reflected favorably on the principal. But Vernon wanted revenge on the man who had snubbed his girl. So, he went to Sallie Jones, the school superintendent, and got permission to float a crazy idea. Instead of buying a memento for the school, what if the students used their class donations to buy their own caps and gowns, thus relieving parents of that burden?

Peeples had served as a page in the legislature twice, back when prospective candidates had to campaign statewide for the positions, so he had watched enough legislators to understand politics. Parents were happy but the principal was flummoxed. He was reassigned the following year.[46]

---

[44] Punta Gorda Historic Mural Society
[45] https://www.myfloridahouse.gov/Sections/Representatives/details.aspx?MemberId=2995&SessionId=42
[46] Conversations with Vernon Peeples, Nov. 2017

A People's History of Charlotte County

Vernon tried divinity school, didn't like it, and eventually graduated from Florida State University. Edna Jane did well in nursing school. By then the parents realized the kids knew better.

Vernon soon got a job in the state transportation department. He and Edna Jane were married in 1956, launching twin careers of public service and decades of living out their teenaged dreams together.

Wedding bells also rang for Christine Goff Maerski. During the war, one of her brothers, who was stationed on a destroyer in the Atlantic, had met a Long Island, New York family while on leave at Coney Island, a popular amusement park.

Goff Family

Wedding photo at the Charlotte Harbour Hotel 1948. Chester R. McDerment, Christine (Goff) McDerment, Reni Goff and Lonnie Goff.

One thing led to another and soon her brother was dating a daughter of the Long Island family. He sent Christine the name and address of the girl's brother. He was stationed in the Pacific. Like many girls during the war, Christine became a pen pal.

"He told me he would come see me as soon as he got home," she said. "He did and we just fell in love and got married." They were married at the Hotel Charlotte Harbor. Then her husband, Chester McDerment, whisked her away to Long Island, where she lived for 60 years.

Even as the war engendered and accelerated the creation of the most private of institutions, it also served as a major catalyst and impetus for public facilities and utilities. The air base, for example, would grow to become the county's major economic engine by the end of the 20th century. Another institution of the war years that county residents enjoy today is the county's first hospital.

Punta Gorda's first hospital was established by a combat veteran and popular local doctor, Dr. Walter B. Clement. Prior to the hospital, county residents had to go to Arcadia or Fort Myers. In 1937, Clement and others began planning a hospital. However, the Great Depression and World War II were more than major

1947

Charlotte Hospital built by the Punta Gorda Rotary Club and community residents with twelve beds

County builds a bridge to replace the old Chadwick structure in Englewood, named for Leo Wotitzky

The Truman Doctrine announced, granting $400 million in aid to Greece and Turkey to battle Communist terrorism

Jackie Robinson breaks Major League Baseball's color barrier when he debuts at first base for Branch Rickey's Brooklyn Dodgers

CENTURY

1948

Florida State College for Women goes coed as Florida State University

Vasco Peeples becomes county commissioner, a post he would hold through 1956

President Harry S. Truman rallies to win his first presidential election over Thomas E. Dewey. Headlines in national newspapers announced a Dewey victory, only to be proven wrong, with Truman's 303 electoral votes to Dewey's 189, with Strom Thurmond, the States' Rights candidate, receiving 39 votes

obstacles, they stifled fundraising efforts. A $20,000 bond issue to build a hospital failed that year, despite the efforts of the Punta Gorda Rotary, which helped spearhead the fundraising drive, and the *Punta Gorda Herald,* which actively championed the issue.

After the war, when Dr. Clement returned home from service as a paratrooper with the 101st Airborne, the hospital drive picked up where it had left off. It was successful and in 1947 the Charlotte Hospital opened its doors.

"The hospital was opened m August of 1947, and I flew back home from a 101st Airborne Division convention in New York for the occasion. One of the first patients we had was one of the Peeples girls {Gussie Baker} who had her tonsils out the first night the hospital was open," Clement recalled during a 1974 newspaper interview.[47]

Upon the hospital's opening, the *Herald* ran a column that read, in part: "Probably there are few people who do not recognize that the opening of Charlotte Hospital Monday, and its immediate and enthusiastic acceptance, is one of the most momentous events in the history of this county."

The writer was Leo Wotitzky, a man whose contributions to the county merit a book unto itself. The late 1940s saw Wotitzky sacrifice his career as a legislator (1938 to 1950) for the future of the state's schoolchildren.

He first came to the public eye as a schoolteacher; he also made a failed run for school superintendent. He was such a good teacher that one of his pupils, Vernon Peeples, modeled much of his

Daily Herald News

Dr. Walter Clement, a major force in the creation of the county's first hospital, dressed for combat before D-Day as a member of the 101st Airborne. Below, a flyer soliciting community support for the hospital. (Florida Weekly)

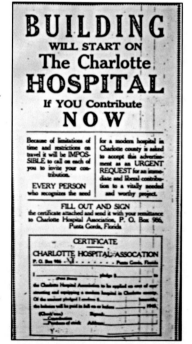

---

[47] *Daily Herald News*, April 30, 1974

Leo Wotitzky during his years in the state legislature.

public service career after the man people invariably called "Mr. Wotitzky." Wotitzky crafted his own political death by championing a fair funding formula for state schools.

At the time, students in some parts of the county, like Englewood, often went to school barefoot. The county's black schools used hand-me-down books so dilapidated students had to read around annotations from years of previous white students.

Wotitzky teamed up with Tallahassee-area legislator LeRoy Collins, an upper-crust Floridian who had married into state aristocracy (his wife was the descendant of a Florida governor). He had the advantage of representing one of the few education centers in the state; an established black college in Florida A&M University and the growing Florida State University, which had yet to reach its potential.

Wotitzky, however, came from a community where education was expensive and undervalued. Black students had to be bused out of town if they wanted to go beyond sixth grade, while several schools, including Englewood's only elementary school, had structural issues like leaky roofs that went unattended for lack of money.

Wotitzky understood that the rich get richer and communities like Charlotte County would never see their children amount to anything unless they had a better shot at education. So he and Collins were able to move legislation through the Florida House and senate creating, for the first time, a revenue-sharing formula by which money from every county would be redistributed to address the wide fluctuations in community wealth.

Here's how Wotitzky remembered the struggle for a fair education funding formula, a fight that still goes on today.

> *I was chairman of the education committee in the House. We enacted what was called a minimum foundation program for schools, for public education, and brought Florida really out of the Middle Ages into a reasonably well-financed public education system where the state, for the first time, went a long way toward funding the public schools of Florida. It's kind of a complex program, but it revolutionized public education in Florida.*
>
> *And I am quite proud of the role that I had in that. In that, people, I guess, who are familiar with the education programs and teaching in the state will know about it. And with regard to that though, it so increased the state funding of public education that we had to find new revenue. And as a result, I wound up as a floor leader to pass Florida's first sales tax, 3 percent sales tax. And that was in 1949. So after that I was defeated for re-election.*[48]

1949

WTVJ-TV (NBC), Florida's first television station, begins broadcasting

WJXT-TV (CBS) in Jacksonville also begins

The first "networked" television broadcasts take place, as KDKA-TV in Pittsburgh, Pennsylvania goes on the air, connecting east coast and mid-west programming in the United States

Second Red Scare in the United States: Celebrities including Helen Keller, Dorothy Parker, Danny Kaye, Fredric March, John Garfield, Paul Muni and Edward G. Robinson named in FBI investigation.

---

[48] *The Florida Civil Rights Oral History Project*, March 8, 2001

CENTURY

1950

Charlotte County population 4,286, an increase of 17.0%

Korean Conflict begins. Six Charlotte County soldiers would die in action

U.S. Senator Estes Kefauver introduces a resolution calling for an investigation of organized crime in the U.S.

Battle of Inchon: Allied troops commanded by Douglas MacArthur land in Inchon, occupied by North Korea, to begin a U.N. counter-offensive.

Although he was one of many legislators who agreed to the measure, as head of several key committees, Wotitzky bore the brunt of blame for creating the state's first sales tax. Vernon Peeples told a reporter that merchants would place containers for the extra sales tax generated by the equalization plan near the cash register, with Wotitzky's name prominently displayed as the reason for the higher prices.[49]

Wotitzky lost the following election. No good deed goes unpunished unless, in this instance, one lives in a college town that values education. Collins, resident of Tallahassee, went on to become governor. Wotitzky went back to law school, then joined his brother, Frank's, law firm and edited the *Punta Gorda Herald*. He passed away in 2005.

After the war, Jones and her family salvaged wood from the barracks and other buildings at the abandoned air base.

"After the base closed those army huts were demolished and people built homes with the lumber and supplies that they salvaged from the army huts," she said. "I do remember that all the family went there and maybe they had to buy those army huts and take them apart. They built my aunt a house on Daddy's land. All of the material to build her house came from the material at the airport." And the abandoned base had a greater utility for young people. "When I was a teenager, that's where we learned to drive, out on those runways," Jones recalled. "You could just drive and drive on those runways and you didn't have to know a thing about how to drive. That was the teenage meeting place."

Aratha Jones

Jones in high school.

Beyond those in-the-moment benefits of the Punta Gorda Army Air Corps base, its legacy lives on in two ways that syncretize the perils and the prosperity of the war years for Punta Gorda. The sacrifices were shared by families like the Baileys, who sent front-line fighters into World War II. And the fruits of victory are enjoyed in part because of an airport bequeathed by the war that has become an economic engine of the county.

In 2007, airport manager Gary Quille found out about the Fighting Bailey Brothers. He was so impressed he convinced the Charlotte County Airport Authority to rename the glittering new terminal after the family,[50] thus aligning the World War II era and Charlotte County's future in a monument to commerce and the fact that freedom is not free.

Plaque commemorating the Fighting Bailey Brothers in the Bailey Terminal of the Punta Gorda Airport.

---

[49] Conversation with Vernon Peeples
[50] Gary Quille, February 2019 interview with the author

PUNTA GORDA ARMY AIR FIELD

Frank Desguin

Early in World War II, Florida Sen. Claude Pepper announced plans to construct a training facility on just over 1,700 acres of land a few miles east of the county stockade at Carmalita and Florida Streets. It would become one of 40 facilities operating in Florida during the war due to the state's wide-open spaces and practically year-round flying climate. The stockade building, with its barred windows, still stands today, adjacent to the horse arena.

After much planning, construction began in early 1943 and included a three-mile asphalt access road. When completed in January 1944 there were three asphalt runways, each 5,000 feet long and 150 feet wide in a triangular configuration, 61 service buildings (hangars, repair shops, mess halls, etc.), 268 hutments with wooden floors, sides, and canvas roofs, and a 20-foot-high control tower.

Interestingly, the first plane to land at the airfield, in February 1943, did so mistakenly. It was a Bell P-39 Airacobra, out of Page Field in Fort Myers. The pilot became disoriented during a night training mission, landing on what he thought was a concrete roadway, but was actually a barely graded runway!

Military personnel began arriving in mid-November 1943 and by the airfield's formal dedication, March 19, 1944, over 1,100 officers and enlisted men had arrived to support an average of 200 pilots in each training group. Pilots were assigned to one of two squadrons, the 502nd Fighter-bomber and 490th Fighter. Maj. Forrest H. Munger was the first commanding officer. Since the Punta Gorda and Sarasota airfields were considered "branches" of Venice's, Munger reported directly to that base's commander, Col. V.B. Dixon. The 27th Service Corps Detachment from Venice Airfield was in charge of base operations.

When you consider many of the servicemen were accompanied by families, one can easily imagine the change it brought to a county with a population of just under 3,700 folks only two years earlier. In fact, Punta Gorda's city council appointed a Fair Rents Committee to handle complaints of rent gouging. Two of the five members were my granddad, Frank Rigell, and county attorney, Earl Farr. And I'll bet the small town's young ladies enjoyed all the newfound attention they likely received.

A United Service Organization (USO) center was established at the Punta Gorda Woman's Club on Sullivan Street and world heavyweight boxing champion Max Baer was part of its first show in January 1944. The non-commissioned officer's club was on Marion Avenue in today's Ace Hardware building, while Page Apartments at Charlotte Street and Mark Avenue in Solana served as Bachelor Officers' Quarters.

CENTURY

Early aircraft were various trainers and the Curtis P-40 Warhawk of Flying Tigers' fame, later replaced by the North American P-51 Mustang, the Air Corps' front-line fighter, in the fall of 1944. Bombing and strafing exercises were conducted on a remote area of today's Babcock-Webb Wildlife Management Area, with aerial gunnery over the Gulf of Mexico. The basic structure of the EAA's (Experimental Aircraft Association) building at the airport's southeastern corner today, was the airfield's three-sided, open concrete bunker used to sight aircraft guns. The airfield also "hosted" about 500 transient aircraft each month.

World War II ended on August 15, 1945, with victory over Japan and the airfield was placed on inactive status September 1, 1945. Its last commanding officer, Lt. Col. R.A. Hanes, declared the field "surplus" in November 1945. Recently arrived German prisoners-of-war then helped dismantle base facilities and equipment. The airfield was turned over to the county in April 1947, although a reversion clause for reactivation remained in effect until late 1969, after which the county deeded the airport to the then Charlotte County Development Authority.

During approximately 22 months of operation, the Punta Gorda Army Airfield trained around 800 pilots crucial to the war effort. Unfortunately, there were seven fatal crashes during those months involving pilots stationed at the airfield.

Flight Officer Edward B. Harrison lost his life on March 9, 1944, due to engine failure during a bombing exercise. Capt. Dorrance C. Zabriskie was killed during a dive-bombing exercise March 31 and 2nd Lt. Harris L. Kimble died in a crash during a routine flight May 26, only 19 years old. The wreckage was found on sand flats six miles west of the field.

A fourth pilot, Lt. Donald R. Smith, was presumed dead after a 7-day search, when the mail plane he was piloting went missing on its return trip from Drew Field in Tampa, Aug. 7. Lt. Robert M. Day was killed Aug. 14 in a mid-air collision during a high-altitude gunnery mission. The other pilot, Lt. Harold E. Hanson, though injured, survived. Capt. Robert R. Sherbondy, a decorated combat veteran, died March 7, 1945, on a routine training flight west of Egmont Key while on temporary duty at Pinellas Army Airfield, and Theodore F. Vander-Heuval died after bailing out of his plane over Fort Ogden Field in July when the engine failed.

THE BAILEY BROTHERS
Don Moore

Lt. Charles Bailey, Sr. was the first black aviator from Florida to become a Tuskegee Airman. He is credited with shooting down two Focke-Wulf-190 German fighter planes in "Josephine," a P-40 Warhawk named for his mother, and later in "My Buddy," a P-51 Mustang named for his dad.

Bailey was an early member of the 99th Fighter Squadron in World War II, one of only 450 black pilots who saw action during the war. The 99th Squadron was assigned to the U.S. Army's 12th Air Force in Europe together with the 100th, 301st and 302nd black fighter squadrons.

Charles' fight with the Luftwaffe began in North Africa. He flew 133 combat missions over enemy territory. Charles and his squadron also saw action in Sicily, Naples-Foggia, Anzio, Rome-Anzio, Normandy, Northern France, Southern France, North Apennines, Rhineland, Central Europe, the Po Valley and the EAME Theatre in Germany.

During World War II, 66 Tuskegee pilots were killed in action and 32 became prisoners of war. The black airmen received 150 Distinguished Flying Crosses, Legions of Merit and Red Stars of Yugoslavia.

The Baileys during a Punta Gorda homecoming. People who knew the Bailey brothers credit their parents, Archie and Josephine, for instilling in their children high standards. They pose with their children and daughters-in law in the photo above. From the left kneeling in the front row: Charles, Carl, Berlin and Harding. Standing at left: Maurice, Josephine, Maurice's wife, Olivia, and Archie.

Before the war, Charles graduated from all-black Howard Academy in Ocala. There was no black high school in Charlotte County. So he lived with family in the Ocala area while going to high school there. For two years, in the late '30s, Charles was enrolled at Bethune-Cookman College in Daytona Beach, one of the few black institutions of higher learning in the state 70 years ago.

While in college Charles enlisted in the Army Air Corps. On April 29, 1943 he earned his wings and gold second lieutenant's bars upon graduation from aviation cadet training at Tuskegee Institute, the premier black college in Alabama. A month later, when the 99th Fighter Squadron shipped out to take part in the Allied Invasion of North Africa, Charles was one of the squadron's pilots.

After the war, he returned to Bethune-Cookman to complete his final two years. He received a degree in elementary education. Charles married Bessie L. Fitch of Punta Gorda in 1946. They had two children, Charles Bailey, Jr. and James A. Bailey. Later he also graduated from the Cincinnati College of Embalming. Eventually the family moved to DeLand, Florida where Charles Sr. taught school for decades. When he retired from teaching he opened the Charles P. Bailey Funeral Home in DeLand.

CENTURY

Carl Bailey

His brother, Lt. Carl A. Bailey, was the first black jet pilot in Florida. He was born September 1, 1929 and died November 23, 1957. Carl didn't serve in a segregated unit like his older brothers in World War II. He was a member of the integrated U.S. Armed Forces. He was one of two black jet pilots from Florida, at the time, who flew F-84 Thunderjets in the early 1950s.

He flew jet fighters at the end of the Korean War after attending Florida A&M University in Tallahassee.

"Some of the older folks around town can tell you about him flying over the Punta Gorda water tower in his jet fighter back then," his nephew, Maurice Bailey, added. "The water tower was right next to where his mother lived in those days."

At 28, and still in the service, Carl was killed while on vacation in an auto accident near Fayetteville, N.C. He is buried next to his father and mother in the Cleveland cemetery, east of Punta Gorda, named for him. Carl never married or had children.

Sgt. Maurice M. Bailey, born on May 16, 1906, was the eldest of the nine Bailey children.

Maurice's son said he entered the Army after graduating from Florida A&M University. He married his wife, Olivia, when they both attended college.

In the Second World War, he was a member of the "Red Ball Express," a primarily black unit that kept U.S. front line troops supplied with fuel, food, and ammunition during the fighting in Europe. As the German lines were crumbling, the "Red Ball Express" supplied a surging Allied advance across Europe.

Cpl. Arthur J. Bailey was a Marine who was at Iwo Jima.

Maurice Bailey

"I don't know what he was doing there, but he was there," Maurice's son said.

His discharge papers don't give a clue either. All they say is Arthur was qualified to drive a light truck and he saw no combat.

When Arthur was discharged from the Marines, he returned to his hometown of Punta Gorda. For a while he was a cook at a local hotel. Then he went to work for General Development Corp., the primary home builder in Charlotte County after the war. Legusta Felder, his widow who remarried after his death, said he was next to the youngest of the Bailey children. Arthur was born March 20, 1925. He died November 14, 1959, according to his former wife, who still lives in Punta Gorda. He is buried in the Cleveland Cemetery, named for his younger brother, Carl.

Arthur Bailey

Pfc. Paul Bailey was a chaplain's assistant assigned to Company D, 2805th Engineering Battalion in the Western Pacific during World War II. While in the Army, Paul received the Good Conduct Medal, the APTO Medal and the World War II Victory Medal.

After the war, he earned a degree in music at Bethune-Cookman College in Daytona Beach, Fla. He also graduated from the Boston Conservatory of Music.

"He could play the piano beautifully," his cousin Margaret Johnson recalled.

A People's History of Charlotte County

Paul Bailey

Paul retired in the 1970s and returned to Punta Gorda to live with his widowed mother until he died on April 2, 1987. He is buried in the Cleveland Cemetery. Born September 3, 1922, he was the sixth Bailey sibling.

E-4 Berlin J. Bailey, Sr. was a member of the U.S. Navy's 3rd Construction Battalion who served in the Pacific Theater during the war. He was at Guadalcanal, the scene of one of the major island battles in the South Pacific.

Berlin was an electrician's mate 3rd class, a trade that served him well after he was discharged from the service. When he returned from war, he established an electrical business in Punta Gorda he operated for more than 50 years. In 1960, Berlin was named to the Charlotte County Citizens' Committee on Education. From 1976 until 1983, he sat on the Punta Gorda Planning Commission.

Lorene, his second wife, taught school in Charlotte County for 33 years.

Berlin Sr. died January 6, 1997. He is also buried in the Cleveland Cemetery. He was the second-born Bailey child. He was born November 24, 1912.

E-5 Harding C. Bailey, Sr. served aboard the USS Mason, a destroyer escort, during World War II, according to his son Harding, Jr. His father was an electrician's mate 2nd class. What made the Mason unique is that it was the first Navy ship with a predominately Negro crew, the Dictionary of American Fighting Ships says. The Mason served in the Atlantic and the Mediterranean.

Following his military service, Harding, Sr. became an educator. He began as a teacher and retired a principal in the Brevard County School District on Florida's East Coast. Harding is the fifth-born child of the Bailey siblings. He was born October 2, 1920 and died August 31, 1984.

Berlin Bailey

Bailey family descendants and other relatives say the brothers did not tell war stories. They also say the brothers' demeanor before and after their military experiences reflected their upbringing.

Harding Bailey

"They were straight-laced," Burdette Cain, the 45-year-old daughter of Harding, Sr. explained from her Melbourne, Fla. home. "They had the value of respect and family life."

Maurice Bailey was a church benefactor even after he moved away. He is responsible for the existing entrance doors on the century-old church.

"He came down here and paid for them," Johnson said.

Several Bailey descendants followed in their elders' footsteps, Maurice's son, Maurice, Jr., enlisted in the Air Force. Harding Jr. is an Army veteran of the Vietnam War. In 1995 Marcia Bailey, Maurice's granddaughter, graduated from the U.S. Naval Academy at Annapolis, Md. Like her forefathers she carried on the military tradition of the Baileys of Punta Gorda.

ENGLEWOOD RESIDENT SHELTERED BY PHILIPPINE GUERRILLAS

Jo Cortes

One of the most harrowing stories of World War II courage and desperation is that of an Englewood woman, Mrs. Kluge. In 1929 Mr. and Mrs. Kluge left for the Philippines and eventually became residents on the island of Luzon. In 1941 they had to seek refuge in the mountains to escape the Japanese invasion.

For 45 months she lived with the guerrillas who often risked their lives to hide the courageous woman, but her husband was taken prisoner by the Japanese and met his death at their hands in 1945.

She then returned to Englewood where she turned her energies to the numerous civic projects.

The Veterans Club of the American Legion stands on ground donated by Mrs. Kluge as a memorial to her late husband

Mr. and Mrs. Herman C. Kluge. Below, March 4, 1943 Sarasota Herald Tribune *article announcing that the couple was behind Japanese lines.*

Former Englewood Residents Are Missing In Philippines

Two former Sarasota county residents, Lieut. and Mrs. Herman C. Kluge, are missing in the Philippine islands, it was learned here today.

Lieutenant Kluge was listed by the War department as missing after the fall of Corregidor and no word has been received from Mrs. Kluge.

Lieutenant and Mrs. Kluge own a home on Lemon bay near Englewood, which is still maintained by a resident caretaker.

Lieutenant and Mrs. Kluge were from Elmira, N. Y., but lived near Englewood several years ago before going to the Philippine islands in 1928 where he was in charge of a large lumber company. They lived at Bagario, Mount province.

The last news from them was in November, 1941. Since then no word has reached friends or the family except the War department's informing the family that Kluge had joined the army as a first lieutenant and was listed as missing after the fall of Corregidor.

Although no word has been received from Mrs. Kluge, the family in New York state hopes for news through the Red Cross. The three sons, Frederick, August and Herman, were being educated in New York state, so escaped the fate of their parents who evidently are in the hands of the Japs.

Cheryl Frizzell

Cheryl (Cherry) Frizzell and her friend, Leroy, at the Frizzell Ranch in 1948. Her world would change forever because her father and grandfather could not reconcile their differences. That disagreement would eventually lead to the birth of Port Charlotte and North Port.

HOME PORT

The Bible paints a vision of when the wars have ended, where every man can sit under his fig or olive tree in peace. Odie Futch doesn't have a fig tree, his is an oak. But he's earned the peace of sitting under his tree on a gentle rise of land not far from the Myakka River in South Gulf Cove. Futch found his peace in the Fifties and early Sixties. His story parallels and dovetails with those of many longtime county residents who experienced the dramatic transition from scrubland to community that marked the postwar years.

Futch was born in 1952 and spent his first years in a rundown part of town that housed a guava cannery. Today the same area, along Cross Street (US41SB), features an exclusive mini-mall and is near the epicenter of Punta Gorda's revitalization efforts.

But Futch recalls neighbors picking fruit from their guava trees and selling the produce to the canning factory as a way to make extra money. Because of his family's precarious existence, Futch said, they moved around a lot.

But then Futch's father got a job operating the fire warning tower in Murdock, near El Jobean.

Odie Futch.

A People's History of Charlotte County

Cheryl Frizzell

The Florida Forest Service's Frizzell Forestry Site.

One of two letters in which A.C. Frizzell laid out the reasons why he was selling his ranch and bypassing Paul, his son, as the inheritor of his land fortune.

Futch's family, like many that lived in El Jobean, Murdock, or what would become Port Charlotte, lived in the shadow of A. C. Frizzell.

"He wasn't a bad old man," Futch recalled. "He kinda took a liking to me because I always was up there with Dad, just a young boy. He called me Hoss because I was so big. I'll never forget we was up there one day and, you know, we didn't have a lot. And they were butchering a cow up there and Old Man A. C., after we'd been working all day he said, 'Hoss, where's your daddy? When he gets loaded up send him over here.' So he gave us the biggest round steak I'd ever seen in my life off of that old cow."

And, more important, Frizzell gave Futch's father a good job, manning the fire tower Frizzell had underwritten. The tower is still there, in El Jobean on the left as one travels SR776 toward Englewood.

Even as Futch and his family flourished, the Frizzell empire was fading, which would change history dramatically. Paul, Frizzell's son, had never been right since the war. In modern times he may have been diagnosed as having PTSD, sad memories of the war that led to drinking, survivor's guilt, irrational behavior, and an avoidance of responsibility. After setting him up in several key positions within his businesses and the ranch, subsidizing his stay in an exclusive sobriety clinic that was anything but, and watching him squander money, A. C. Frizzell came to a hard decision.

In 1954 he sold out, leaving Paul and other family members with pieces of his land empire. From that point on, the Frizzell colossus swiftly came apart.[51]

But maybe his heart wasn't in it. One day, while sitting around on what was left of his holdings, he mused about what would come.

1951
Korean War: Third Battle of Seoul: Chinese and North Korean forces capture Seoul for the second time (they had lost Seoul in the Second Battle of Seoul in September 1950).

Jackie Brenston "and His Delta Cats" (actually Ike Turner's Kings of Rhythm) record "Rocket 88" at Sam Phillips' Sun Studio in Memphis, Tennessee, a candidate for the first rock and roll record.
It is covered on June 14 by Bill Haley and His Saddlemen.

---

[51] Cheryl Frizzell, p. 211

1952

Groundhog Day tropical storm forms just north of Cuba, moving northeast. The storm makes landfall in southern Florida the next day (the earliest reported landfall from a tropical storm).

Republican General Dwight D. Eisenhower defeats Democratic Governor of Illinois Adlai Stevenson (correctly predicted by the UNIVAC computer).

Inter-service feud about air power ends as Army and Air Force agree to limit Army aviation to a fixed wing weight limit of five thousand pounds empty and unlimited capacity for helicopters.

Melinda Frizzell

A portrait of A.C. Frizzell's final home in Murdock. An electrical substation and a Days Inn occupy the site, located directly across from Lowe's on SB US41. Below, the real estate operation in El Jobean eventually run by Frizzell's daughter-in-law. (Cheryl Frizzell)

"One day there will be a house for every cow," Frizzell said.

By the late Fifties, the Frizzells had begun a slow fade to anonymity, eccentricity, and sometimes even the butt of practical jokes.

"When I was in school there, high school, he had two horses as you pull into his driveway off of 41, he had two male

horses standing up on their hind legs like that and you can imagine what it looked like, all males," Odie Futch recalled. "And for fun every once in a while me and the boys would go over and paint their peckers all red. That was all we done evil back then, us boys just having a good time out doing something like that," he said with a laugh. "We'd go over there, right across from Lowe's, that's where he built that house for Miss Dorothy."

Miss Dorothy was Frizzell's second wife, a woman he had met while carousing at the notorious Acline Wine Place, better known as Ma's or the Alligator Bar. Upon A. C.'s death in 1961 Dorothy Frizzell and Patti, a foundling the couple had adopted, inherited much of Frizzell's wealth. His son, Paul, received much of the El Jobean holdings. His problems, however, continued and he divorced his wife, Sandra Elizabeth. She in turn set up a real estate operation and began selling the El Jobean property her husband gave her as part of the divorce settlement. Frizzell's grandchildren are still remembered fondly by old-timers. Odie Futch recalls riding with them on the school bus to Charlotte High School, where Paul played football

A People's History of Charlotte County

Melinda Frizzell

Robert Preston Frizzell, also known as Randy, was A.C. Frizzell's nephew. His dad, Johnnie Frizzell, followed A.C. to Florida and later worked for him. Randy started riding for the ranch when he was 10. That's him on the right with the smallest horse. Below right, Missie Harper, Joyce Harper and Nellie Frizzell, Randy's mom, outside what used to be known as the quarters, housing on the site of the Town Center Mall in Murdock which A.C. Frizzell had built to house black ranch workers.

one year. And Chris Goff Maerski, at age 97, still remembers Paul as "the little prince. "He had this little horse that Mr. Frizzell had given him," she recalled. "He would ride that horse down to where we all played and let us all take turns riding him."

Robert Preston Frizzell, a nephew of A. C., started riding for the ranch when he was 10. His family's example speaks to the generosity A. C. Frizzell showed toward family members. Randy, who now lives in Tallahassee, still does well renting out a prime piece of Murdock commercial property near the Town Center Mall his father inherited from Frizzell.[52]

Years later Cheryl Frizzell, the oldest of Frizzell's grandchildren, would write a book about her grandfather that placed him squarely in his times, revealing much that had gone untold about both the man and Charlotte County during the first 40 decades of its existence.

---

[52] Robert Preston Frizzell, Interview

1953

President Harry S. Truman announces the United States has developed a hydrogen bomb.

71.1% of all television sets in the United States are tuned into I Love Lucy, to watch Lucy give birth to Little Ricky, which is more people than those who tuned into Dwight Eisenhower's inauguration

Dial system of 1,000 telephones switched into service at Punta Gorda. First call is made by Mayor E.J. Mccann to his sister in New Jersey.

Sallie Jones retires after 18 years as superintendent

1954

Cattle baron A.C. Frizzell sells 82,000 acres of his Charlotte County range to Yellowknife Bear Mines, Ltd., and Chemical Research Corp. of Canada- in partnership with Mackle Brothers Construction Co. of Miami.

The U.S. Supreme Court ruled in the Brown v. Board of Education case that school segregation was unconstitutional. Many Florida resisted the decision, prolonging desegregation until well into the early Seventies.

The Tallahassee bus boycott began to desegregate that city's public transportation system

But even as one empire died another was born as the dream of "$10 down and $10 a month" created the county's largest development.

Many servicemen home from the wars wanted their little tree under which to sit and make war no more, so millions of returning GIs were battering an already overburdened housing market.

And the conglomeration of firms that had purchased the Frizzell land legacy had a plan to make those hungry homebuyers happy. Frank E. Mackle III, in his history of the family's enterprises, writes:

The first major ad campaign for $795.00 lots in Florida for "Ten dollars down and ten dollars a month" began to be placed in 1957.

The national advertisements would include a "cut-out" coupon asking for more information about Port Charlotte.

When the coupon came in to the Miami office a brochure went out by mail to the customer with Reservation Coupons (usually three at a time) which - with the attachment of a ten-dollar bill - would reserve a home site in Florida. Receipt of the Reservation Coupon and the ten-dollar bill was followed up with a contract for a specific lot to be signed and returned.

The results of the new national advertising program were phenomenal!

Coupons - along with the ten-dollar bills - came pouring in by the postal bag load!

Bill O'Dowd tells the story that in the early days the Mackles - giddy with their success - would actually open the envelopes themselves in the office that they shared!

Bill remembers Elliott excitedly yelling "I got triple!" - when he would find thirty dollars and three coupons in one envelope!

Above, Frank E. Mackle III, curator of his family's legacy (Mackle Family); left, a Tampa Tribune profile of A.C. Frizzell; below, the ad that launched a thousand dreams (Charlotte County History Services)

A People's History of Charlotte County

Charlotte County History Services

The big news in 1954 was the sale of a huge chunk of A.C. Frizzell's land empire to a consortium of arcane origins. All would soon become clear. One note: That's U.S. Cleveland in the lead photo, handing out awards to young Scouts. He was an active participant in local scouting activities.

1955
Mackle Brothers clears land and builds four model homes along Tamiami Trail north of Charlotte Harbor. Investors reorganize as General Development Corporation.

Development named Port Charlotte. Advertising blitz launched in northern and foreign cities offering $600 home lots for $10 down and $10 a months. Sales skyrocket.

Marian Anderson is the first African-American singer to perform at the Metropolitan Opera in New York City.

> Soon the huge volume of returns required an entire mail order department to be set up.
>
> The quarter-page advertising experiment soon turned into a grand "mail order" land sales business. As time went on the simple ad and "fulfillment material" grew more and more sophisticated.
>
> Soon national advertising expanded to international advertising and contracts were being mailed all over the world. I was collecting stamps at the time and a fringe benefit was that Dad would bring exotic foreign stamps home by the hundreds.[53]

Because of the success of the coupon program, General Development soon found itself turning into a land sales company that backed into the community building business. But the Mackles took the commitment seriously and built so well, many of their homes still stand.

They developed amenities such as the Cultural Center, which grew out of a desire on the part of residents to do more than look at sunsets. They built a water

---

[53] http://themacklecompany.com/femjrstorypublic/10-generaldevelopment1954-1957.htm

CENTURY

1956

Charlotte Hospital is ready for its first major expansion. A new south wing is connected to the main building by a walkway, increasing the patient capacity to 38 adult beds, four bassinets and two pediatric beds.

The Johns Committee - named for Senator Charley Johns; investigated Communists and homosexuality in the state

Elvis Presley releases his first gold album in the United States.

City Lights Bookstore in San Francisco publishes Howl and Other Poems by Allen Ginsberg

Charlotte County History Services

General Development started building southwest of US41 and marked their spot with a tall lighthouse. They built a similar edifice in North Port when they began work there. The tower fell during Hurricane Donna.

utility and, at least while such things were under their jurisdiction, tried to build main roads and other infrastructure.

And, as discussed in Sandra Witzke's article on Port Charlotte's first civic organization, they contributed time, money, and facilities to fledgling community groups.[54]

Construction of Port Charlotte started in October 1955, a year after the deal was done. The first building in Port Charlotte was at the intersection of US41 and Elkcam Boulevard. Construction of model homes was begun in December 1955 on Martin Drive. In October 1956, James Renshaw, his wife, Kathryn, and daughter, Connie, moved into their home at 102 S. Easy St. to become the first family in Port Charlotte.

For Odie Futch, General Development Corporation was a job dropped from heaven. He went to work for them right out of high school. Soon the slugger was slinging cement and managing men.

Right away, he ran into a problem that persists decades after GDC collapsed in bankruptcy. Developers had to build and maintain roads and infrastructure for a set period of time to ensure their safety and workmanship. County inspectors

---

[54] Witzke, Sandra, *Garden Trowels On a Mission: Port Charlotte Garden Club*, 2019, p. 16

Charlotte County History Services

By the end of the Fifties, the southwestern edge of Port Charlotte looked like this. The long wharf at lower left is part of the future beach complex, which county government now operates. The road leading left then turning to recede into the upper left corner is Harbor Boulevard. Below, 58 years after their installation by GDC, 17 miles of old iron pipe had to be replaced. GDC's gone, so the job fell to the inheritors of the former developer's water system, the Charlotte Harbor Water Association.

1957
Legislature passes an interposition (HCR 174) to reject Brown v. Board of Education decision by the U.S. Supreme Court; rejected by Governor Leroy Collins.

Seminole tribe of Florida formed as a political entity.

1957–58 influenza pandemic (also called "Asian flu"): Influenza A virus subtype H2N2, first identified in Guizhou province of China, spreads to Singapore. It reaches Hong Kong by April and the United States by June, killing at least 1 million people worldwide.

were responsible for monitoring such work and eventually approving its reversion to county government for maintenance and repair.

"Well, back then there wasn't anybody around here when the streets were put in," he recalled of GDC's early days. "I don't think the county ever came out and accepted them or not but it was theirs then. Later, when the area started developing in the Seventies and people started moving down and buying them lots and building a home in those out farther reaches, they'd say, 'Oh, General Development; they sold us this property and look at the streets. They don't even maintain anything.' Well, it wasn't ours. That's what we tried to explain. It belonged to the county."

CENTURY

1958
Alfred M. Johns and Wilber H. "Bud" Cole buy sand flats at Punta Gorda. They dredge 55 miles of canals for fill to raise ground level four feet while providing saltwater access for boaters.

Deed restrictions spur upscale construction at Punta Gorda Isles and Burnt Store Isles.

Punta Gorda library moves into its own building

The first of Leonard Bernstein's Young People's Concerts with the New York Philharmonic is telecast by CBS

In Sarasota County, where commissioners and inspectors probably were stricter, government attempted to nip the problem in the bud by requiring performance bonds before new work could be done in what was then called North Port Charlotte. In reaction, company officials in 1958 moved employees into town and put them on the town governing body. Not surprisingly, the commission then voted to incorporate. When county officials complained that the move was designed to circumvent the stringent development code, the new city's commission argued that community growth alone informed the decision.[55]

But in Charlotte County, still recovering from the dislocation of the Great Depression and the contraction of the postwar period, standards weren't so high. Initially that wasn't a problem, but as the company grew wealthier, the Mackles felt that quality was being compromised. After a failed effort to take back control of their company, the Mackles sold out in 1962. Years later, the only vestige of

Charlotte County History Services

The Fishery in Placida, Englewood's largest example of a vertically integrated fishing operation, during the late Fifties.

their once-ubiquitous presence was their signature quirk, common in every community they developed, of a street named Elkcam, Mackle spelled backward. Their name would return to the news in 1968, after Barbara, a daughter of Robert Mackle, was kidnapped. The kidnapper was apprehended in El Jobean.

But even as the land in between suddenly appeared to have a bright future, the skies were cloudier in Englewood. A concentration of the fishing industry, which started as a lifesaving phenomenon during the Great Depression, had become a way of life for many fishermen. Just as A. C. Frizzell left a legacy of peonage in what became Port Charlotte, so had the fishing industry become a sort of fiefdom,

---

[55] Marshal Grove, *p. 11*

A People's History of Charlotte County

Diana Harris

Built in 1928, torn down in 1978, this handsome school building became a victim of hard times that reflected Englewood's decline. 1972 photo by Woody Thayer.

Above, a very young Ellison Haddock; below, Calvin Haddock.

controlled by a few families fortunate enough to have sustained themselves and prospered during the harsh and turbulent Thirties and Forties.

Many fishermen, like the workers in Frizzell's industries and ranch, lived in company housing, used company equipment, and basically owed their soul to the company fish house.[56] However, many of the fishermen, particularly those supporting families, would have been hard-pressed without the vertical integration of a place to deliver their catch and a place to live. It made for a hard life in a poor community, one in which children went barefoot to a school that leaked.

As Odie Futch began his career and Englewood began a slow adjustment to a new reality, two children south of Punta Gorda were moving toward an appointment with destiny. Ellison and Gertha Haddock, along with their older brother, Calvin, lived on Burnt Store Road, on the site of the company that fed his family, the now-defunct Pinellas Gladiolus Company.

"I don't consider my family a major contributor to this area," Haddock says. "However, I know my dad came here in 1938 and he was born in Parrish; it's in north Florida. My mom is from around Albany, Georgia."

1959
Charlotte Hospital changes its name to Charlotte Community Hospital to better identify itself as a facility dedicated to serving the entire community.

General Development starts development of North Port Charlotte.

Charlotte Harbor Spa, the grand lady of Punta Gorda since 1886, is destroyed by fire.

The Daytona International Speedway completes construction.

Nylon tights, popularly called pantyhose or sheer tights, first sold on the open market as 'Panti-Legs' by Glen Raven Knitting Mills.

---

[56] Diana Harris, p .76

CENTURY

1960

Population is 12,594, a 193.8 percent increase since 1950

First U.S. troops sent to Vietnam

Hurricane Donna ravages most of U.S. eastern seaboard and does considerable damage in Charlotte County.

First Presbyterian Church wrecked, burns during rebuilding efforts

Punta Gorda adopts a new charter.

Cultural Center in Port Charlotte created by General Development Corporation

Charlotte County History Services

Gladiolus beds on the Frizzell land holdings in Murdock, where Pinellas Gladiolus once rented land. Circa 1950s.

From the time he was born, Haddock says of his father, the man worked hard.

"If he got hurt he'd put a little something on it or my mom would bandage him up and he would be back to work the next day; he'd just walk it off," Haddock said. had that rarest of jobs for a black man; a position of responsibility and independence that he held for 30 years. He was the groundskeeper, caretaker, and irrigation foreman for Pinellas Gladiolus Company's Burnt Store Road holdings.

"They were based out of Ft. Myers and he went down there to work, too," Haddock said. "But on the Burnt Store Road operation, he made sure the fields were wet enough and the flowers were growing. That's what he did. We lived there rent free, so the only thing was really electricity and gas for the gas stove."

His father is still a hero to Haddock, particularly because the man, who never spent a day in school, bequeathed to his children a belief in the value of education.

"My dad was illiterate, and my mom only went to fifth grade, but most parents back then valued education so much that they wouldn't allow their kids to drop out," Ellison said. "They wouldn't allow their kids to say, 'Hey, I don't feel like going today.' or 'I've got a stomachache.' 'Here, take this and go to school,' they'd say because they realized the opportunities they missed by not going to school."

Ellison and Gertha Jean Haddock didn't know it at the time—and neither did their parents—but they were being prepared to be sacrifices in the struggle for civil rights. The experience would affect them differently, as it would the small group of black children whose education marked the cusp of segregation's end and integration's beginning.

Near the end of its long life, the newly renamed Charlotte Harbor Spa tried a new ad campaign that could hide the fact that the city icon's best days were long past.

THE HOTEL CHARLOTTE HARBOR CHECKS OUT

Glenn Miller

Punta Gorda has never seen anything like it before or since. On August 14, 1959, the most famous hotel in the county's history burned to the ground, leaving little more than a smoldering heap of rubble and ashes.

It was gone. Utterly. And forever.

Flames were visible more than 25 miles away as the building that was constructed in 1887 and opened as the Hotel Punta Gorda was consumed. Firefighters rushed in from three counties, from Arcadia and Ft. Myers and Fort Myers Beach. Onlookers feared the fire would spread to the rest of downtown. Firefighters struggled for five hours to keep flames away from other buildings.

All that may have saved Punta Gorda from further destruction that humid night was a fortuitous change in wind direction.

Sherra Poppell was there, witnessing it from a safe distance as a 6-year-old, then beginning her first week of grade school.

"They thought it was going to take the whole town," Ms. Poppell said.

It was quite a sight for a small child.

"I was kind of scared," Ms. Poppell said. "I didn't know what was going to happen."

Betty Jo Lees was living across the Peace River 55 years ago.

"Somebody said the old hotel was on fire," said Ms. Lees, a 1955 graduate of Charlotte High.

Somebody was right.

The fire was a huge regional news story, one the *Fort Myers News-Press* splashed across its front page the next morning with a big photograph and this headline: "Flames Raze Old Charlotte Harbor Hotel."

The paper reported that the "giant structure" was totally destroyed and that there were "no casualties."

Reporter Rufe Daughtrey wrote that Homer Monson, who had just arrived in port with a cargo of fish at the Punta Gorda Fish Company, first noticed the fire at 2 a.m., and jumped in a car and sped to a fire station to spread the alarm.

He notified engineer Derrill E. Moore, who was on duty at that time. It was a scary night as the hotel, which was made of native pitch pine, blazed away in the summer heat.

Firefighter Earl Davis told a reporter that, "the heat was intense and we had to keep the firemen sprinkled so they could stay close enough to keep water pouring into the building."

The heat wasn't the only worry.

"We kept water pouring steadily on a 400-gallon tank of fuel oil to prevent an explosion," Mr. Davis told the newspaper.

That prevented an explosion but couldn't save the grand old hotel.

"A blackened chimney towered bleakly out of the wreckage of the kitchen," Mr. Daughtrey wrote. "Steel columns for the elevator were doubled by the heat into hairpin shapes."

The cause of the fire was immediately a mystery and remains so. Hotel caretaker Floyd Goodpaster was suspected of being involved in starting the fire and was given a lie detector test and was subject to what The News-Press termed "three days of grilling."

They couldn't pin anything on the 48-year-old Mr. Goodpaster about the fire and three days later came the news that he was cleared of any suspicion of starting the fire.

That's how the grand hotel's life ended — under plumes of smoke and an unresolved investigation.

By 1959, of course, people were traveling by jet planes and driving over the Peace River in cars and watching television and listening to radios.

None of those things existed when the hotel opened in 1887.

A People's History of Charlotte County

Florida Weekly

The Hotel Charlotte Harbor, built as the Hotel Punta Gorda. The hotel was purchased by Barron Collier and Cornelius Vanderbilt in 1924. They enlarged, remodeled and renamed it the Hotel Charlotte Harbor. In its later years, it was known as the Charlotte Harbor Spa.

The fire destroyed it 72 years after it opened at what was then the southern terminus of railroad service on Florida's west coast, which was provided by the Florida Southern Railway.

The hotel was built by Henry Plant, a towering figure in Florida history. He built other grand hotels on Florida's west coast much like his east coast counterpart, Henry Flagler, built on the other side of the state.

In the early 20th century, though, the hotel wasn't always considered an historic treasure.

In historian Vernon Peeples' "Punta Gorda and the Charlotte Harbor Area, A Pictorial History," this comes through in a quote from more than a century ago.

Mr. Peeples reported that the Punta Gorda Herald said this in 1910: "The big unsightly building known as the Hotel Punta Gorda continues to be an eyesore and an incubus to the town and there seems no prospect that it will ever be anything else. … The huge old hulk standing idle and ugly for nine years past is actually a curse to the community."

1927 announcement of Barron Collier's remodeled Hotel Punta Gorda, now the Hotel Charlotte Harbor. Below, a matchbook cover from the era.

But the building survived despite hard times. Mr. Peeples wrote that there were some years back then when the hotel didn't even open.

Over its 72 years of life, the hotel was known by various names. Barron Collier, whose name is perhaps best known for Collier County and the Collier Inn on Useppa, bought the building in 1924, which had closed in 1914, and renamed it the Hotel Charlotte Harbor.

It was renovated and modernized, a swimming pool was built and the hotel reopened in 1927. Two clay tennis courts were constructed in 1930 for one of the iconic athletes of the first half of the 20th century — tennis player Bill Tilden.

Tilden, who was as famous as Babe Ruth, Jack Dempsey and Red Grange in the 1920s, won a tournament in Punta Gorda in 1931.

Mr. Collier died in 1939, and his heirs sold the hotel to G. Floyd Alford in 1944 and he, in turn, let Martin Fleischman take over the mortgage in 1956. Mr. Fleischman re-named it the Charlotte Harbor Spa, which remained its name until its fiery death.

The hotel was one of 20 grand hotels built in Florida in the 19th century, back when the state's population was a tiny fraction of what it is today. In 1890, for example, Florida's population was 390,000. In the 2010 census it was 18.8 million.

Yet, in towns across the peninsula, similar hotels were built. There were the Alcazar and Ponce de Leon in St. Augustine. There was the Belleview Biltmore Resort & Spa in Belleair, a short drive north of St. Petersburg.

There was the Palm Beach Inn, which was later re-named the Breakers.

And more — the Fort Myers Hotel, the Kissimmee Hotel and the Ocala House and the Tampa Bay Hotel. The Tampa Bay Hotel, which is now the site of the University of Tampa, opened in 1891, four years after the Hotel Punta Gorda.

The fate of Punta Gorda's famed hotel was not unique in the state's history. Other grand old Florida hotels from the 19th century were also destroyed by fire. The Hotel Continental in Atlantic Beach, the Seminole Hotel in Winter Park. The Kissimmee Hotel and two in Jacksonville — the Windsor Hotel and the St. James Hotel — all were lost to fire. Now, 55 years later, the images of Aug. 14, 1959, are still seared in the memories of those who were in Punta Gorda that night.

"I've never seen a fire like that," Ms. Poppell said.

Neither has anybody else in Charlotte County history.

The hotel, though, lives on in 2014 in a mural in downtown Punta Gorda on the side of the Charlevoi Condominiums.

There, the grand old building can still be seen, 127 years after it was built and 55 years after it burned to the ground.

The mural, like the hotel it re-creates, is another symbol of Punta Gorda's pluck. The original hotel mural was destroyed by Hurricane Charley on Aug. 13, 2004, one day short of the 45th anniversary of the fire that destroyed the hotel. The middle of August has not always been kind to Punta Gorda, sending first fire and then a hurricane.

But the town recovered from both August catastrophes. An historical marker about the Hotel Punta Gorda was placed in 2009 on the site of the old hotel on West Marion Avenue near Taylor Street. Photos of the hotel can be found on the Charlotte County Historical Society website.

Most of the people who witnessed the fire are gone, as gone as the hotel itself. But for anybody who wonders about the grand old place, just walk or drive by the Charlevoi Condominiums and look up, up at a Florida landmark, one destroyed six decades ago.

Originally published in Florida Weekly, August 14, 2014

CHANGING INDUSTRIES SHAPE ENGLEWOOD

Diana Harris

Mercury Marine's high-powered engine and marine operation, once located at the tip of Cape Haze at the top of this photograph, represented the new wave of Englewood businesses. The Fishery is at the bottom of photo (Diana Harris)

By 1960 Englewood could no longer be described as that sleepy little fishing village on Lemon Bay that nobody knew about. Looking back on Englewood history, it appears that the early '60s was a watershed period and the start of a new era.

A town needs industry and commerce to make it work. And as a town's industry changes, so do the people and the face of the community. Englewood was starting to see some big changes by 1960. By that time, our area had already witnessed several industries that had flourished, receded and disappeared, and a new longer-lasting one was emerging, tourism.

The first industry was the ill-fated lemon and citrus business, which was wiped out by killer freezes in December 1894 and January 1895.

CENTURY

Diana Harris

In the foreground are rails of the narrow-gauge Woodmere railroad. In the background is a main street of the segregated workers' quarters in this circa 1920s photo.

The next industry appeared on the coattails of World War I. Because of the war, a tremendous demand for lumber had been created. Woodmere Lumber Company, located where Waste Management, Inc. is now, on SR776 to Venice, once was one of the largest lumber operations in the Southeast.

Reforestation was an unknown word in the lumber business in those day, so when the beautiful, dense virgin pine forests were cut down, the timber and turpentine people moved on, leaving behind a denuded landscape and a handful of people who settled in Englewood.

Commercial fishing, the industry most associated with Englewood, reached its apex during the WWII years. Records indicate about 2 million pounds of seafood were shipped out annually during the war years.

In the late 1940s, Lemon Bay's clam industry was considered the second most profitable in the whole state. But right after WWII, as beef became more plentiful, the national demand for seafood dropped.

Another blow to local commercial fishing was the effect of Lemon Bay slowly silting in. Interestingly enough, as early as 1935 this had been noted. Florida politicians that year introduced a bill in Congress urging that some new opening into Lemon Bay be made in order to create more of a tidal flow. That fight continued until 1950, when it was finally given up. However, as commercial fishing declined, sport fishing grew more important to the town. The waters were still rich enough that the area enjoyed an outstanding reputation among sportsmen. The tourists were beginning to come more often, stay longer, and bring their families. A demand was soon created for marinas that offered boat storage, boat sales, tackle shops, motels and restaurants. Soon the vacationers turned into property owners and the real estate business started to grow.

The resulting demand in the building trade began to totally change the face of Englewood. The older buildings were almost entirely wood frame structures, set up off the ground a foot or two. Most had small fireplaces and front porches. They were plain and simple in design but charming and inviting. After WWII masonry or concrete block homes started to be built.

An almost totally new Englewood was emerging. Jobs and businesses were different and the town even looked different. A new era was dawning and would bring with it great change.

PUNTA GORDA GARDEN CLUB

Mary Yeomans
President, Punta Gorda Garden Club

For over seventy of the 100 years that Charlotte County has existed, the Punta Gorda Garden Club has been active in the Charlotte County community. The club was organized in 1949 and became a part of the Florida Federation of Garden Clubs in 1950. Meetings were held in members' homes and included a guest speaker at each meeting. Activities in the beginning included decorating a city Christmas tree, providing prizes for the best decorated homes during the holidays, and planting a memorial tree for Arbor Day. Also, a campaign to keep Punta Gorda clean – Don't Be a Litter Bug – was publicized.

The red hibiscus was chosen as the club flower as a salute to the city's history. In 1926 the city council passed an ordinance proclaiming Punta Gorda as "The City of Hibiscus," and 2200 red hibiscus were ordered and planted throughout the city.

Much of the work of the club is based on accomplishment of its objectives which appear on the club website: www.pggc.org. The goals of the club are to promote the beautification and improvement of Punta Gorda and the surrounding areas, to encourage the growing of flowers, plants and shrubbery in public and private places, and to cooperate in the conservation of natural resources, and promote education in all of these areas.

Photos Punta Gorda Garden Club
Top, 1951 show. Above, Marian Bandler and Elise Haymans decorating Bandler's home for the annual Tour of Homes.

Beautification of the community is accomplished in a number of ways. Several public gardens have been designed and planted by club members, including the Quiet Garden at the Woman's Club on Sullivan St., the Heritage Garden at History Park, and the Elise Haymans Butterfly Garden in Charlotte Harbor Environmental Center. Members of the club have worked weekly for years on garden maintenance at these and other public gardens located in the community such as the old Punta Gorda Library, Laishley Park, and more recently, the Peace River Botanical and Sculpture Gardens. Plants have been installed at all of these gardens along with the Blanchard House Museum and many Habitat for Humanity homes. The club's most recent effort is a partnership with TEAM Punta Gorda in the America in Bloom project in downtown Punta Gorda in which consultants advise on ways to beautify the city. Planters have been and will continue to be installed and maintained.

Club members participate in community cleanup efforts each year such as the International Coastal Clean Up and the Great American Backyard Clean Up. These are organized by the Keep Charlotte Beautiful organization, which is part of Keep America Beautiful. These efforts harken back to the first cleanup campaign – Don't Be a Litter Bug!

CENTURY

Flower shows have been held over the years with the first taking place in 1951 at the Woman's Club on Sullivan Street. In 1959 the show spanned two days – 3:30 – 10:00 pm March 5 and Friday, March 6 from 11:00 am to 9:00 pm! The suggested donation was 50 cents. Recently the Flower Shows have been held in Lenox Hall at the First United Methodist Church for one day from 1:00 until 4:00 and no donations are collected. The public is invited after the judging has concluded. Times have certainly changed!

A traditional holiday celebration in Punta Gorda is the Holly Days Home Tour, presented in early December each year. Four homes in the Punta Gorda Historic District and the First United Methodist Church are decorated for the holidays using mostly natural materials. In recent years over 1800 tickets were sold for this event. This has grown to be the primary fundraiser for the club, which provided over $12,000 in donations to local organizations that are involved in the fields related to the club's goals in 2020. Among these are the Peace River Botanical Gardens, the Peace River Wildlife Center, ECHO Farm, Keep Charlotte Beautiful, and Avon Park Correctional Institute Garden Therapy Program. In this unique program, inmates are trained in horticultural methods and prepare for a career to be followed upon their release from incarceration.

Also, scholarships are awarded to selected college bound students from Charlotte County who will be studying in the fields of environmental science, horticulture, landscape design, and other related subjects related to the goals of the club. In 2020, $18,000 was awarded to six aspiring students.

A National Garden Club Blue Star Marker was dedicated in 1968 and is still located in the median on Route 41 at the split near Carmalita Street. This plaque was refurbished by the club in 2016 and replaced by city staff. A second Blue Star Marker was installed in 2020, located at Veterans Park across the street from the courthouse. Blue Star Markers remind us of the unselfish dedication of our Armed Service members.

Florida Weekly

Vic Desguin and Elise Haymans are crowned 2016 King and Queen of Hibiscus During the annual event Bill Crosland.

PGGC is also involved with youth in environmental and gardening programs. For years volunteers taught students about the importance and planting of trees at the annual Arbor Day event held in Punta Gorda for 2nd grade Charlotte County students. Partnerships have formed throughout the years at all levels of schools. Recently club members worked with students from Charlotte High School who have tended a plot in the History Park Community Garden and others worked with horticulture classes at the Florida Southwest Collegiate High School. Students at Sallie Jones Elementary formed a club called "Lil Diggers." This involvement with the youth of the community continues to evolve as needs change, but PGGC attempts to fulfill the needs of educators and students in Charlotte County.

Throughout the seventy or so years the Punta Gorda Club has existed, it has infiltrated many facets of our community and made this a better place to visit and in which to reside. Here's to another 70 years!

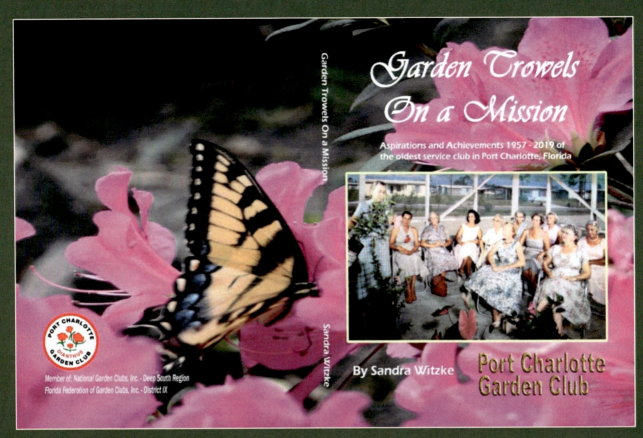

Sandra Witzke's scholarship and insight into the dynamics of early Port Charlotte offers a surprising look at the power of a few good women with trowels.

THE PORT CHARLOTTE GARDEN CLUB
Sandra Witzke

"As long as one has a garden one has a future; and as long as one has a future one is alive."
Frances Hodgson Burnett, In the Garden, 1925

The story of the Port Charlotte Garden Club for all intents and purposes was set in motion just a few years after the area's transformation from cowboy ranches, pasture grass and the cattle business. Financial potential was seen by eager land developers which resulted in loads of infrastructure improvements. All was then followed with paved streets, newly dug canals and cleared lots to replace the existing dirt roads, drainage ditches and grazing land.

Massive international advertising campaigns by Mackle Brothers Construction and the General Development Corporation in the mid-1950s, promoted individual lot sales to retirees from all areas. They mapped out 25,000 lots in the Port Charlotte area and reached out to the cold northerners to buy a lot for only $600 with just $10 down. Houses cost between $5900 and $17,990 and 1000 homes were built in 1958.

Housing in Port Charlotte was even marketed via color ads in Life Magazine in March 1958 and February 1959. In fact, to make the Port Charlotte development more appealing to the northern retirees, Mackle actually named one of the streets, Easy Street. As a result of all the hype, scores of new residents began arriving to build homes.

CENTURY

While these homes were rapidly being built, new friendships were forming just as fast. Neighbors excitedly arrived from a multitude of areas in the country and eagerly became settled in their new surroundings. Sadie Bailey was one of those new residents, building her house on Waterway Circle, not too far from Easy Street. She was a long-lime widow, had been a caregiver for her mother and also worked at the VA Hospital in Fort Custer, Michigan. The dream of retirement was coming true. She bought into the marketed installment land sale campaign and was thrilled to have the opportunity to move south to the much warmer climate of Port Charlotte and begin a new life.

Coming from Battle Creek, Michigan, she most likely was a gardener who was accustomed to plant growth and blooms that occurred in just the summer months, then were tucked beneath a blanket of snow for the remainder of the year. Sadie soon recognized that she wasn't alone in the aspiration to learn of new gardening routines and so many new plant choices. In addition, she acknowledged that not only her immediate neighborhood, but the budding new community could also use some dedicated guidance in beautification.

Sandra Witzke

Sadie Bailey

Full of energy and enthusiasm, and not content to sit idly at home, this exceptional woman made it her mission to share her inspirations with others. Beginning with her own neighborhood, she actually went door-to-door to personally chat with many early Port Charlotte residents in an appeal to start a garden club. After weeks of talking and visiting with interested people, the group met for the first time on October 24, 1957 with 18 women at the new Port Charlotte Community Building, near Easy Street.

The first meeting was attended not only by the new interested Port Charlotte residents, but also by the Florida Federation of Garden Club (FFGC) Director of District 9, Mrs. M. C. Kayton of Wauchula. As representatives of the sponsoring club, the Punta Gorda Garden Club president, Mrs. Ruth Allison, along with Mrs. Farr and Mrs. Maxwell and several other gardeners of Punta Gorda were also present. The name, Port Charlotte Garden Club, was proudly chosen, and the guest speakers enlightened regarding the various activities that a garden club could do to increase beauty and interest in the community. That first gathering had to be so exciting!

In the newly created constitution, the club objectives stated that the "Port Charlotte Garden Club shall promote the beautification and improvement of Port Charlotte; to encourage the growing and showing of native plant material; to co-operate in the conservation of natural resources; to study the art of flower arranging and to foster the practice of good horticulture in all its phases." These words are still respected to this day.

* * *

In observance of Florida's Arbor Day, a Cherry Laurel tree became the club's first tree planting on January 17, 1958, taking place at the Port Charlotte Community Center, the center for the club and other civic activities. According to the club minutes that day, "The services were well attended, despite the cold and windy day. I'm sure we'll all be very proud of it and enjoy watching it grow. At Christmas time it will be a nice tree to light and decorate." Spade work for the event was done by Mr. John Rogers, president of the Port Charlotte Civic Organization and Mr. LeGier, a Mackle Company representative.

A People's History of Charlotte County

Nathaniel "Doc" McQueen, Charlotte County's long time Extension Agricultural Agent of that era gave compliments regarding the tree choice adding, "The Cherry Laurel tree is a very hardy tree which will withstand freezes and needs no pruning and, if properly cared for, would be a source of enjoyment for the folks here and for years to come and would remain as a visual reminder of the handiwork of God."

Rev. Ralph Fink read the well-known poem, "God Planted a Garden" by Dorothy Frances Gurney (1858-1932).

In conclusion, Mrs. Bailey fittingly dedicated the tree to the "future beautification of Port Charlotte" and announced that a plaque would be furnished and installed at the base of the tree by the Mackle Brothers Company. Photos of the happy moment were taken by Mr. Nice, a Mackle Company photographer which were later proudly displayed in the newspaper.

* * *

During the 1960s, more and more residents were now entering the Port Charlotte area. The General Development glossy color magazine ads and brochures claimed, "How can you afford to stay up north when it costs so little to live in the sun? Get your own home for as little as $225 down and $52 a month." The Mackle-built homes were being promoted for retirement, vacation or investment and the population was increasing dramatically. In fact, the Charlotte County census figures of 1950 indicated a population of 4,286 with a whopping 193.8% increase in 1960 to 12,594 people.

Sandra Witzke

Being the earliest service club in the area, the garden club was continuing to flourish and gain new members, recording 145 members by 1961. In efforts to show the growing comradery within the new community, General Development cleverly used color photographs of a Port Charlotte Garden Club meeting and also one of the club's outside events in their numerous brochures as a marketing strategy. The Port Charlotte Civic Association had also formed which gave residents a greater voice in city government and it too was aiming to provide more interest for the new residents. So much was definitely happening in the area.

In accordance with the club's persistent beautification goal of Port Charlotte, education seminars were arranged and held at the community center; Palmer Nursery in Osprey and the club partnered to provide garden classes which were attended by club members and interested residents. Types of plants, growing zones and aspects of landscaping were just a few of the topics by the speakers. It surely had to be a win-win situation by both increasing club membership and by advertising the nursery's business.

1965 sales brochure published by PGI/ Punta Gorda Isles Civic Association.

THE BIG CHANGE

"I've seen fire and I've seen rain," sang James Taylor. In the Sixties, Charlotte County would see its share of both. And no community would be as transformed by fire and rain as Punta Gorda.

It began the day the hotel died by fire, at the end of the Fifties, almost like a fiery punctuation to a decade of dislocation. By that time, Aaron "Jim" Marshall's life was a metaphor for the uncertain times. His itinerant minister of a father had suddenly been felled by illness while working a pastorate near Venice. The family opted to return to Indiana, but Jim decided to stay put. He moved in with the Hughes, who owned the grocery store where he worked as a meatcutter and jack-of-all-trades.

Across the water lay the new colossus, a burgeoning tract of homes that seemed to rise as fast as their prices fell. Jim met a girl, the daughter of a General Development executive. The man saw where his daughter's eyes were fixed, so he offered Marshall a job at a dollar an hour. But Jim wanted more and left the area, only to return years later driving one of the last trains to enter Venice, at the end of Southwest Florida's rail age.

But in between, a lot of things happened. Amid the fire and the rain was a scene of love, enacted on a quiet vista of palmettos, fiddler crabs, and glorious dreams. Al Johns, a former CIA operative and present banker/developer based in Miami, drove the woman who would be his wife to a point overlooking Punta Gorda west, toward what is now the PGI tidal basin. There, near the western edge of the peninsula called Fat Point he spoke of his dream to create a high-end development that would dwarf anything done before. [57]

His date must have believed in him. Three children and thousands of homes later, Al Johns proved to be as good as his soaring words as PGI changed Punta Gorda from a sleepy fishing village into something completely different.

Florida Memory

Visitors to Punta Gorda During the late Fifties and early Sixties were greeted by this sign of the times.
Below, the powers-that-were at Punta Gorda Isles.

1961
Charlotte County Art Guild organizes.

Charlotte County board of education agrees to participate in establishing Fort Myers Junior College, name changed to Edison Community College in 1971. Florida Legislature established Edison Junior College (EJC) and appropriated funding for a permanent campus. It is now called Florida Southwest State College.

The first American astronaut, Alan Shepard, was launched into space from Cape Canaveral Space Center (later called Cape Kennedy).

---
[57] Gaye Johns Brownie Interview, October 2021

1962
Punta Gorda dams Shell Creek to create reservoir for municipal water supply.

First Presbyterian Church rebuilds.

St. Joseph-Bon Secours Hospital opens at Port Charlotte.

Ranger 3 is launched to study the moon; it misses the moon by 22,000 miles.

Danny Thomas founded St. Jude Children's Research Hospital.

Gaye Johns Brownie as May Day queen with her king, future football star Burton Lawless; right, Judi Duff Addison needles Santa. Below, the friends in 2020.

Part of the reason for PGI's growth and durability has been its early family presence. Gaye Johns Brownie and Judi Duff Addison are friends for life who met as two of the first girls in PGI. Their first job was to raise and lower the flag at the development's sales office every day. Their first adventure entailed almost drifting out to sea on an ill-advised cruise from the yacht basin.

But childhoods like theirs, and the investment made in such formative years by the thousands of parents who moved to PGI, gave the community a grounding that endures. Although few people would call PGI or the subsequent spin-offs that dot Southwest Florida family communities, that's what PGI was at a time when Punta Gorda and other communities around Charlotte County seemed to some to be a children's paradise.

Steve Frizzell, who was born in 1949 and lived on Olympia Avenue in Punta Gorda as a child, remembers a much different community from the city's modern ambience.

A People's History of Charlotte County

Cheryl Frizzell

Steve Frizzell, his brother, A.C., and sister, Cheryl.

"The kids pretty much had the run of the town," he recalled. "We could go anywhere we wanted. We would run through people's back yards. Nobody cared. Everybody was just very friendly and for the most part just thought of the kids as just kids out playing and having a good time."

Frizzell remembers the excitement of his family having the first television on the block.

"I do remember the TV station in Fort Myers a little more because it had a show there called the Cousin Vern's show for kids every Saturday morning, and I remember one day the four of us were all on the Cousin Vern Show one day and that was a big deal," he recalled. "There was a summer recreation program down at the park on the bay there. There was a library right there and a park and the coaches from the school ran the summer recreation program. The kids would all go down there and they would have organized activities. The coaches were there looking out for the kids. So parents were working and kids were at the park in the program. They would do field trips a couple of times a week. I remember we did a field trip to a bowling alley over in Charlotte Harbor. That's where I learned to bowl and I ended up loving the bowling and I bowled for years."

Frizzell describes a waterfront, one teeming with townsfolk instead of tourists.

"A little further down was where they had the Little League baseball diamond," he said. They also played men's softball and women's softball and that. There was a lot of activity going on o the waterfront."

Historian Lynn Harrell, whose work appears throughout this volume, opines that stricter zoning laws in the aftermath of Hurricane Donna put an end to the kid-centered universe. Harrell says that when mixed-use zoning was forbidden in downtown, families could no longer live above shops. Adjacent neighborhoods were rezoned medical or commercial. When the families left, Punta Gorda began a slow 30-year decline.

Probably the fondest memories of Odie Futch's life were made under the fire tower where his peripatetic family found security and Futch was fortunate to grow into himself. He had started playing Little League ball then, but he still hadn't grown into his size, so he was clumsy and uncoordinated. He recalled how after dinner,

1963

Barbara Mackle, daughter of Robert Mackle, is kidnapped and buried alive in Georgia in a ransom extortion. Abductor Gary Krist flees with the ransom to Hog Island in Charlotte Harbor where he is captured. Miss Mackle rescued.

George Wallace becomes governor of Alabama. He defiantly proclaims "segregation now, segregation tomorrow, and segregation forever!" He was wrong.

President John F. Kennedy is fatally shot by Lee Harvey Oswald, and Governor of Texas John Connally is seriously wounded

The Boys of Summer

PORT CHARLOTTE ROTARY REDS
MANAGER, Ben Lowe COACH, Bob Feist
Mike Dwyer, Mike Barley, John Upsahl, Larry Correll, Bruce Smith, Larry Zeeman, Stanley Lowe, Chris Taylor, Loren Wright, Otis Futch, David Raybuck, Steve Reilly, Rik Jesse.

PUNTA GORDA KIWANIS YANKEES
MANAGER, Jack Connelly
Ricki Inden, Donnie McFarland, Jackie Connelly, Dale Hadley, Garry Moran, Don Houghtaling, Fred Hindman, Lane Deitrick, Wayne Bennett, Jim Savasek, Jim Doyle, Nick King, Sid Johnson, John Smith, Eli Winesett.

Otis Futch Slams 1st Homer

Otis Futch, the Reds' huge first baseman, got his first full uniform in three years with the Little League and proceeded to pay for it with the first homer of his career—a whomping blast over the left field wall.

Coupled with four other hits for the Reds, it was enough to pass the Indians with a 9-7 score. Wedell was the winning pitcher, serving up only three hits.

Wedell got a double, and Skotko got the only extra base hit for the Indians, a triple to the center field corner. Opsahl, the Reds shortstop, got that unusual Little League play—an unassisted double play.

his dad would come down from the fire tower and they'd play catch, with his mom fielding balls and the two parents offering instruction and support. By then his dad was coaching Little League ball, so he knew what he was talking about and Odie listened. It became a family effort. When he visited his grandparents in Punta Gorda, his grandfather would take him down to Seminole Drugs and buy him a milkshake. The old man would tell the soda jerk to put a whole egg in it to build his grandson up. Odie Futch still pauses and catches himself as he recalls the old man looking at him, face beaming with pride and love, as he urged his grandson to drink up and get strong.

A People's History of Charlotte County

The old Little League field on Punta Gorda's waterfront. Below, Futch with his big rig during his General Development days.

It worked. Little League baseball back then was a much more intimate affair in Punta Gorda. The fields were located right on the waterfront, between where the children's section of Gilchrist Park and the YMCA building sits today. Futch became a slugger, hitting multiple home run records high into the Peace River—a local car dealership gave a boy a silver dollar every time the little leaguer accomplished that feat—and becoming the wheelhorse of his team.

The Scout house was located near the ball field, so Odie joined the Scouts, again a pursuit much more intimately woven into the society of Punta Gorda back then. That was when families often congregated downtown for the ball games, scouting events, or just to enjoy the park, before the city's emphasis turned toward retirement living and tourism.

Little League is still big, but much of the action takes place out of the mainstream, at the huge county complex on Carmalita Road east of Punta Gorda or at the assorted Little League fields around the county The fields reflect a welcome and major commitment by the county toward youth facilities but lack the central locations and community support youth sports once enjoyed Odie Futch graduated from high school and went right to work for General Development Corporation. Residents of the Springlake area have him to thank for the pilings and abutments along the inland pond.

Sports taught Futch to work with others, so he was able to rise from work gang to crew chief to foreman. But he knows his rise to a life he is proud of started on his field of dreams some 60 years ago.

1963

Vietnam War – Battle of Ap Bac: The Viet Cong win their first major victory.

Cape Canaveral renamed Cape Kennedy by President Lyndon Johnson, who also established the Kennedy Space Center at the site, located in Brevard County.

Black student Harvey Gantt enters Clemson University in South Carolina, the last U.S. state to hold out against racial desegregation.

1964

Federal Department of Transportation approves extension of interstate-75 to Naples after appeals from Charlotte County civic leaders and others. Construction moves slowly in segments.

Edison Junior College's first formal commencement ceremonies were held for a graduating class of 67 students.

St. Augustine race riot, white men with baseball bats attack NAACP youth groups staging sit-ins

Florida Atlantic University in Boca Raton and the University of West Florida in Pensacola open.

Punta Gorda Isles Civic Association

Part of the reason for the burgeoning sense of community in new developments like PGI was the activism of newcomers like Pete Bontsema, who organized the antecedent of what is now the Punta Gorda Isles Civic Club. Every year Bontsema would create giant postcards with Christmas themes which he placed along the sidewalks of PGI. The idea grew so popular City Hall borrowed it and soon made the cards an annual display in the city's Gilchrist Park. But that wasn't the only infiltration from the new community. Soon PGI executives were sitting on the City Council, effecting community change, and in doing so beginning a process that would end in PGI literally swallowing Punta Gorda.

The change was gradual and, at least based on early sales tools, somewhat unexpected. One 1970s ad described:

"A place where you can look out of your window and see grass and trees and water. Instead of somebody else's window. Punta Gorda Isles . . . designed for independent people who prefer leisure outdoor living. Away from crowds.

A People's History of Charlotte County

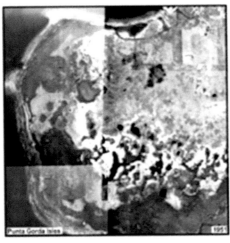

This series of aerials supplied by Punta Gorda government shows how PGI grew from the 1950s through the end of the century.

And the private clubs, boating, fishing, golf and tennis that go with it. People who know a good thing when they see it.[58]

All that would change as PGI blossomed and eventually swallowed Punta Gorda. Today all save one of the City Council seats are held by members from

---
[58] *Port Charlotte Daily Herald News*, 4-30-74

1965
Cultural Center operations transferred to Charlotte County adult education department.

What is now Bayfront Hospital adds a 13-bed intensive care unit, a new laboratory and a 60-bed extended care facility.

New campus of Edison Junior College opened on an 80-acre site off Cypress Lake Drive, with Building B (Leonhardt Hall), Building C (Robinson Hall, and a maintenance building that contained showers and locker rooms for physical education and athletics.

Dr. David G. Robinson inaugurated as second President of Edison.

CENTURY

Sonja Wright

1966
Charlotte Hospital becomes Medical Center Hospital. Administrators say the change is being made because "we are serving an area, not just one county."

Claude Kirk elected Florida's first Republican governor since Reconstruction.

Part of Babcock-Webb Wildlife Management Area set aside for secretly training Cuban exiles for aborted Bay of Pigs invasion.

Charlotte Hospital purchased by Medical Center Hospital.

Tamiami Trail expanded to four lanes.

When the irrepressible Mary Nightingale noticed that black school children didn't get lunches, she became the lunch lady, bringing her own snacks for the students at the Baker Academy in addition to her school bus driver duties. Martha (Russell) Bireda is the girl accepting a bottle of milk.

PGI or the adjacent western communities the development spawned. Punta Gorda supports and maintains seawalls and other amenities built by the PGI developers and readily annexed the community.

As the *Washington Post* reported, Hurricane Donna nearly wiped out the canal network being built in 1960. During a commemorative story celebrating PGI's 20-year anniversary, the writer noted that the storm, coupled with a state crackdown on dredging, almost crippled the company at its start.[59] But steady growth, feeding off the postwar boom in Florida in-migration, spurred success.

PGI was indeed an idea whose time has come. At the turn of the century, its population of retirees drawing remittances from investments helped shield the city from the worst effects of the pandemic and economic downturn. That pain, not surprisingly, was felt more by the restaurants and other businesses and service amenities that have come to depend on PGI money for survival.

As walls were going up in Charlotte County, walls also were coming down. The 1954 Supreme Court Brown vs. Board of Education decision was felt keenly in Florida and much of the South. Many resisted the Court's mandate that separate but equal facilities were unconstitutional. Charlotte County, by virtue of its relative poverty and its proximity well below the Mason-Dixon line, offered a prime example of what separate but equal looked like.

---

[59] https://www.washingtonpost.com/archive/realestate/1978/04/01/punta-gorda-nears-21/da364398-1cb3-40cf-a69d-8ff2accbbeda/

A People's History of Charlotte County

All photos Sonja Wright

At the time, Charlotte High School in Punta Gorda was the only county secondary school. Students from Englewood were bused or drove daily around the crescent of SR776 to US41 and Punta Gorda.

But for black children whose parents wanted them to be educated beyond grammar school, the journey to the classroom was even more arduous. The only black school, the Baker Academy, was a converted Army barracks located at the present site of the Cooper Street recreation center. The curriculum consisted of manual arts for the boys, domestic training for the girls, and enough traditional subjects to enable students to read, write, and do simple calculations.

"They really expected us to fail," Ellison Haddock, a member of the last class to pass through Baker Academy, said. "All of our books were pass-me-downs. They had already been used, you know how they put the names in the books? Those were the books we got and those were the good books."

He chuckled at the bittersweet memory. "And they weren't even second hand; more like 15th hand."

And if a black student wanted to go on to high school, the county financed an interlocal agreement by which black high school students were bused to Ft. Myers, to Dunbar High School. That commute could last for two hours. Black students from Englewood would be driven to the Baker Academy, where a

1967
Florida Legislature approves pari-mutuel betting with proceeds to be allocated to counties. Charlotte County authorizes expenditures for a War Memorial Auditorium (completed 1969, and a public health center at Punta Gorda, 500 feet of gulf beach at Englewood, and $200,000 for a new Cultural Center at Port Charlotte.

Building E (Learning Resources, Doris Corbin Auditorium, Auditorium Gallery) completed at what is now Florida Southwest State College.

1968

Complete revision of the state constitution, which consolidated the numerous boards and commissions into more streamlined Departments and Divisions, such as Departments of Natural Resources, Environmental Regulation, Education, State, Agriculture, Commerce, and Transportation.

Florida is the scene of the nation's first statewide teachers' strike.

Florida Technological University opens near Orlando (later renamed University of Central Florida).

schoolteacher would drive them down to Dunbar for classes and drive them back at night to begin the whole process in reverse.

Parents with greater means sent their children to relatives who lived in communities with high schools that welcomed black children or paid to have them educated in a black private school.

Judi Duff Addison experienced integration twice, first as a primary school student who didn't know what she was looking at and later as a woman, brought face to face with her father's role in integration.

She recalls being at the old Sallie Jones building in 1963 when Charlotte County became one of the first southern school districts to open public education to all races, looking across the street at a parade of cars and a large group of people clustered around the high school. She knew something big was happening but didn't know what. Decades later, at an old timers gathering for longtime Punta Gorda residents, she was approached by the city's doyenne, Gussie Baker.

"She wagged her finger at me and told me she had something to tell me about my father. Addison's father was Omar Duffy, the go-to guy for PGI projects. As a City Councilman and an employer of black men on a variety of PGI construction sites, Duff walked in both worlds.

Baker told Addison that Duff was a go-between during the secret struggle for integration that would make Punta Gorda one of the first high schools in the state to integrate. Credit for the courageous move goes to private citizens like Baker, then a mom of primary school children, and a farsighted superintendent of schools, Hugh Adams. Sonja Wright, author of *Down the Street,* an account of black life in Punta Gorda, remembers integration from a different perspective. Her mother, Bessie Mae Haynes Thomas-Bryant, worked with her brother, Booker T. Haynes, and John Henry Allen, leader of the local NAACP branch, to find black students both morally and academically strong enough for the challenge. Wright, who was in the third class of black students to enter Charlotte High, wrote this tribute to the pioneers:

Gertha Haddock

Felix Johnson

Jolivet Thomas

Sonja Wright

The first black students to graduate from Charlotte High School in 1965 were Gertha Haddock, Jolivet Thomas and Felix Johnson. A year later, Louis Birden, David James, Ronald Middleton, Isaac Thomas and Judy Lloyd became the second group of black students to graduate from formerly all-white Charlotte High School.

At the end of the 1964 school term, the school was fully integrated. After several years, once the state of Florida began complying with the Brown vs. Board of Education decision, the Baker Academy became a pre-school and day care, while Dunbar became a middle school.

The parents of the first black students to integrate Charlotte High School knew they would be exposing their children to ridicule and possible violence. For that reason, after a series of community meetings they picked the brightest and the most even-tempered among us to break the color barrier at Charlotte High School.

My brother was one of those people. His example not only inspired future generations, he also inspired me to follow him to Charlotte High School.

For the next several years the black community sent its best and its brightest to Charlotte, hopeful sacrifices in a war that never ended, an effort to realize American values of equality and justice. The results were mixed and the verdict is still out.

Among the pioneers were Judy Lloyd Jones, homeless advocate and shelter operator, Sonja Wright, Isaac Thomas, Ron Middleton, and a host of others. Few of the graduates found a place in the governance of the city or in the affairs of Charlotte County. Thomas, a scion of a powerful religious family, served in Vietnam, had a troubled return, and later became a pastor and director of the Cooper Street Recreation Center programs. But most of the graduates followed routes such as that pursued by Wright who,

1969
Seventh-Day Adventists acquire Medical Center Hospital. The Board of Directors of Charlotte Hospital Association, Inc., gives the facility to Sunbelt Adventist Health System. The hospital remains non-profit and Sunbelt assumes ownership and management of the now 148-bed hospital.

The Tet offensive of 1968, also called the general offensive and uprising of Tet Mau Than was a major escalation and one of the largest military campaigns of the Vietnam War.

1970

County population is 27,559, a 118.8 percent increase over 1960

Weekly Punta Gorda Herald goes to six days a week.

First nursing class graduated from what is now Florida Southwest State College.

Walt Disney World opens, with Magic Kingdom as its first park.

Reuben Askew elected governor.

realizing there was little opportunity in the area for young black people, built a career in Georgia State government.

They had varying experiences but there were some commonalities. For example. Middleton recalls how sports helped bridge the racial gap for him. Likewise, Ellison Haddock became a basketball star, so he made friends easily with members of the team. But even then, he was cautious.

"There was not a whole lot of social mixing," Haddock said of the times. "I do remember that the guy who I was co-captain with on the basketball team invited me to his house. This was about the time that, "Guess Who's Coming to Dinner?" came out with Sidney Poitier, and everybody thought it was a big joke that he invited me. But I was scared to go because it was an all-white neighborhood, I didn't know anybody other than him. I didn't know his mom or his parents. So I think I wound up giving some excuse or something and I don't think I went."

Gertha Haddock's experiences weren't as humorous. As a high school student she weighed almost 300 pounds and claimed she threatened to sit on any white students who messed with her. All of the Haddocks were big, which helped.

Although she graduated with honors, Gertha haddock could never find her place in Punta Gorda. She found a job with the state and lived most of her life in

Diana Harris

Arcadia. She now lives south of Punta Gorda, bedridden and tended to by her daughter. When she recalls her experiences and the life that followed, she told a visitor something her father had taught all of his children:

"Never trust white people," she said.

A People's History of Charlotte County

Across the river and west of Punta Gorda, Englewood faced its own challenges of change. A longtime dream, first of wartime planners and later of sports boaters and sailors, was to build a protected coastal waterway that would girdle the country.

During the early Sixties, the idea gained traction and came to Englewood. Dredging in the area began in 1962. According to "A Historical Geography of Southwest Florida Waterways":

Two dredges and crews operated concurrently. One dredge began at "The Bulkhead" at South Tampa Bay and worked southward to complete improvements to Venice in 1965; the other dredge worked northward from Gasparilla Sound through Lemon Bay, reaching Red Lake by 1965. The five-mile connector channel linking Red Lake and Venice was completed in 1967.[60]

Oldtimers claim the dredging forever ruined the fishing in Lemon Bay and created perennial silting problems at Stump Pass. The development helped spur growth in Englewood and opened up the area to sports fishermen. The Intracoastal's impact has yet to be fully measured. What's certain is that the growth in sports sailing and boating was the first in a series of blows that would decimate the community's thriving fishing industry.

1970

Diana Ross and The Supremes perform their farewell live concert together at the Frontier Hotel in Las Vegas. Ross's replacement, Jean Terrell, is introduced onstage at the end of the last show.

The American Football League and National Football League officially merge under the NFL's name.

A jury finds the Chicago Seven defendants not guilty of conspiring to incite a riot, in charges stemming from the violence at the 1968 Democratic National Convention. crossing state lines to incite a riot.

A Historical Geography of Southwest Florida Waterways Vol.

Pre-dredging and 1990s view of the waterway. Above, Stump Pass, in upper right, off the coast of Grove City. (Charlotte County History Services).

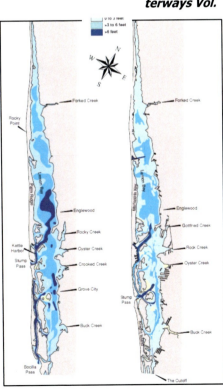

---

[60] http://www.sarasota.wateratlas.usf.edu/upload/documents/03HistoricalDevelopment.pdf

Charles Peck

SONG FOR RUTH
Michael Haymans

Heaven's on fire
Just look at that flaming sky.
Heaven's on fire
Still Peace River washes by.
On Grandma's porch rock and sway.
Watch the birds fly and wade.

Florida backwoods
Sparkman twinkles in her eyes.
Florida backwoods
Moved to town around 1935.
Tarpon schooling on the bay
Near Punta Gorda is where they stayed.

Raised a family of her own
Many more along the way
Beautiful daughters
And Robert's pretty in his own way.
Mom's Marina is where they play.
Bring the grandkids round to stay.

Worked hard all her life
Tax collectors earn their pay.
Friends abound
You know the ones won't let you down.
Cleavland Methodist she prays.
Smells the flowers along life's way.

Cancer dancer
Swirls and twirls through our lives and town.
Faith in God
Nothing bad long keeps her down.
Ruth says, Where you go I will go.
Lord, where you stay I will stay.

Heaven's on fire
Just look at that flaming sky.
Heaven's on fire
Still Peace River washes by.
On Grandma's porch rock and sway.
In Grandma's smile we're going to stay.

Heaven's on fire
Just look at that flaming sky.

THE GIRL IN THE PHOTO

Lynn Harrell

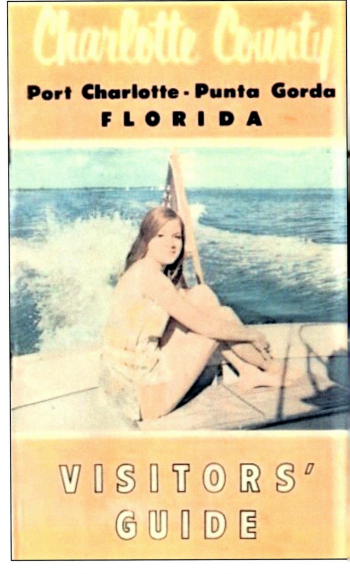

Lynn Harrell graces the Chamber of Commerce annual magazine cover. Left, John Henry Allen.

All photos Harrell Family Collection

My family moved to Punta Gorda in 1958, when the Charlotte Shopping Center was built on Olympia Ave. It was a forerunner of today's enclosed malls.

Anchor stores, Belk-Lindsey, Thrifty Drugs and B & B Grocery, had connecting doors inside so shoppers could go from one to the others without leaving the building. The Belk store was the first full-line department store in Charlotte County and the only store with an open second-floor mezzanine. It was reached by a wide double stairway.

My mother had transferred from the Ringling Belk-Lindsey in Sarasota, as had the store manager, Robert Davis. All the other employees were hired locally. And I didn't realize at the time, with segregation still enforced, that "Mr. D" had bucked the norm. Belk's had a blended staff.

Among the first people hired were two black folks—John Henry Allen, an Air Force veteran who'd served in Korea and was president of the local NAACP, and Mrs. Julia Hamilton, a skilled seamstress well-known in the community. John managed the stock room; Miss Julia sold fabrics and sewing notions and did custom tailoring of men's and women's fine apparel. They would become close family friends.

Mom had found a home for us on the corner of Cross Street (now US41SB) and Virginia Ave. She'd spotted the "For Rent" sign on a previous trip and sent the landlord a check before telling Dad about it. It was a shabby two-story with an odd layout of tiny rooms. When we arrived, Dad looked it over and shook his head. He wasn't impressed. I recall "ugly" and "unsuitable" among his comments. It was also too small, only two bedrooms, upstairs. There were five of us then; my parents, Charles and Leila Harrell (aka Chuck and Lee), me, and my two older sisters. Toni was 18 and about to be married, Marla was 9 or 10, and I was 5.

Sale day at the Punta Gorda Belk's.

Mom pointed out the convenient location – the employee entrance to the new Belk's was a few blocks up Virginia, the school Marla would go to was two blocks away, and one block south was Sacred Heart Church. We were Methodists, but Toni's fiancé was Catholic, and she'd undergone all the steps needed to convert so they could be wed in a Catholic church. Mom had talked to the priest and he'd be happy to do the ceremony. Dad wasn't so happy, but agreed that we'd stay put, for a while. So, Mom and Dad bunked downstairs, Marla and I shared a bedroom and Toni shared the other with her wedding gown. It took up half the room.

The new Belk's opened on schedule, Dad was hired by Green's Fuel Gas as a service tech, Marla started school and I trailed after Toni as she revamped the wedding plans. Then, Marla's school burned down. A local landmark, built in 1911, the "Little School" held all grades until Charlotte High was built, then it served the lower grades. Two new elementary schools opened just before we moved here, Sallie Jones and Baker Academy (that segregation issue again). Baker students had all switched to their new school, but the transition to Sallie Jones was ongoing. Marla's class was the last one left. Luckily, no one was there when the fire started. A circus was in town and school was let out so students could attend. The building was a total loss–one of many landmarks we would lose in the coming decade.

A few months later we moved to another old place, on the corner of Olympia and Booth Street. It was built in 1925 as the dream home of a wealthy young couple, William and Mary Smith Knight, and years later turned into a tourist lodge.

It was called Walled Garden. The house was stately, graced with wrought iron trim and a red shingled roof. The grounds were amazing, an overgrown botanical garden dotted with fountains and statues, shaded with tall specimen trees. A massive Banyan towered over a small cottage in the backyard, former servants' quarters that became my playhouse. The north half of the property held the house and gardens and was surrounded by a six-foot-tall red brick wall. The driveway ran alongside the south wall from Booth Street to a garage behind the house. Across the driveway

Walled Garden

from the garage was an old carriage house, and beyond that a wire-fenced grove of mixed citrus that took up the south half of the property.

The inside of the house was amazing, too. High ceilings with fancy crown molding, push button light switches set into brass plaques, a cobalt blue pedestal sink and mosaic tile floor in the hall bathroom, a full butler's pantry, pull-down attic stairs in the hallway, and too much more to list here.

My grandparents, Oden and Ecil Stout, drove down from Bradenton to visit soon after we moved to Walled Garden and Grandma asked me if I liked my new school. I said I wasn't going to school because I was too little. She was upset. She taught me to read when I was three and I was very good at it. She marched into the kitchen to speak to my mother. I listened in from the pantry.

Mom explained that she'd tried to enroll me when she called to enroll Marla, but my birthday was two weeks past their cut-off date for starting first grade, so I would have to wait another year. Mom hadn't told them I was reading on an adult level, or that I'd already started school in

Bradenton, because the secretary had hung up on her. Grandma told Mom she would take care of it.

After Mom left for work the next morning, Grandma and I walked to Sallie Jones. Grandma told the secretary we were there to transfer me from Orangewood Elementary in Manatee County, and that my transcripts would be

A postcard view of the Peace River Lodge; below, my grandparents in the grove.

sent later. There's a lot more to the story, but the upshot was, I walked to school with Marla the next day as a proud new member of Mrs. Englehardt's first grade class!

We'd been at Walled Garden over a year when Dad came home from work one day and said we had to move again. The owners of the property had finalized their plans for it. He didn't tell me it was owned by Medical Center Hospital and the plan was to bulldoze the whole estate to expand their facilities. Instead, he said he'd seen an interesting, big old place upriver that he was going to check out.

And so we moved to another unique historic place. Not as elegant, but nonetheless remarkable, and definitely big. Peace River Lodge was built in 1884 by Dr. Alfred T. Holleyman as a hotel, back when Cleveland was the end of the railroad line. It had 20 bedrooms and 10 baths upstairs, a dining room that sat more than 50 people, a kitchen equipped with two massive cast iron wood-burning stoves and a dumbwaiter for transporting dishes and linens between floors. There was a player piano in the front parlor and the main hallway was lined with displays of tarpon scales signed by former hotel guests, some famous, who'd caught the "Silver Kings." The lodge sat on an acre facing the river, with a 100-foot dock in front and a boat ramp at the end of the driveway that ran alongside the building.

Some of the events that happened while we lived there were fun, some weren't. Among the fun ones, my parents bought their first boat, Mom held a family reunion, Marla and I discovered that I could fit in the dumbwaiter, and my grandparents sold their Bradenton home and stayed with us while building a new house south of Alligator Creek. I learned that my grandmother could play piano, that manatees are very fond of banana peels, and it helps to open the damper first when cooking on a wood stove.

The first of the bad things happened on August 14, 1959. My grandparents were visiting, they hadn't yet sold their house. I woke in the middle of the night smelling smoke, hearing men's voices downstairs. Dad and Granddad were checking all the rooms for the source of the smoke. I went to Marla's bedroom, she was awake too, and we went downstairs. Mom and Grandma were standing by the front porch door.

Dad and Granddad had just gone outside, and Dad called to us from the end of the dock. "We're safe, it's not us. Come look!" From out on the dock, to the west we could see a bright orange glow streaked by flashes of flame, with thick black clouds of smoke billowing above. "It's the Spa," Dad said softly. We stayed on the dock and watched for a while and then went back to bed.

We were all up soon after sunrise. After breakfast Mom, Dad, Marla and I piled into Mom's station wagon. We were going up to St. Petersburg to see Toni and her husband. The smell of smoke was still heavy and got stronger the closer we got to town. We turned from Hwy 17 (Marion Avenue) onto Highway 41 and passed the smoldering ruins of the Charlotte Harbor Spa. Twisted spires of metal, former fire escapes, poked up from piles of rubble and wisps of smoke still wafted up, keeping the sky dark and hazy over downtown.

Postcard featuring a night view of the Hotel Charlotte Harbor in better times.

It was a quiet ride, Dad drove, Mom snoozed, Marla curled up on the back seat and I was stretched out in the back. When we started up the incline of the Sunshine Skyway bridge I looked south towards home. You could still see smoke rising up into a dark cloud that hovered over the remains of the once-grand hotel.

It had opened in 1887 as the Hotel Punta Gorda and was purchased in the 1920s by Barron Collier and Cornelius Vanderbilt, who'd enlarged it, refaced it in Mediterranean style, added many amenities and changed the name to the Hotel Charlotte Harbor. New owners had recently rehabbed it as a health spa. It would be replaced by the Punta Gorda Mall and Charlevoix condos. A poor substitute, in my opinion.

The really bad thing came about a year later. After the Spa burned, my parents worried about the Lodge. It had its own water supply, but they knew if fire broke out the old wood-frame structure would be gone, fast. They'd had an opportunity to buy it but decided instead to buy a brand-new house across the river in Harbour Heights, a subdivision that was just starting up. The closing took place on Friday afternoon, Sept. 9, 1960.

Surveying the damage at the "new" home after Hurricane Donna.

Belk's was usually open late on Friday nights, but when Mom got back from the closing, Mr. Davis and John Henry Allen were taping up the storefront windows. Mr. D had heard on the radio that the tropical storm meandering up the Gulf had gained strength. It was still predicted to bypass Charlotte Harbor and make landfall farther up the coast, but Mr. D wasn't betting on that.

Mom was home early, Dad was late. Green's Fuel customers were getting nervous, wanting their tanks

topped off. We had dinner, watched some television, and went to bed. The plan was to pack up some provisions in the morning and go to Harbour Heights to wait out the weather, since a new cement block house was surely safer than the creaky old lodge.

First thing next morning, Dad was called into work. They had a backlog of service calls. Change of plan – we'd go to Harbour Heights when he got back. But meanwhile, the storm grew into a hurricane. Her name was Donna. And by the time Dad got home rain squalls had started and wind gusts were breaking branches off the trees. He pulled up next to Mom's car and one of the Australian pines lining the driveway crashed down behind him. We weren't going anywhere.

Donna was our first hurricane and she was scary. Wind howled, flying debris thudded against the walls and broke through windows, the water tower fell, the dock buckled and as its planks flew off, the water drained out of the bay. We'd hunkered down in the front parlor. Dad removed the doors from unused upstairs rooms and nailed them up inside the tall parlor windows. When the front doors to the porch started to blow inward, we wrestled the piano up against them. The power went out and the room was dark. When the eye of the storm passed over, Dad went out a side door and did a quick survey around the building. "It's bad," he said when he came back in, "but the roof's holding."

Donna's second half kicked in, but by then we felt fairly secure in our bunker. Mom had made a kitchen run, bringing back sandwich makings and a couple of oil lamps. When it was finally over we all went outside. Dad was right, it was bad. But the roof had held and we were all okay.

The next morning, Dad was in the driveway contemplating the fallen pine when a big panel truck drove up and stopped on the far side of the tree. Two of his coworkers got out, and after determining that we were safe, pulled an old-fashioned two-man logging saw out of the back of the truck. I'd never seen such a thing before! They sawed through the tree trunk in two places, in line with the edges of the driveway. Then they rolled the center section off to the side and asked Dad for the keys to the work truck. They'd come to rescue the company vehicle, not us!

Charlotte County Government

Harbour Heights—a fine location but only one way in or out.

They drove off with both trucks and we took the station wagon to Harbour Heights. Not many houses had been built yet, but trees had blown down and debris was scattered around. We pulled up in front of our new house, it looked fine. We headed up the walkway to the front door. As Dad pulled out the keys, Marla poked me and pointed to a large pile of rubble in a vacant field across the street. There was a broken beam sticking out of the heap with a hanging lamp dangling from it. Mom turned around to see what we were looking at.

"That looks like our dining room lamp," she said. Dad unlocked the door, stepped in and said, "Leila, come here." Turns out, Mom was right.

That was our dining room lamp. Donna had demolished the screened porch and entire back wall and ripped off most of the roof.

We rented a small house on McGregor Street while the new house, and much of downtown, was rebuilt. There was a lot of damage in Punta Gorda, buildings wrecked or destroyed, the city playground was demolished and many of the old trees were uprooted. New developments like Punta Gorda Isles, Port Charlotte and Harbour Heights had fared better, partly because the buildings were newer, but also because there weren't that many homes built yet.

Hurricane Donna hadn't bypassed the bay, obviously. She'd escalated rapidly and then changed course, veering sharply east, churning through the harbor, heading upriver and beyond. Donna is the only storm in recorded history to sustain hurricane-force winds from Florida through the Mid-Atlantic states and into New England. The name "Donna" was retired.

In October, we were still on McGregor when Sallie Jones died. I read her obituary in the paper. She was a teacher for many years, the first female Superintendent of Schools in Florida, and my school, Sallie Jones Elementary, was named for her. The odd thing is, she'd been a neighbor, living catty-corner to us when were at Walled Garden. Miss Sallie was very kind, I had visited her often, but I had never known her last name. I cried, sad because I knew her, but even sadder because I hadn't known her at all.

Living in Harbour Heights was quite a change for us. Everything was new and modern, except the Clubhouse. It was built in the 1930s by a retired Army Air Corps General, Charles Danforth, and resembled the officer's club in Panama. The developers of Harbour Heights had turned it into a community center, adding an Olympic-sized pool and other amenities. It's still there, now owned by Charlotte County. The pool was filled in and replaced with tennis courts.

Our house was very nice and full of modern conveniences. We had an intercom system, central air, a breakfast nook and Dad's favorite gizmo – a blender built into the kitchen countertop, perfect for making milkshakes! In time, we added a pool. But there were drawbacks, it was a pain having a party line phone, and the distance from town caused some problems. Marla and I rode the same school bus, but I was assigned to Peace River Elementary, the first school built in Port Charlotte, while she rode on to junior high in Punta Gorda. She could attend after school activities and walk to Belk's to ride home with Mom. If I didn't catch the bus, I was stranded in Port Charlotte. I didn't like the school or my teachers, I was sick a lot and my grades tanked. Mom took notice, and somehow arranged a transfer. I rode the bus all the way to Charlotte High and walked across the street to Sallie Jones.

A fun event occurred in May 1963, the "Route 66" production crew rolled into town and filmed an episode of the popular TV series. Along with series stars Martin Milner and Glenn Corbett, "Shadows of an Afternoon" featured guest stars Ralph Meeker, Miriam Hopkins, Kathryn Hays, Michael Conrad, and Cliff Hall. Local folks served as extras and participated in crowd scenes, and a good time was had by all!

We lost another landmark in 1964, the downtown movie theater on Marion Avenue. Built in 1917 as the Plaza Theater, showing silent films, it was re-equipped for "talkies" in the late 1920s. The Desguin family bought it in 1936, remodeled and renamed it the "New Theater." Marla and I went there many times, stopping at the Seminole Drugstore on the corner for penny candy. I saw my first "horror" movie there, "The Blob," and had nightmares of man-eating Jell-O for weeks afterward.

Many other events happened in the 1960s and I trust others will tell those stories. These are the ones I recall the best, the ones that shaped my life. The '60s brought many changes to the county, some good, and some bad, all irreversible. Most newcomers don't understand that there's no returning to "normal" after a community is ravaged, whether by intent, such as arson, or in the name of progress, such as destroying historic buildings to make room for modern ones, or by forces of nature, like hurricanes. Torn fabric can be mended, wounds eventually heal, but the scars remain forever in our collective history. Happy 100th Birthday, Charlotte County.

NEW LIBRARY COMES TO PUNTA GORDA

Tony Farina

In 1967, Vernon Peeples chaired a meeting to propose a Friends of the Library group. The meeting was held at the old Punta Gorda Library that was located at the corner of Retta Esplanade and Cross Street.

Attorney Kenton Haymans, was chosen by acclamation as the temporary chair to form a Friends of the Library group. Included in the meeting were the Punta Gorda librarian, two Charlotte County Commissioners and the Mayor and Vice Mayor of Punta Gorda. In 1967, the Friends of the Punta Gorda Library was given unofficial auxiliary status with the intention of being used to "promote the library and to bring it before the community in the most favorable light and to aid the library in funding for books and other items and perform other unofficial acts on behalf of the library."

Since that February day in 1967, the Friends of the Punta Gorda Library have lived the mission set forth by aiding the library and by extension, the entire community as the library has always been and will always be the center of the community.

When the library moved from the small, cramped quarters downtown, to the building on Henry in 1974, the Friends were there helping. They donated the flag pole and were honored at a dedication ceremony

2020 Board of Directors of the Friends of the Punta Gorda Charlotte Library. Susan Cravens, Celia Eames, Lois Modrow, Sara Benson, secretary; Katie Mazzi, bookstore manager, striped jacket; Georgia Buda, Minerva King, president; Virginia Caldwell, Penny Shattuck, Nancy Lewis, Judi Beaumont, Jerri Marsee, Geri Saunders, author Marie Benedict, Teresa Coady, vice-president; Tony Farina. Not pictured are Hank Bauman, treasurer, Berna Goldberg, Jane Fitzpatrick.

In 1977, under the leadership of Chairman U. S. Cleveland, Vice-Chairman Robert Wilford, Secretary Deanna Patterson and Treasurer Robert Eliott, an application for incorporation was made to the State of Florida. On August 9, 1977, the Certificate of Incorporation as a non-profit under Florida Statutes was issued to the "Friends Library of Punta Gorda, Inc." making the group no longer an unofficial auxiliary group, but a bona fide non-profit giving the group the standing and recognition it deserved.

Since that time, the Friends have been active participants supporting the library with funding for programs and providing equipment or support as needed. The bookstore, which is filled with donations from the community and from withdrawn materials from the library itself, has raised, on average, $25,000 a year that is put back into the library.

In 1999, the Friends bookstore started as just a small shelf in the Henry Street location and it eventually grew to the full store that is staffed 100 percent by volunteers. In 2016, at the first public planning meeting for what would become the new library hosted by the architect and the county, the overwhelming consensus of the public was that the Friends bookstore needed to be included and it needed to be bigger. Both wishes were granted and the space at the library on Shreve is beautiful and a reminder that the community appreciates the hard work and dedication of the Friends.

The Friends raise money through events like the literary luncheon that brings in world class, best-selling authors. They collect membership dues from the thousands of Punta Gorda residents who became Friends. There have also been several generous legacy gifts that help fund the Friends' mission. Through these fundraising efforts, the Friends have given hundreds of thousands of dollars to the library for everything from youth and adult programming to landscaping and equipment and furniture in the Mary Knowlton Teen Room. If one were to consider the time spent by the thousands of volunteers over the years would be well into the millions of dollars if those hours had been paid.

The Friends of the Punta Gorda Charlotte Library have been actively helping the community grow for over half a century and they plan to stay involved for years to come. Their impact on the library in particular and on the community as a whole is immeasurable. As long as there is a library in Punta Gorda, the Friends will be there, helping to make sure they can be the center of the community.

POWELL'S NURSERY AND LANDSCAPING

Sandra Witzke

Established since 1963, Powell's Nursery and Landscaping at 6366 Elliott in Punta Gorda has subsequently been the everyday life of Carl and Jo Powell along with their son Joseph and his wife Amanda. Being a native Floridian and growing up in Punta Gorda, he has great historical memories of the area.

After his discharge from the Army, Carl worked as an auto mechanic, then for Kelly's Nursery before settling into his own desired nursery business on Elliott Street. At the time there were only three plant nurseries operating to include those of Ehrenfeld, Lewis and Laishley. Kelly was a landscaper and also had a small nursery.

The Powell's first home on the same street was a small framed home with the electricity originating from one little metal ceiling light outlet from which an extension cord went into all the other rooms. It met their needs, as well as the outhouse in the back. At the time, only a few scattered homes were in his neighborhood and maybe 20-30 homes in the beginning of Punta Gorda Isles.

In an effort to create adequate space for a business, he was able to purchase two acres farther down the street from owner, Fred King. However, the middle acreage between that area and his home was owned by Florida Light and Power. With persistence on Carl's part, FPL relinquished the land to him, thereby tying the property all together.

In time, he acquired more land across the street to accrue his current almost 10 acres. All was needed to provide room to grow and propagate new plants, plus create an area for displaying the numerous trees and various vegetation for sale to commercial landscapers and to homeowners.

Now in his eighties, Carl states, "Jo and I, along with Joseph have worked hard our entire lives. I never had anything as I grew up poor. So every time I had a nickel, we put it right back in the ground, because if I never had it, I'm not going to miss it."

When asked about trends in the agriculture business he reminisced. Pineapples were a big enterprise at the beginning of the century, but all were out of the area by the early 1900s. Apparently celery was then tried for a while, but due to its better growth in a mucky soil, that operation did better farther south in the Glades. The growing of gladiolus flowers was quite popular and profitable in the Punta Gorda and Fort Myers areas up until the early 1980s. Large fields in south Punta Gorda were located on the west side of Tamiami north of Taylor Road and downward towards Burnt Store Road. This Pinellas Gladiolus Company was a big employer for both men and women in the various facets of the huge operation.

The harvested plants from the many acres were basically green stalks when taken to the warehouse to be sorted, bundled with rubber bands, and cut before being loaded into trucks and taken to the airport. Growers knew the color of the eventual blossoms, but all were shipped green so the new blooms would be in the hands of the receiving florist. At their destination airport, the orders were picked up by delivery trucks to be distributed to the various florists.

It was apparently a lucrative business, however, farmers began to sell their land to eager developers. They found that the land was more valuable than the flowers and that ended the gladiolus business.

CHARLOTTE COUNTY HISTORICAL CENTER SOCIETY

Frank Desquin

The Charlotte County Historical Center Society has deep roots in the community. Beginning over 50 years ago in 1969, the Society was started as a private nonprofit organization, called the Youth Museum of Charlotte County. Founders School Superintendent Dr. Hugh Adams and Peggy Desguin started the museum to address the need to extend classroom history lessons for area children. The museum had several locations over time, including a vacant fire station on East Marion Avenue in Punta Gorda. In 1975, the Youth Museum moved to the then vacant county library building on the corner of West Retta Esplanade and US41 south.

In 1989, the name and focus of the museum changed to reflect the growing appeal to all ages, becoming the Museum of Charlotte County. The organization relied on private contributions and state and local government grants for the museum's operations.

In 1995 the museum name was again changed, this time to the Florida Adventure Museum. That same year the Society hosted the first Florida Frontier Days festival.

In 2002, the Charlotte County Board of Commissioners voted to take over the museum operations. The museum was renamed the Charlotte County Historical Center (CCHC) and moved to Bayshore Road, Charlotte Harbor. The Society then began doing business as the Charlotte County Historical Center Society. It remains a separate non-profit dedicated to helping preserve and promote Charlotte County's rich history.

Over the years the Society's main fundraisers became annual events – Florida Frontier Days, the Hibiscus Festival, and the Lobster Bake. All three are highly anticipated and strongly supported by the community. This has allowed the Society to continue its mission of supporting county-based history programs, services, and projects.

A group of children gathered for a Halloween parade. In original caption, Joyce Tate is identified as standing far left, Oneita Spragar is second from left; Galvin (no last name), is the boy with the goat at center front, and Wanda Whitaker is the girl at center left background wearing a crown. 1959 photo by Woody Thayer

WHEN ENGLEWOOD WAS KIDS' TOWN

Diana Harris

Pat Smith's generation may have been the last to grow up in the unspoiled little town of Englewood where everybody knew and looked after each other.

By the mid-60s, the large population increase had started. Life, for better or worse, would never be the same again in Englewood.

Pat was 3 when her family moved here. Her father owned a gas station on W. Dearborn Street.

"Englewood was a special and unique place to be a child," said Pat. "When I was growing up here in the '50s everyone always pulled together for the kids. Each parent had their own style, but they all took great responsibility in helping raise us. Every parent donated something."

A People's History of Charlotte County

Top, Pat Smith; middle, Florence White Geary; bottom, Max Bernd-Cohen.

Outdoor activities were greatly emphasized, sailing, swimming, fishing and shrimping. But many of the parents tried to inject a bit of culture whenever possible, worrying that their children would be deprived of a bit of worldly sophistication growing up in tiny, isolated Englewood.

Florence White Geary was a descendent of the Gottfried family. She was born in Kansas in 1909. As a child she, with her family, came often to Englewood.

Eventually she moved here with her father when she was in her teens. She spent the rest of her life living in a home on the bay in the New Point Comfort area.

She lived to be 90. Florence was a gifted piano player and became the town's piano teacher. Florence took great pleasure in the children she worked with. She taught several generations of Englewood children to play the piano even though their parents sometimes were unable to pay her.

In the 1940s she formed and coached a popular singing group that became known as "Florence's Choir Girls" that sang in churches and other locations. The small book of poetry Florence wrote of Englewood "This Fair Spot," is out of publication but has become a collector's item.

Another talented adult who cared was artist Max Bernd-Cohen, who felt the children should be learning something about the art world.

"Max Bernd-Cohen would show us his paintings, furnish all the supplies and encourage us," remembered Pat Smith. "Of course, at first we were shocked to see nude models in his studio—we were just kids and, Wow! But I think it enhanced our character."

Little did Pat or her friends realize at the time that Max Bernd-Cohen was a renowned artist whose paintings hung in world famous museums. There were undoubtedly many who would have given anything to have been able to take painting lessons with him.

"Mr. and Mrs. William Vanderbilt were Manasota Key residents," Pat said. "They were always great to the kids. Billy Vanderbilt was our age. Little did we know then what an important family he came from. The only important thing we knew about Billy was that he had a swimming pool, which most of us didn't. But we didn't hang out there too much; his mother wasn't a very good cook. My mother was a better cook, so everybody chose to come to my house when it came to eating.

"The Vanderbilts were extremely generous about letting the local children ride the horses in their private stables. I can remember riding on the beach and also the beach road, 'course there was no traffic then.

"All the kids had small sailboats called prams. Mr. Bob Johnson built them for us and Mr. Hoadley was our sailing instructor. He was world-famous for his sailing.

"Sometimes we would want to go to the beach. We would just swim across the bay. It was much shorter than walking. The Intracoastal Waterway hadn't been built yet so there was no boat traffic. Most of us were great swimmers. Along with tap, ballet and acrobatic dance lessons held at the Woman's Club, square dancing at the Rec. Center, schooling in etiquette and public speaking, the Wedgwood China lessons Mrs. Lasbury gave us; we were quite well rounded in our activities, especially for such a small town. And besides that, all the kids in town could use chopsticks correctly. The "in" restaurant was the Chidori, a wonderful Oriental place in Grove City.

"When we were growing up in the 1950s, every parent tried to do their part to educate us," recalled Pat Smith. "Mrs. Leah Lasbury, for instance, decided that for us to be proper young ladies, we should know about Wedgwood china and how to drink tea correctly. So she loaded up her station wagon with about 12 Girl Scouts and off to the Wedgwood Inn in St. Petersburg we went.

Nancy Czerwinski and an unidentified friend ride their decorated bikes during Children's Bicycle Parade in the first Pioneer Days, 1956. Photo by Woody Thayer

"As we approached the Skyway Bridge, which none of us had seen, much screaming and ooohing and aaahing started. Sandy Lampp put her head out of the small vent window, and got it stuck. Mrs. Lasbury couldn't pull over on the bridge so she's crossing it with this car full of hooting and hollering Girls Scouts and one has her head completely outside the car.

"Mrs. Lasbury lost control momentarily—who could have blamed her? She swatted poor Sandy with a newspaper several times and accused all the Scouts of not being proper ladies.

"We talked about greasing Sandy's ears—I think we did spit on them—to pull her back in. By the time we got to the Inn we had settled down. We learned that day Wedgwood China was expensive and very nice and we should be proper when we ate off of it. Mrs. Lasbury also taught us to use the proper silverware, how to order in a restaurant and how to curtsy."

"There were always little adventures in Englewood when we were growing up here in the 1950s," said Pat Smith. "For instance, where Indian Mound Park is now was a big play area where we would go to swim. The mound wasn't connected to the shore then. The Englewood kids found endless amounts of human bones there, because it is a burial mound. I would take leg bones and skulls home and put them in my mother's bird bath. When I got older I realized the significance of my bone collection and donated it to Venice High School. We probably destroyed a lot for the archaeologists who came later, but we didn't know any better then.

"The older kids had a game at New Year's always. It was often raining at that time of year. The game was to go across the old rickety bridge and hit their brakes hard and see if they could spin their cars, right in the middle of the bridge (half of the bridge remains today as the Bill Anger Fishing Pier). Well,

Prams in action. Below, Bob Johnson.

probably four or five cars went off the bridge doing that. We were all excellent swimmers and spent a lot of time in the water. We used to jump off the old wooden bridge and dive down to the cars that had gone off the bridge. When the new (Tom Adams) bridge and the Intracoastal Waterway came in, they finally took the cars out.

"We took tap, ballet or acrobatic dance lessons held at the Woman's Club, plus square dancing at the Rec Center. We had schooling in etiquette and public speaking. A lot of us kids had small sailboats called prams. Different businesses in town would sponsor each boat and that paid for the materials for Mr. Bob Johnson to build them for us.

"I've never forgotten Bob Johnson's advice to us kids. He taught us to be outspoken and to adventure into things. Always ask questions. Do treat people nice. Voice our opinions and be good citizens. Always ask and do and take a stand. Remember money isn't the most important thing in life—it's getting along. Looking back, I was so fortunate to have grown up here in Englewood at the time I did."

CENTURY

Arlene Kinkaid in front of the county schools' speech department/Arlene Kinkaid

1970s

THE NEW PEOPLE

In 1968 Arlene Kincaid, her husband, Jim, and their sons Mark and Jeff packed up, left their native Indiana, and took I-75 south as far as it would go. This was before the Interstate's extension, which meant that at some point they left the highway and travelled the poorly paved single-lane road that constituted Tamiami Trail through Port Charlotte.

She may not have known it at the time but Kincaid, who tells her story later in the book, was one of thousands of people, many with families, who swelled the county's numbers to figures unimaginable during the lean years of the Thirties.

Between 1970 and 1990, Charlotte County's population would essentially double every ten years. From a population of 27,559, the number of residents increased to 58,460 a decade later and 110,975 as of the 1990 census.

Historian Howard Melton of Arcadia once remarked that the railroads brought industry to Southwest Florida, but the automobile brought people. And people like the Kincaids weren't tin can tourists or sunshine soldiers making seasonal escapes from snow and cold.

These weren't folks hankering for a dollar and a dream, they were men and women with professional capabilities who were bringing their skills to a raw community. The '70s is when Port Charlotte grew civilized, when it was in its glory years as the place to be. They were modern pioneers who traded in their wagon trains for station wagons and minivans. And they would revitalize Charlotte County.

A People's History of Charlotte County

Daily Herald-News/6-15-72

The Herald was able to expand from a weekly tabloid to a daily broadsheet because of pages like this one, chock full of housing-related adds.

Daily Herald-News, 10-1-7

Their presence alone sparked change, as developers, realtors, merchants, and bankers rushed to fulfill new needs and meet new demands. Social and infrastructure services suffered as well as roads, as governments unequipped for the welcome upsurge, worked to meet the strain of happy news—too many people.

Aratha Jones by then had come back to Punta Gorda with her husband and settled down. Filled with the confidence of having managed her household around the world, she took a job in a realtor's office and soon began selling homes herself. As a licensed realtor, she said, the times were right.

"I was in real estate after my husband returned and I sold real estate to some of the officers who had been flight students at the airport," she said. "Many of the people who live in PGI are ex-military from flight training at the airport."

Jones had never intended to go into real estate, but after caring for a family of three on military bases around the world, she found she just wasn't ready to sit at home and bake cookies.

Sales frenzy had struck and there was plenty of demand. Builders flocked to meet the housing needs.

"Everybody was moving here so housing was probably the most lucrative business that you could be in, especially if you had land like Mr. (Vasco) Peeples—he was selling his own land and developing his own land, you know Charlotte Park and all of that?" Jones said.

1971

Atlantic Coast Line Rail Road discontinues passenger service.

Health and Physical Education Building completed as Fort Myers Junior College's name is changed to Edison Community College.

The Baltimore Colts defeat the Dallas Cowboys 16–13 in Super Bowl V to win the National Football League championship. The Colts scored the winning points on a 32-yard field goal by Jim O'Brien with five seconds remaining.

Walt Disney World opens in Orlando, transforming Florida's economy and surrounding Central Florida.

CENTURY

1972
CH&N Rail Road suspends operations.

Both the Democratic and Republican presidential nominating conventions are held in Miami.

The Miami Dolphins play a perfect season, winning every game they played that year, including the Super Bowl.

1973
The Arab Oil Embargo sent gas prices through the roof. Between 1973-1974, prices more than quadrupled, leading to calls for energy independence.

Roe v. Wade: The U.S. Supreme Court overturns state bans on abortion.

One of the most high-powered sales teams of the seventies was that led by Realtor Monroe Randol and his wife, Theola. Randol, who first came to town selling GDC homes, grew disenchanted with the developers and branched out on his own. His timing was right as the housing market took off like a rocket. He was active in many county governmental and booster organizations and, near the end of his life, led an unsuccessful effort to incorporate Port Charlotte.

Peeples created several developments on the southern part of the Punta Gorda peninsula east of Punta Gorda Isles. Like Peeples, Jones knew the lay of the land and that gave her an advantage she was quick to utilize.

"For me, my biggest asset was that I was from Punta Gorda—I knew the area—most of the people that I worked with at Century-21 were transplants from the North who were just filling their time, so they would be completely lost. I always knew exactly what part of the woods I was in—and there was a lot of woods back then!"

One of the biggest bits of news back then was the news. the *Punta Gorda Herald*, seizing on the land boom, decided to become a daily and expand its coverage area. The newspaper made their story front-page news and enlisted the help of Florida's playboy Governor Claude Kirk to ballyhoo the new product.

But progress has its own price, oftentimes ignored in the rush to improve. One small change that had a major impact on an often-forgotten segment of the community was the creation of Ponce de Leon Park.

Judi Duff Addison, who grew up in Punta Gorda, described how the community baptismal font was lost.

"So Sam Burchers decided that it was off of the PGI side of the harbor and it was totally undeveloped, but there was an area there that was not overgrown with mangroves," she recalled. "So he decided that we needed a marketing tool, a monument to Ponce de Leon. My dad's role with PGI was superintendent of special projects. Dad was given the project. Now Dad was a jack of all trades in that he could fix a little bit of electrical, he could fix a little bit of plumbing. He was a master carpenter, so he built a monument."

She described how her father, Omar Duff, had Judi and Gaye Johns Brownie, her best friend, collect shells that were used in the original base of the monument.

But there was one problem. Judi lived in one of the first homes built in PGI, along Marion Avenue, and she used to regularly see carloads of black worshippers heading out to the area for baptisms.

"Lo and behold at 12:30 in the afternoon all of the cars would be heading to Ponce de Leon Park for immersions," Addison recalled. "I always called it Ponce's place. And then the community started referring to it as Ponce Park or PGI Ponce Park. I do know that before they put the seawall in it was very easy to go out into the water for the immersions."

Barbara Thorp Gunn, a reporter with the Punta Gorda Herald during the 70s, left an evocative account of a baptism she witnessed firsthand.

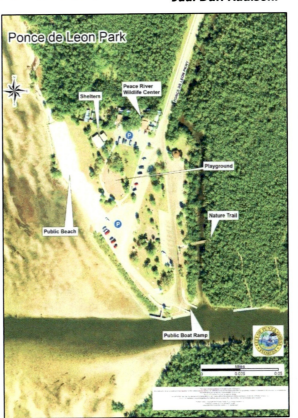

Judi Duff Addison.

Ponce de Leon Park/City of Punta Gorda.

1974
Charlotte Community Hospital builds a new three-story addition, expanding patient capacity to 156.

Edison Community College establishes Charlotte County branch in rented rooms over Sunnydell shopping center stores. Provost is Claude Pridgen

1975
Watergate scandal (United States): John N. Mitchell, H. R. Haldeman and John Ehrlichman are found guilty of the Watergate cover-up.

In response to the energy crisis, daylight saving time commences nearly 2 months early in the United States.

For six months I was the women's editor at the local daily newspaper. It was while in this position that I did a photostory, first of its kind done here, of a

CENTURY

1976
Albert Gilchrist and new Barron Collier bridges opened over Charlotte Harbor.

Edison Community College faculty elected to organize for collective negotiations.

1977
Construction begins on I-75 section and harbor bridge in Charlotte County.
Punta Gorda Fish Company, last of the wholesale fish companies, ceases operation.

City leases the municipal dock to radio personality Earl Nightingale for Fishermen's Village consisting of restaurants, shops, timeshare apartments and marina.

colored baptism held in the Peace River....Here on the shores of the river, members of the Church of the Living God assembled one cool Sunday morning for their annual baptism service. Here I waded right out alongside the participants, who were dressed in white gowns made of coarse cotton...The Amens and hallelujahs from those on shore, the expressions on the faces of the eight young women as they were immersed by the Reverend and then slowly brought to the surface, shall long linger on my mind.[61]

Ellison Haddock recalls when the park was the black parishioners' baptismal font.

"See Punta Gorda Beach, which is at the end of PGI, what is that - Ponce de Leon Park now?" he recalled. "That was the beach. There was no other beach. And we used to do baptisms there. But there was like a whirlpool. We had to avoid that and the people would go out and stake out the path to get out to where that happened. Because nobody had a pool. Nobody had a baptismal. And so even though we had churches that was the way you got baptized, it didn't matter what denomination, that was the baptismal."

Haddock said the black community soon learned to make do with Berlin Bailey's pool. Bailey, one of the fighting Bailey brothers, and his wife, Lorene, had done well. Bailey was an electrician and his wife Lorene was a schoolteacher. They were able to buy one of the first pools in the area, which soon became the community baptismal font. So black people accommodated and didn't make a big deal about it.

Ellison Haddock.

"It just was a whole lot easier and more controlled because we knew the people in the house," he said of the community baptismal font. "The only thing we had to worry about was parking in somebody else's property or something."

The monument helped spur the creation of the Conquistadors, a local men's group, and helped lead to the publication of "Boldly Onward," a book by historian Lindsey Williams that perpetuates the Punta Gorda colony story, which is still open to historical interpretation.

As a recent news story describes it:

The Royal Order of Ponce de Leon Conquistadors out of Charlotte County recently donated a new bronze bust of Juan Ponce de Leon to Punta Gorda as part of the city's ongoing renovations at the park, which was established in the 1970s.

---

[61] Barbara Thorp Gunn, *Call Us Colored*, p. vii-viii, 1978

A People's History of Charlotte County

The Conquistadors were formed in the late 1970s to commemorate the Spanish explorer for his discovery of Florida and landing on the shores of Charlotte Harbor in 1513 and attempting to establish a colony somewhere on Charlotte Harbor in 1521.

"You can debate from now until whenever of exactly where (Ponce landed) but the suspicion is that it's around this Charlotte Harbor area," said Kent Kretzler, Conquistador chairman at a Nov. 4 City Council meeting "I can honestly say that he was the very first snowbird." [62]

Non-Agricultural Employment Trends Years 1970-1984

Employment Category	1970	% Dist.	1980	% Dist.	1984	% Dist.
Charlotte County:						
Construction	520	9.8%	3,160	22.6%	2,164	12.6%
Manufacturing	160	3.0%	380	2.7%	414	2.4%
Transportation/Public Utilities	300	5.7%	480	3.5%	715	4.2%
Wholesale/Retail/Trade	1,340	25.4%	3,290	23.7%	4,648	27.0%
Finance/Insurance/Real Estate	920	17.4%	1,740	12.5%	1,588	9.2%
Service/Government	2,040	38.6%	4,820	34.8%	7,699	44.7%
Total Employment	**5,280**	**100.0%**	**13,870**	**100.0%**	**17,228**	**100.0%**
Region:						
Construction	11,600	10.0%	22,410	12.3%	26,108	11.4%
Manufacturing	6,480	6.1%	12,270	6.7%	13,971	6.1%
Transportation/Public Utilities	5,180	4.9%	8,500	4.7%	9,744	4.2%
Wholesale/Retail/Trade	24,620	23.1%	53,260	29.2%	69,271	30.2%
Finance/Insurance/Real Estate	8,080	7.6%	15,850	8.7%	19,068	8.3%
Service/Government	30,300	28.5%	69,770	38.2%	91,722	40.0%
Total Employment*	**106,380**	**100.0%**	**182,430**	**100.0%**	**229,432**	**100.0%**

*Employment figures and percentages may not equal totals due to the withholding of data for certain counties.

Source: Previous SWFRPC Data; State of Florida, Department of Labor and Employment Security; and Halcyon Ltd.

In 1966, roughly at the mid-century mark of Charlotte County, the latest version of the periodic comprehensive plan had this to say about local demographics.

The population of Charlotte County by race and sex, per decade, from 1930 to 1960 as shown in Table 3, has changed significantly since 1930. The 1930 Census showed 784 non-white persons residing in Charlotte County. This number declined to 673 in 1940, declined again to 672 in 1950, and increased to only 725 in 1960, less than the number of non-white persons recorded in 1930. Consequently, the percentage of the total population accounted for by the non-white population. has consistently declined each decade from 19.6 percent of the population in 1930, to only 5.8 percent of the population in 1960. [63]

---

[62] Charlotte Sun, 11-19-2020
[63] 1966 Charlotte County Comprehensive plan draft, p. 11

1978

First class (nursing) of Vocational Training Center convened at St. Joseph Hospital. Full-course building and campus open 1980.

Bob Graham elected governor: in 1986 he would be elected U.S. Senator.

Old Capitol saved from destruction, would later reopen as a museum

1979

Charlotte Sun newspaper started at Port Charlotte by Derek Dunn-Rankin

Florida's first execution since the U.S. Supreme Court ruling allowing them to resume.

1980

County population is 58,460, an 112.1 percent increase over 1970

Good Shepherd Episcopal Church builds its present sanctuary in Punta Gorda

Mariel boat lift; increase in Cuban immigration to Florida.

U.S. President Jimmy Carter announces that the United States will boycott the 1980 Summer Olympics in Moscow because of the Soviet invasion of Afghanistan.

Operation Eagle Claw, a commando mission in Iran to rescue American embassy hostages, is aborted after mechanical problems

This photo shows the Atlantic Coast Line (ACL) train depot in Punta Gorda. Built in 1928, the depot was purchased by Fred Babcock in the early 1970s when passenger service was discontinued and the depot closed. Mr. Babcock later donated the property to the Punta Gorda Historical Society. It has been restored and now contains an antiques mall with multiple vendors. Below, The ubiquitous US Cleveland outside the dilapidated station prior to renovation. Restorers decided to keep the signs noting "separate but equal" white and black sections of the station as a tribute to real history.

The snapshot of the county Census data from the era show a sharp decline in agricultural, forestry, and other gang labor types of employment, which traditionally employed a majority of blacks who had jobs. That may explain the drop in the black population.

There was one final harbinger of change in the '70s, this one a decline. Both the Charlotte Harbor & Northern and the Atlantic Coast Line ceased operations in Southwest Florida. Boca Grande would close as a phosphate port and begin its transformation into a luxury community. Punta Gorda, once the southernmost railhead on the north American railroad system, no longer had passenger rail service.

But it did have a railroad station, which was donated to the local historical society by Fred Babcock.[64]

---

[64] Jo Morrison, *Babcock Ranch and Tales of Bygone Days*, p. 104, 2005

WHEN RAILS RULED THE ROAD

Before there was a Tamiami Trail, I-4, or an I-75, the easiest way to get across the state was by train Railroads did the heavy lifting, carrying phosphate, cattle, lumber, and other goods from the interior of the state to the southwest coast. The Charlotte Harbor and Northern, which ran from Mulberry to Boca Grande, was built in 1907 as a phosphate carrier. It was acquired in 1925 by the Seaboard Air Line railroad, which merged with the Atlantic Coast Line Railroad in 1967. The merged company became the Seaboard Coast Line Railroad. Tampa Bay's facilities eventually outclassed those of Boca Grande Port, which closed in 1979. The railroad left behind monuments such as an enormous steampunk geared and ratcheted drawbridge mechanism off Placida, or the wooden fishing pier on the north side of El Jobean Road (SR776).

The Florida Southern came to Punta Gorda in 18 after founder Isaac Trabue outbid Hickory Bluff by offering a sizable chunk of land to the railroad, which built the iconic Hotel Punta Gorda. Railroad workers later teamed up with Trabue's enemies to steal the town and incorporate it as Punta Gorda. The Florida southern was sold to the Atlantic Coast Line Railroad in 1902. The Atlantic Coast Line became the Seaboard Coast Line Railroad after the 1967 merger with the former rival, the Seaboard Air Line Railroad. Punta Gorda is graced today with an Atlantic Coast Line Railroad station, another legacy of the railroad importance to the county's growth.

PORT CHARLOTTE IN THE SEVENTIES

Arlene Kinkaid

Tamiami Trail in the 70s. before it was widened and resurfaced.

In January 1968, after selling our business and home in Lebanon, Indiana, my husband, Jim, our two sons, Mark and Jeff, and I headed south for Port Charlotte, Florida.

I started work for the Charlotte County Public Schools in the fall of 1971. Mark and Jeff were students at Peace River Elementary. In the fall of 1971, the CCPS student count was just over 4,100 students. There were no Meadow Park, Myakka River, Kingsway or Vineland Elementary schools. There was no Port Charlotte or Punta Gorda Middle School and no Port Charlotte or Lemon Bay High.

I was assigned three elementary schools. The only two at that time were Peace River and Neil Armstrong Elementary in Port Charlotte and Sallie Jones Elementary in Punta Gorda. Peace River and Sallie Jones were overflowing with students at that time. Therefore, I drove a mobile unit to those two schools, plugged in behind the cafeteria for electric, and had the speech students come to the van for therapy. The van had an AC unit for cooling and heat. Yes, some days in the winter it was chilly enough to turn on the heat and almost daily the AC had to be on.

The speech van was set up as a very small portable room with a table in the middle and two school bus seats against each wall so it could seat four students comfortably. There was a small table behind the driver's seat where a mirror was placed for the students to see the proper placement of their speech helpers to help make a correct sound. And I had a chair to sit in at the end of the table nearer the driver's seat. There was a file drawer and a small storage cabinet to keep records and speech therapy activities such as cards that I had to make for each sound. At that time, the school supply manufacturers did not produce any speech therapy games or activities.

I drove the van for a few years and then construction of homes and businesses began to decline, thus many families had to leave Charlotte County to find work wherever they could. The drop in school population enabled me to give up the speech van and have a room within the school buildings. Thus, the speech van went to the maintenance workers in the school system.

The Speech Therapy program had been started a few years before I started working for the county by a Mrs. Marie Springman. This knowledgeable elderly lady would eventually serve East Elementary and the Baker Academy in Punta Gorda. We worked together for about three years before her retirement. We did all the yearly hearing testing required by state. We tested each student in grades K, 1,3,5,7, and 10 at all the schools.

I was the first speech therapist to work at Liberty Elementary when it opened in the 1980s with Mr. Bob Alwood as the principal. I retired in December 1995, only to return to work at Liberty in the spring of that school year. I continued to do a steady job of subbing for the next 11 years.

Some things I remember about Charlotte County back then:

In 1968, there was only one traffic light on US41 and Harbor Blvd. in Port Charlotte.

Where CVS now stands at the corner of US41 and Harborview Road, was Pond's Dodge. It was rather small compared to today's auto agencies.

My husband, Jim, worked there with a fella, Ferdie Hilenski, whose wife, Louisa, was principal of Baker School in Punta Gorda. Baker, at that time, was a PreK and kindergarten school.

A small shopping center at the corner of US41 and Harbor Blvd. was the main shopping area for Port Charlotte residents. In the center was a Kwik Chek (Winn-Dixie), Neisner's Department Store, a Sears catalog store, and a drug store with a lunch counter. (There was a handicapped gentleman who rode a three-wheeler bike and would have his lunch at the counter.) There were some other small stores, one of which was where the local residents paid their utility bills.

In the mid-1970s a fire almost wiped out the shopping center. The reason given for the spreading fire was there were no firewalls between the connecting stores. It was so sad to think of the loss of jobs and of the many Christmas gifts that were stored at the Sears catalog store, not to mention the main shopping area for the Port Charlotte residents.

On the route south on two-lane US41 just before crossing over the Peace River bridge there was a small gas station on the Harbor where everyone bought their milk. The milk was in a glass bottle, usually a gallon, and you had to wash and return it for the next purchase.

Merit Gas Station was at the southwest corner of US41 and Edgewater. Ralph Shaefer was the owner and a friend of ours, and a life saver during the gas war in the mid-70s.

Scoop Hartwig owned a few gas/service stations. One was located on the corner of US41 and Harbor Blvd. Our son, Jeff, worked there for a while when he was a student at Charlotte High School which was the only high school in the county at that time.

BUILDING CHANGE

Peter Taylor

When I first moved to this town the only place to eat was the Port Charlotte Diner. That was the only restaurant. Then later on we used to go to Mr. B's Restaurant. Tamiami Trail was a two-lane road. It was the main north-south road. Now, of course, during season it's tough to get up and down 41, even after it was widened.

Back then, Punta Gorda had a strip joint near where the Turtle Club is today. There was a Bible Bookstore over the bridge. Barber shops were closed on Saturday. Sleeping dogs were lying in the middle of 41. It was a dead town.

General Development Corporation was the spark that ignited a boom. There was high unemployment before GDC. Nobody was doing anything, and when we advertised for workers they stood in line. There were 100 people in line. The general superintendent that I hired, Albert Albrecht, was one of those people. I had lunch with him the other day, I have known him for 40 years, and he was the winning candidate of all those that stood in line.

CENTURY

Peter Taylor

Taylor ran a railroad spur to the Murdock depot of his building operation, the warehouses of which later became a flea market and kids playground.

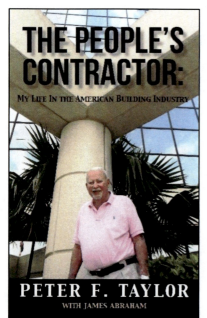

And the building inspector for North Port also applied for a job. He's dead now. He was a little prick, about 5-foot tall, big cigar. His father was the sheriff so he dressed in sheriff's clothes except for the badge. He's the one who would turn down a house if the outlet plate was a little crooked or if the sidewalk was dirty.

We were the largest private employer at that time, with more than 375 people. As I mentioned before, Taylor Contractors of Florida combined with ERB Lumber Company and another individual. We formed a partnership, and that partnership signed the contract with General Development to build homes here.

You know they sent the president of GDC to jail; he worked for me in New York when I was senior vice president at Levitt. He was sued by homeowners. Part of the sales program was buy a house.

Fellow says, "I don't need a house."

GDC tells him, "You're going to retire in five years. Buy the house, rent it out. At the end of five years you give it a coat of paint and move in. You'll have a retirement house at a price five years old."

"Geez, that's a hell of a deal," said the unsuspecting guy. "I'll take two."

They had sales offices all over the country, even in Guam. So they'd buy a house. Say it cost $30,000. But when the guy tried to sell the house, he found it was only worth $25,000.

I was president of Chamber of Commerce and I brought GDC's president over to one of our breakfast meetings. He said in front of the whole group that the marketing cost is one-third the cost of the house. They had New York salesmen, Port Charlotte salesmen, and headquarters people. That's a lot of overhead.

So people felt they were getting screwed paying this high price. There was no value in the house for the marketing efforts.

In a nutshell, they were overpriced. It would cost $20,000 and they were selling for $30,000. Somewhere that $10,000 difference doesn't add value to the house.

But you can't avoid the fact that it's 30% for marketing. That's a huge expense. But they had sales offices and salesmen all over the place, and that's the way they ran their store.

A SHORT PERSPECTIVE ON BIG CHANGE

Maryann Mize, CCIM

Much has changed in Charlotte County since I moved here in 1989.

And one of the most memorable was recalling the change to the Charlotte County center for Edison Junior College, now known as Florida SouthWestern State College.

Malcolm Brenner

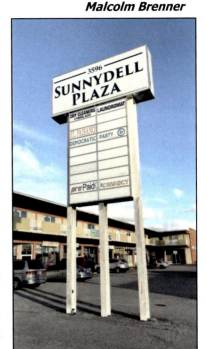

Today when you visit the beautiful campus off Airport Road in Punta Gorda, it's hard to imagine that in 1974 the first classes for what started out as a junior college were held in Sunnydell Plaza, 3596 Tamiami Trail, Port Charlotte.

From that humble 1974 beginning at Sunnydell Plaza, the campus grew. In 1990 the Charlotte County campus moved into a new interim location in Punta Gorda. That location, 2445 Shreve Street, was the home for the Charlotte County Center from 1990 until the new campus was completed in 1997.

This beautiful campus location on 80 acres of land donated by Charlotte County on a long-term lease now includes a robust learning experience for those seeking both a two-year and four-year degree and also houses a collegiate high school.

In conclusion, education has long played an important role to our community's quality of life. Having access to a vibrant Charlotte County of Florida SouthWestern State College campus is a wonderful asset to current and future residents of the community.

And don't forget that it all started at Sunnydell Plaza.

Maryann Mize is senior vice president and senior credit officer at Charlotte State Bank & Trust.

FROM THE KITCHEN TO THE CORNER OFFICE

...we don't see as many wild hogs and quail running through our yards but we enjoy a much more vibrant community for our families.

Craig DeYoung
President, Charlotte State Bank & Trust

My first job in PC was a dishwasher at a restaurant that was located in the Promenades Mall in Port Charlotte. I rode my bike to work from my home near Peachland Boulevard and rarely came across a car in the travels as it was in the mid-70s and traffic was not a real issue.

I started in banking in 1980 at a community bank working in the loan operations area and trying to learn as much as I could. My boss was leaving on maternity leave at which time I would be on my own to run the loan operations department with very little experience. Over the years I was a loan collector (including handing repossessions), indirect auto lender, consumer lender and commercial lender. In 40 years of banking in Charlotte County the changes have been incredible.

We went from a lazy retirement town with very little development and commercial growth, to US41 being built out. Many of the buildings and projects done in the '70s and '80s already have seen their useful life come to an end and have been redeveloped into new up to date buildings. The same thing has happened with the residential growth in the area. We went from vast miles of vacant land with roads nobody drove on to tremendous growth throughout the community. For those who lived here since the early '70s or before, we don't see as many wild hogs and quail running through our yards but we enjoy a much more vibrant community for our families. This trend will continue as we are no longer the sleepy southwest Florida community nobody knows about. The secret is out, we are a tremendous place to work, live, raise our families, and retire.

I am very thankful my parents chose Charlotte County as their retirement spot in 1972 and as the youngest sibling that came down here from Chicago with them, I was fortunate to have my teenage years and entire adult life to have my children and now see my grandchildren enjoy a wonderful community.

OF DAIRY QUEENS AND GDC

Jeff Fehr

Above, an enduring Port Charlotte icon; below, a 1960s postcard view of the community/ Charlotte County History Services.

My introduction to Charlotte County was in the late '60s when I traveled from Miami to visit my dad, who was living in Venice. I remember Tamiami Trail as a narrow two-lane road with an old drawbridge spanning the beautiful Peace River. Heading north from the river there was a single traffic light at Easy Street, as I remember the only light until reaching Venice 30 miles north. Only a handful of buildings existed including an iconic "A" frame Dairy Queen that is in the same location today. Tired of living in Miami, in 1974 my wife and I moved to Port Charlotte, which I saw as an opportunity to open a small business that could cater to the rapidly growing population generated by strong marketing of the area by the General Development Corp. Due to the fortunes of timing, luck, and hard work my wife and I raised our family, started a successful business and have retired, choosing to remain in Charlotte County, living on the Peace River overlooking the bridge that replaced the drawbridge that was part of the earliest memories of my first visits to the area.

Jeff Fehr is a real estate investor and appraiser.

Don Gant's family became a growth industry after moving to Charlotte County/The Gant family.

A GOOD PLACE TO RAISE A FAMILY

Don Gant

My first introduction to Charlotte County was when I worked here during the summers as a teenager. As a native Floridian, I loved the pristine waters and could tell that a lot of people would someday call this home. In 1972 I moved to Charlotte County after graduating from University of South Florida. It was more evident than before that this was a growing community with lots of business opportunities and miles and miles of beautiful shoreline. As a sportsman, this was a big draw for me. And now, 48 years later, Charlotte County still offers the same thing to new families. It is still full of business opportunities and still surrounded by beautiful Charlotte Harbor, a jewel unlike any other on the west coast of Florida.

Donnie Gant is a retired commercial real estate broker.

TO BUILD A COMMUNITY

James Anderson

While visiting family in Charlotte County during the '70s, I knew I wanted to be in construction and the rental space business. So I decided to move to Port Charlotte.

In the late '70s and early '80s it was apparent that the plotted lots were readily available from the initial GDC buyers. At that time GDC, Ruth Richmond Homes, and a larger builder from Ft. Myers had a huge sector of the new home market. Several Charlotte builders began to emerge. Then, after the Great Recession of the mid-2000s national builders arrived on the scene.

In the '80s and '90s with a new baseball stadium (and a big-league spring training team), the new five-story county office building, the opening of the regional mall, the continued widening of US41, a new vocational and high school, the population growth of the WWII citizenry and the solid economy, generated a boom town atmosphere. GDC's efforts had reached a critical mass and the Port Charlotte subdivision's population was forging ahead.

The critical mass and a boom town mentality produced the opportunity for contributing, for self-growth, and for creating a great place to live. A few examples of this include a Little League field on Harold Avenue that sprang up before a county-funded parks and recreation department, volunteering and supporting new vocational and high schools that had limited funding at the time, organizing a new Charlotte builders' association of 500-plus members from a former regional system. Other milestones included volunteers building a Moose Lodge under the coordination of Lee Odom, watching national restaurants emerging on US41, and many, many other great developments. It was an exciting period. Charlotte County should be proud of its history and the opportunities people have available for a fulfilling life.

James Anderson is a prominent builder.

THE PEN IS MIGHTIER THAN THE SNOW SHOVEL

Mary Williams left a snowy Indiana to visit Charlotte County in 1979 and stayed to chronicle the community. For many years she wrote a popular column for the *Sarasota Herald-Tribune* and was a part of the golden age of newspaper coverage of the region during the '90s. Her daughter, Betsy, became a news and contract photographer and her granddaughter, Miki Matrullo, opened her own real estate firm in 2020.

GROWING UP IN PGI

Gaye Johns Brownie

I was lucky to have grown up in a very loving home. Things were quiet. I don't remember my parents raising their voices. We had rules and were taught respect. Don't interrupt. No matter what, be honest. Be home by six for dinner. Call if you are going to be late. Keep your voice down. I had a hard time with that one. Don't make fun or judge anyone, you don't know what their life is like. Be nice to everyone. Don't do anything to embarrass yourself. You are going to live here for a long time, and you always want to be able to look everyone in the eye. In my mind it was not so much about me, but I didn't want to do anything to embarrass my parents.

Our mom was great! She and my dad were very much in love. All she wanted was to spend time with him and her family. She ran the house and loved to clean. She was always there for us, and she would not let anyone mess with her children. If she went off for the day she would always be home when we got

All photos Gaye Johns Brownie

Dad, Mom, Kevin and me in our PGI yard.

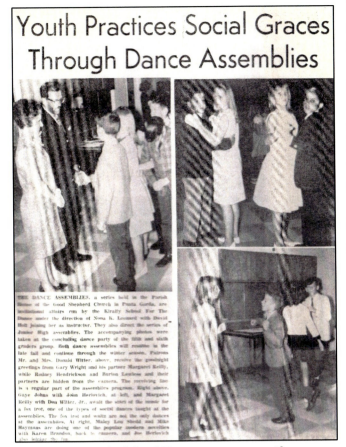
Gaye Johns and Michael Haymans, among others, practice etiquette.

home from school. I think I was 21 before I ever came home to an empty house. I was also in college at that time.

In late elementary we got horses. I'm sure this was for our pleasure and to keep us out of trouble. Well… one day we were told that we weren't allowed to play cowboys and Indians. It wasn't good for the cows. We scared them when we were on horseback trying to round them up.

Judi Duff Addison and I used to ride the horses out to Ponce de Leon Park. There were a couple of old concrete picnic tables. We would ride our horses up to one and take our shoes off. We would unsaddle the horses and take them swimming.

We did a bunch of racing on Tract A, now known as Jamaica Way.

Judi and I decided one day we were going to go build a fort back on what we called the sand flats. This area is down Bal Harbor maybe a little to the right of where the strip mall is now. We gathered up a bunch of sticks and tied them to our saddles and off we went. I don't actually remember us building a fort, but we had a great time playing in the dirt, picking up sticks and playing with Spanish moss. There are chiggers in that moss known as red bugs. They would get under your skin. That was OK because if you got one you could paint your skin with clear nail polish and they would go away.

One day Judi and I decided we were going to barrel race on the same barrels at the same time. We just about killed each other.

One afternoon I was in the tack shack where all the food and supplies for the horses were kept and I hear Judi hollering. I ran out to see what the matter was. I'm jumping up and down. She won't tell me what's wrong. As that turned out she had stepped on a nail that was in the board I was jumping up and down on. That definitely called for a tetanus shot.

Judi and I took a lot of dance classes from Mrs. Leonard, including ballet, tap and toe dancing. I later took more ballet in college.

Mrs. Leonard, (not sure about the spelling of her name), also set up an etiquette class. The girls had to learn to set the table. We all had to learn what silverware to use.

When we were learning to dance the boys sat on one side of the room and the girls on the other. The boys had to walk across the room to ask us to dance. They would take our hand and lead us to the dance floor. I don't remember the dance we were taught, but probably something like the box step.

CENTURY

Judi and my first job was to put up and take down our American flag every day. It was at the entrance of PGI. We each got fifty cents a week. I remember being very proud to do this. We by no means would let it touch the ground and we folded it properly. Respect!

When I was in sixth grade I was crowned May Queen. Burton Lawless was my king. Our music teacher, Mr. Moss, taught us a dance to wrap the May pole with ribbons. As a young adult I used to substitute Mr. Moss's class.

There was an A&W root beer stand on 41 south in Punta Gorda. We loved to go there. They had car hops and I thought that was really cool. Next door was a roller-skating rink where Judi and I spent a lot of time.

We did a lot of water skiing. We would try to ski from PGI to the bridge and on out to Harbour Heights. If you could make it to the bridge your legs would feel like jelly. Harbour Heights was a blast! Out at the railroad trestles there was a rope hanging from a tree. Kids and families would swing out over the river and let go. Later years, among other places, we rode Sea Doos out there. Then they changed the speed limit to a no wake zone out there.

Don't forget the Breezeway. This was a hamburger joint on 41 and McKenzie. Without question the best hamburgers in the world. This was owned by Mr. Peden.

We all hunted and were taught to shoot and respect guns. I hit my first bullseye at six years old. I don't remember what kind of truck my friend Kelley had in high school, but he had a gun rack in the back window with guns. One of his teachers went over to talk with him and asked Kelley to come over to his truck. He wanted to show Kelley his guns. Oh my, how times have changed.

Man vs. machine

Champion arm wrestler Kevin Johns of Punta Gorda pulls two trucks and a trailer with his left arm during a demonstration at Palm Chevrolet in Punta Gorda on Wednesday. The combined weight of the vehicles, which were in neutral, was more than five tons. The Florida State Arm Wrestling Championships will be held Saturday at the Town Center Mall in Port Charlotte beginning at 1 p.m. Brian White column / 1C

THOMAS A. PRICE/News-Press

He loved racing cars. A bunch of guys would go out around Collingswood Boulevard in Port Charlotte to race, where streets had been laid out but no houses had been built. They would be sure not to have much gas so the car would be lighter. Then they would take some of the air out of the tires to give them more traction. All the guys were quite serious about this.

My younger brother, Kevin loved hanging out with his friends. They would go out on the weekends and catch hogs. They went mudding on four wheelers. They actually liked getting stuck in the mud and having to pull each other out.

At 22, he opened Kevin's Gym on 41 in Punta Gorda. Kevin won a total of nine world champion arm wrestling matches. The Hawaiian World Cup International in 1988 was the first one. There were several in California around that time. The last one was in Tokyo, Japan in 1992. In his early to mid-thirties he was supposed to arm wrestle a fire truck. That couldn't be arranged so Palm Chevrolet tied three Chevrolet Suburbans together and he arm wrestled that and won.

Kevin liked to give positive motivation speeches to young people about health and fitness. Then he would break boards and bend steel rods over his head to impress the little tykes.

I can't think of any better place to have grown up other than right here in good old Punta Gorda.

THANKSGIVING REMINISCENCES OF A TARPON'S GLORY DAYS

Paul DeGaeta

Half a century ago - exactly 50 years ago around this time of day, Coach Fred Goldsmith's 1970 Tarpons were getting ready to claim our school's first Coral Coast Conference and District Titles. We were down at North Ft. Myers playing a very good Red Knight team.

Most of us who played on that team are still close. Charlotte has gotten used to winning as a program. But back then, we were the only high school in the county. Tarpon fans ranged from South Punta Gorda Heights to Boca Grande and Englewood and North Port. So, it was an incredibly big deal. So next time you're in the Tarpon Gym - look up at the Football banner. This is the date that starts all those other ones.

Here's a shot from that day the *Ft. Myers News-Press* ran on their sports cover. Burton Lawless, Jeff Gilmore, me and Harold "Mackie" Mack are flying downfield - of eight feet among us, only one is on the ground. I think this was the first-ever SWFL high school football game held on Thanksgiving Day. There were probably 6-7,000 ringing the field including a number of Vietnam Vets recently returned or home on leave.

CENTURY

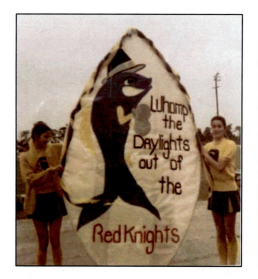 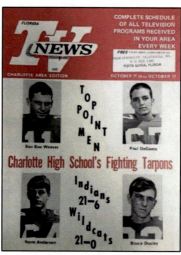 

Marcia Barnett Harrell and Danette Brancaccio-Dorotich, two Tarpon cheerleaders, hold the banner we ran through coming onto the field for the 1971 Turkey Bowl on Thanksgiving morning at Tarpon Stadium! Note the Pilgrim Hat on the Fightin' Tarpon. As Danette posted on Facebook: "What better way to celebrate Thanksgiving but with another win for the Tarpons!" Boo Boo's Tarpon Letter Jacket showing our Coral Coast Conference and Regional Champion Patches - Mine was lost in Dodge City, Kansas.

When the *News-Press* (before their tourist editors redefined the boundaries of SW Florida) asked Coach Goldsmith what the Tarpons were going to do about Coach Ron Hoover's stud fullback, Mike Rubinski, Goldsmith never hesitated. He said the Tarpons would answer with middle linebacker, Harold "Boo Boo" Weaverski (whose last name is actually Weaver).

Burton Lawless put a big hit on their fastest do-it-all player, Roosevelt Dorris on the opening kickoff that got his attention the rest of the game. Our defense was awesome - Marlon Runkle, Ed Stepp, Reggie Carr, Dale Russell, Robert Horton, Ben Graham, Pete Whisenant, Bruce Dooley, Boo Boo and Burton. Boo Boo also led our offense as QB. Our backs, Harold Mack, who the *Miami Herald* nicknamed "Mack the Knife," John Herlovich and Kenny Poteet had great games behind the ground and pound O-line (Dale Russell, Wendell Woolum, Norm Anderson, me, Randy Sisk and TEs Jeff Gilmore and Burton). I love them all!

You won't find many teams who stayed as close as this one over 50 years - we've been best men in each other's weddings, godfathers to children, and lifelong close friends.

Coach Goldsmith has checked on us over the years. He even came down for the ceremony when Burton Lawless presented Charlotte High with the NFL's Golden Football to each high school player who played in a Super Bowl. So I texted Coach Goldsmith reminding him of this day so long ago. His reply: "Thanks Paul it means a lot to me that we can share those special moments like it was yesterday. God bless you and all Tarpons. My all-time favorite team."

That's high praise coming from a 2-Time NCAA Coach of the Year at Rice (Sports Illustrated COY 1992) and Duke (Bobby Dodd COY 1994). He was also HC at Slippery Rock and Lenoir-Rhyn. Coach served as an assistant at Florida, FAMU, Air Force. He finished his career in North Carolina at Franklin High School in 2011.

I always said Fred Goldsmith blew into Punta Gorda like Hurricane Donna and was gone just as quick. He was here for only two seasons. He notched our first winning season in years then brought us to the state semi-final game. But he was a force of change for our program and eleven of us from this team got the opportunity to play college football. Burton Lawless went to three Super Bowls with the Dallas Cowboys.

Congressman Connie Mack and State Representative Vernon Peeples were on hand to open the present Barron Collier Bridge, the second to bear that name.

CULTURE CLUBS

In 1985 Bob Roberts arrived in Charlotte County, fleeing a divorce and the cold of yet another New York City winter. He was a realtor who had bought and sold in the mean streets of the Northeast, and Charlotte county was like a wide-open frontier to him.

Roberts soon became a top salesmen on the front lines of the housing boom. He also was shrewd enough to join the Republican Party as it took over Southwest Florida. At the time, county Republicans were led by several factions, the strongest of which were east of the Myakka River and led by military veterans. Tom D'Andrea was a former pilot who once flew bait missions to draw North Vietnam's surface to air missiles into the air. His counterpart was Rufus Lazzell, a double winner of the Silver Star

CENTURY

1981
I-75 bridge completed over Charlotte Harbor and Charlotte County accesses opened.

County commissioners move administration offices to new building in Murdock.

The first space shuttle launches began at the Kennedy Space Center in Cape Canaveral.

1982
Florida was one of fifteen states to fail to ratify of the ERA Constitutional Amendment.

Florida News Service begins in Tallahassee.

Walt Disney World opened its second attraction in Orlando, EPCOT.

Bob Roberts

for valor who fought in Korea and then went back for more in the Vietnam War. Roberts, a Marine who still shakes his head when he remembers what he saw in Korea, fit right in—until an inadvertent endorsement.

Back then, in the late '80s, Vernon Peeples was the last remaining Democratic legislator from Southwest Florida. The Republican resurgence was lapping at his heels. Roberts, who by then was also president of the local realtors board, was standing at the back of the room as Peeples was being honored for legislation that benefitted the group.

"Come on up, Bob," said the presenter. Bob did, just in time to get photographed shaking Peeples' hand. That marked the end of his presidency.

"A party man called me up and told me to come out to an emergency meeting," Roberts recalled. "I drove all up and down some back roads in the county somewhere until I found the place. They let me in and we went into this dark room. All around it were the officers of the party."

Tom D'Andrea barked out a few orders in his gravelly voice and shoved a piece of paper at Roberts. It was his resignation.

Today, Roberts laughs at the incident. But it spoke to the military precision and singularity of purpose that the Republicans brought to their successful campaign to become the only party of importance in the area.

Lindsay Harrington, now a successful realtor, was a Republican foot soldier during the Eighties who rose to city and state leadership. How serious was he about politics? Just ask his wife.

Lindsay Harrington

"Debbie and I had just started dating," Harrington said. "So I asked her, 'Would you like to go out waving signs with me?'

'Sure I'd like to go,' she said.

'I'm going to Lehigh on a Saturday,' I said.

"She says, 'Let's go.' So we went down there. Debbie had on a wide-brimmed straw hat. I had on a baseball cap, I think. Debbie's on one side of the road and I'm on the other side. People were driving by blowing horns, waving, smiling—at her! They thought Debbie was the candidate."

But voters soon learned to pick the right Harrington as he and his mentors built an unstoppable political machine, the first such operation in modern county history.

A People's History of Charlotte County

Sarasota Herald-Tribune

Tom and Diane D'Andrea

"My campaign managers, Tom and Diane D'Andrea, were quite influential in helping to strengthen the party," Harrington recalled. "Diane worked for Ronald Reagan's campaign and Tom once worked at the Pentagon. I think they are the ones who brought about the biggest change. I ran for city council and won in 1988 and at the same time I ran for chairman of the Republican Party and defeated Darol Carr for chairmanship of the party."

His victory soon locked up Punta Gorda for the party. Then Harrington and his change-makers set their sights higher. Harrington names Dave Bittner, an able captain in the Republican ranks who served in the state legislature, as his mentor. Working with Bittner, Harrington went on to become Punta Gorda mayor and later served in the legislature, defeating Vernon Peeples and ending Charlotte County's presence in the statehouse.

Harrington himself is now a behind-the-scenes power broker, a Republican one should get to know before tossing a hat or a toque into the ring. And he loves giving advice, particularly this basic bit of wisdom for the first-time campaigner—put your boots on the ground.

"You know it took a lot of work on the ground, a lot of door-to-door," he said. "I did 10,000 doors, door-to-door Charlotte and Lee County. I even waved signs in the rain in Arcadia and people would drive by and crack their window. But hey, rain or shine you wave signs.

"I used to sit down at Route 80 and Route 82 down in Fort Myers just east of the Interstate and it's six lanes coming into town off Palm Beach Boulevard and I would sit there and have my easel set up with my sign and then I had a hand sign I would hold it up every so often to the different lanes of traffic.

"And then I'd count cars. I'd count the drivers that waved yes or gave a thumbs-up, you know. But the best fun was little old ladies. They'd come down the road and you'd be standing there and they would not dare look at you. It's like 'I'm voting for you if I look at you!' I had more fun at that."

At the turn of the century Charlotte County and most of Southwest Florida was a red enclave thanks in part to men like Harrington. And despite the obvious problems with one-party rule, one sure benefit accrued to Charlotte County. Prior to the rise of men like Harrington, any officeholder was lucky to win a second term. Politics were personal, they had no coherence. The San Casa Road

1983

Old Barron Collier bridge over Charlotte Harbor replaced with a twin of Gilchrist Bridge and restricted to north-bound traffic.

Wheel of Fortune begins with hosts Pat Sajak and Vanna White.

Motown celebrates its 25th anniversary with the television special *Motown 25: Yesterday, Today, Forever*, during which Michael Jackson performs Billie Jean and introduces the moonwalk.

The Space Shuttle Challenger is launched on its maiden voyage.

President Ronald Reagan signs a bill creating Martin Luther King, Jr. Day. a federal holiday.

1984

Edmund Kulakowski Observatory established and named for former ECC astronomy and geology professor.

ECC Retirees Association formed.

President Reagan announces that the United States will begin development of a permanently crewed space station.

1985

Charlotte County Art Guild builds Visual Arts Center at Punta Gorda.

Englewood Community Hospital opens.

Ronald Reagan sworn in for a second term as President of the United States.

Gang from Englewood, Rufus' Raiders from Punta Gorda, or the Sewer Rats from Port Charlotte, were single-interest groups with dedicated leaders and fired up followers. They had the single-issue firepower to dethrone a commissioner or councilman who voted the wrong way. And the revolving door of the sheriff's office swung by its own rules, thus adding to the slipshod politics and governance of a revolving door type of governance.

But the Republican ascendancy marked a permanence in local politics. Party structure provided a ladder by which the best and brightest—or the guy with the most friends and money—were vetted before seeking office. Strong war chests and a dedicated organization helped keep folks in office, thus ensuring continuity in state, city, and county government.

By the end of the era Frank Desquin was left as the only Democratic officeholder in the county. Sheriff Bill Clement, whose rise and fall was marked with a celerity remarkable even for the revolving door of the office he won and lost at the end of the 1990s, would prove an anomaly. Through old family ties and loyalties forged through years of shared struggles and fine times, the Desquins held on to a popularity that transcended one-party rule. So the Desquins would come to represent a small blue oasis of small "d" principles in a red sea of Republicanism.

Ironically, the local Republicans would prove more amenable than Charlotte Democrats in grooming and supporting successful minority candidates. John Murphy, a black transplant from Detroit who had worked as a UPS executive, once told the author that Rufus Lazzell gave him one operative bit of advice when he came to town—register as a Republican. So the lifelong Democrat switched parties and soon became one of three liberal councilmen on the Punta Gorda City Council during the '90s.

And Bob Roberts? He parlayed his Republican connections into business opportunities to become one of the area's top realtors and an honored member of the Chamber of Commerce. He was the first black president of Leadership Charlotte, a networking and informational series sponsored by the Chamber.

Because of the groundwork laid by Harrington and others, Southwest Florida recently elected its first black congressman, a Republican.

Politics, however, didn't end at the Myakka River. L.A. Ainger, son of an Englewood pioneer, parlayed his father's grocery store that he inherited into a political base. His spade work continued the efforts of Pete Buchan, Englewood's first Sarasota County commissioner, who helped secure Buchan Field and bring road improvements to his community.

Englewood was long the red-headed stepchild of two counties. Because of its position athwart Sarasota and Charlotte counties, coupled with a strong Boca Grande—Lee County influence, Englewood was too far from the administrative centers of the three counties to receive its share of public services. Consequently, Englewood had its own volunteer fire department and the Woman's Club was once the town's library. L.A. Ainger, along with state politicians from the area like Jack Tate, another merchant, managed to steer much-needed dollars to the town between the counties. Mac Horton, who married Ainger's daughter, would go on to bring even more recognition and infrastructure to Englewood.

Peace River Manasota Regional Water Supply Authority

The main utility of the Peace River Manasota Regional Water Supply Authority, acquired from General Development Corporation after the company went bankrupt. Below, the authority's coverage area.

In a heartening sign of intergovernmental cooperation, Charlotte, DeSoto, Hardee, Manatee, and Sarasota counties joined in 1982 to create the Peace River/Manasota Regional Water Supply Authority. Hardee County withdrew a year later. The Authority reflects sound state planning aimed at regionalizing water supplies and discouraging "water wars" between jurisdictions drawing from the same source. The Authority acquired General Development Corporation's sprawling facility on Kings Highway north of Port Charlotte in the '90s. Prior to that, the group spent much of its time learning how to work together and drafting plans to utilize the area's major sources of water.[65]

Taking a page from Punta Gorda's periodic efforts to reinvent itself, community leaders in Englewood set out to do the same. They decided to market and glorify the past to encourage business traffic, harking back to when their eponymous designation was the town center.

In 1984 Old Englewood Village Association (OEVA) was founded as the Dearborn Merchants Association, a non-profit civic organization. The Association works with Sarasota County Government and the Englewood Community Redevelopment Agency (CRA) to promote commerce and development. A year later the Lemon Bay Historical Society was incorporated as a non-profit organization "for the specific purposes of perpetuating the legacy of the past [and] honoring the pioneer settlers of the Lemon Bay area."

1986
Barbara B. Mann Performing Arts Hall opened.

Space shuttle Challenger exploded over Cape Canaveral shortly after take-off. The disaster halted the NASA shuttle program for several years.

1987
Charlotte County Stadium opens in cooperation with the Texas Rangers for spring training and regular-season farm team games.

CH&N Rail Road abandons right-of-way.

---

[65] https://www.amwa.net/assets/Platinum%20Peace%20River%20Application.pdf

CENTURY

1989
Trailer homes on Punta Gorda's municipal waterfront moved out. Contract for public-private development awarded to Classic Properties of New Orleans.

County's largest shopping mall, Port Charlotte Town Center, opens at Murdock.

Charlotte Sun and Punta Gorda Herald-News merge as daily Charlotte Sun Herald under leadership of Derek Dunn-Rankin

Peter Taylor builds County Administration building at Murdock is enlarged with five-story annex

Florida Correctional Institution opens on Oil Well Road.

The group sponsors what has become one of the community's biggest events, Pioneer Days.

Culture became big business during the 1980s, as government largesse, the decline of traditional industries, and a growing cohort of wealthy or well-off retires helped spur not a renaissance but a birth of the arts in the region.

The flowering represented the coming of age of the county, as residents moved from subsistence living to a higher standard of life buoyed by home ownership and the post-WWII economy.

For the first time, both governments and private entities promoted, paid for, and sustained long-term efforts to raise the cultural temperature.

A document produced by Punta Gorda's planning department describes that city establishment's blunt reaction to the community's downward slide.

In December, 1986, "Centennial Fever" broke out in Punta Gorda as the community celebrated its 100th birthday. During the year-long celebration, the Medical Center Foundation renovated the A. C. Freeman Home and listed it on the National Register of Historic Places. The City dedicated the first block of its Streetscape Program, and the Revitalization Committee completed work on a local historic resources survey, a building facade improvement loan pool, and a beautification awards program.

On November 15, 1989, Punta Gorda City Council made a finding that slum and blight

(Logo and description from the Lemon Bay Historical Society web page)
Bob Cashatt, artist
The grubbing hoe over the man's shoulder was used to clear scrub palmettos. The cabbage palm tree furnished protection from the elements and food. The fronds were layered like shingles on both walls and roofs of shelters. The center fronds of new growth were woven into hats and the heart of the palm is a delicious food, both as a salad and as a boiled dinner. Fishing was the main industry and source of food, depicted by the fisherman in the boat with the net over the stern. The sailboat brought supplies into the bay. The sunset depicts the beauty of Lemon Bay and the Gulf.

A People's History of Charlotte County

Charlotte County History Services

As Punta Gorda suffered a downturn through the 80s, Punta Gorda Isles boomed. Colony Point is in the foreground of this aerial of the community.

1990

County population is 110,975, an 89.8 percent increase over 1980

School Board administration moves from Punta Gorda to Murdock.

Punta Gorda Council and County Commission appoint a Community Redevelopment Authority to manage waterfront development

World headquarters of Improved Manageability, Profitability and Control (IMPAC)—a large management training company—is located at Punta Gorda. Charlotte Center moved to new interim location in Punta Gorda.

conditions existed in the redevelopment area. They established a Community Redevelopment Agency on December 7, 1989 via resolutions.

Since late 1986, 17 downtown businesses have spent an estimated $1.3 million on interior and exterior renovations. September, 1988 also saw the creation of the Downtown Advisory Board (DAB), Greater Punta Gorda Business Alliance (GPGBA) designed to serve as the private sector's key downtown redevelopment organization.

With a strong downtown revitalization effort already in place, the City of Punta Gorda has now turned its attention toward establishing a Community Redevelopment Agency with the aim of adopting a redevelopment plan for its downtown area and using tax increment financing to fund the projects and programs contained in this plan.[66]

In the decade to come, the marriage of culture, neighborhood development, ecotourism and historic preservation would coalesce to set the city on a peninsula on a path to create the community that ushered in the new century.

---

[66]https://www.ci.punta-gorda.fl.us/home/showpublished document/1356/636020307987530000#:~:text=Then%20in%20December%2C%201986%2C%20%22,National%20Register%20of%20Historic%20Places.

CENTURY

LIZ HUTCHINSON-SPERRY AND THE BLOOMING OF LOCAL ARTS

Liz Hutchinson is the queen and sustainer of local arts. A founding member and driving force of the Visual Arts Center, she has drawn national and international acclaim for her work. She has run an annual art pilgrimage to Giverny, brought national artists to Punta Gorda, and has served as a patron large and small to a multitude of artists.

How did the Visual Arts Center come to be?

We decided the first thing we were going to do was go to the county. Now in those days, at that time decades ago the bulk of the population was in Port Charlotte. That's where everybody lived. And Punta Gorda Isles was being built and there were people there, but surely not the bulk. So then we decided that we would do a door-to-door canvas to see first of all if there was any interest in that kind of thing. And I'm not sure of the numbers but I think I'm fairly safe in saying easily 90% of the people were in favor of an arts and crafts center in the community.

A People's History of Charlotte County

Where was the door-to-door survey conducted? Throughout the county?

The survey that we did was just in Punta Gorda. We walked it. It was interesting because so many people were interested. And we collected $50,000 in this little community to go towards building a Visual Arts Center. Now it was a different community at that time. You have to understand the houses were not the mansions they are now. It was primarily a community of retired working-class people. Not vice presidents and company owners and all that business. So we had $50,000, community interest, and I remember thinking, "Man, we've got a tiger by the tail here."

So we decided we would go to the next County Commission meeting to ask for a site. After we made our little presentation he looked at us and he said, "You all think we've got nothing better to do than give away land?" And I thought, "Hmm."

But all was not lost. A week later we were at one of our board meetings and the city manager from Punta Gorda called.

"I understand you people are interested in building a Visual Arts Center," he said. "How would you like that piece of ground across from Fishermen's Village?"

Well I about fainted dead away. "We'd love it," I remember babbling. "It would be wonderful."

He said, "Okay. We'll work something out. It will be a loan because the city retains the ownership of the land but we maintain the right to build on it."

Man alive. Well that information went through the community like wildfire and it looked like we were going to be able to build a Visual Arts Center.

Well the next thing that happened, I can't tell you a time, was Wayne Goff called. Now I knew Wayne because we had talked with him about building a house. Nice guy. Terrific guy. And the phone rings. I answer it.

"I understand they gave you that piece of ground across from Fishermen's Village."

"Yeah."

Wayne B. Goff was a fourth-generation descendant of the Goff family who were original settlers of Englewood. A 1957 graduate of Charlotte High School; he remained an active CHS supporter throughout his lifetime. Goff graduated from the University of Florida, College of Planning, Design, and Construction.

He began his career with E. I. DuPont, then formed Goff Construction, Inc. in 1960. He was Builder/Developer of Punta Gorda Isles (1970-1984), and owner and President of Church Growth & Building Consultants.

He donated his services as general contractor for many churches, the Performing Arts Center, Habitat for Humanity Punta Gorda, and the Southwest Florida Vietnam Memorial Wall in Punta Gorda and Punta Gorda History Center. He was instrumental in building Port Charlotte "U", an adult education school for retired residents, into the Cultural Center of Charlotte County.

Henry Lhose, left, the mover and shaker in getting land for the VAC from the City of Punta Gorda and the driving force in getting artists to support the idea of a teaching/exhibiting art center. Roseann Samson, left, a school administrator who made art a mainstay in public education. Right, Rebecca Durig, at center, and friends as they open a wing of the VAC named in her honor. Her maiden name, fittingly enough, was Hall. (All photos Michele Valencourt).

"How'd you like me to be the general contractor for that building for $25?" he said. "This community has been very good to me and I've been trying to think of a way to pay back some of that good will that people have pushed my way."

From there, help poured in. Names that come to mind include Linda Plug, architect Bernie Rowan, Rita Blaisus, Rebecca Deurig, Henry Lhose, Michelle Valencourt and others who were instrumental in founding and sustaining the VAC.

A person who has received very little recognition (in my opinion) is Roseann Samson. She was Assistant Spt. Schools and was instrumental in promoting, funding, coordinating the Performing Arts Center at Charlotte High. She was also, incidentally, president of the VAC's Endowment Trust. Big arts in school supporter but largely forgotten

Everybody else. I mean that. When we built the VAC, we really felt the City of Punta Gorda needed that kind of facility. I mean, where were you going to hold any large meetings back then? The business clubs used to use the Visual Arts Center for their annual meetings and things like that, and that was important. You don't want just artists coming in the door. You want the whole community.

SEA GRAPE GALLERY

Bonnie Benande

Sea Grape Gallery is a non-profit cooperative art gallery that was chartered in 1988 by 21 local artists including Marion Burmeister who had a vision for an art gallery in Charlotte County to showcase fine art and provide a professional setting for local artists to display and sell their work. For over 33 years, Sea Grape Gallery has been a mainstay of the City of Punta Gorda business community.

For all these years, Sea Grape Gallery has supported the local community by

Bonnie Benande, Marion Burmeister, one of the original owners of Sea Grape Gallery who started the gallery back in 1988; and Barb Albin.

organizing fundraising events for local charities, providing financial and artwork donations to these charities, and has awarded a yearly scholarship to a local high school student. During Hurricane Charley, Sea Grape Gallery was unable to open its doors for 15 months. However, the Gallery was able to continue its operations due to financial donations from customer supporters and local merchants who donated temporary operating space to ensure that the Gallery continue being an important and valued member of the business community.

Sea Grape Gallery is proud of its long-standing community status and its charitable mission for all these years.

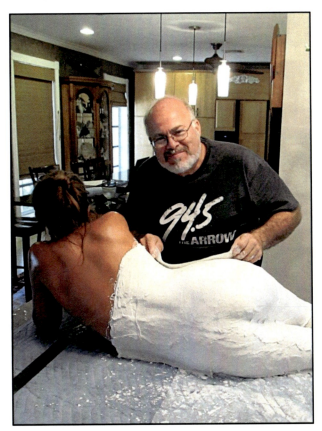

Dedo's mastery of malleable sculpting material had made him an expert at body casting.

HOMEGROWN: THE CHARLOTTE COUNTY CONTEMPORARY ARTS SCENE

Art bends toward its own and in a community with as large a working-class base as Charlotte County, oftentimes the best work can be found where, as Simon and Garfunkel once sang,

"Laying low, seeking out the poorer quarters
Where the ragged people go
Looking for the places only they would know"

So to find the cutting edge of art in a minimum wage community, go to the heart of town. In the county's largest community, Port Charlotte, live two artists who exemplify a specific urban, gritty, Charlotte County style of art—and whose backgrounds offered little clue to their futures as visionaries.

Their work is not only eclectic, but made to sell, as both Rod Becklund and Dedo are salesmen as well as artists. Becklund is an assiduous salesman who works out of his garage, doing everything from mass-producing waterbird statues to painting storefronts at Christmas time. Dedo's background is in home construction, which serves him well in designing innovative ways of bringing durability and verve to his work.

A third example of the local new wave is the work of Patricia Turner. Politics is art to Turner and her work speaks to issues as complex as racism and as contemporary as tomorrow.

Dedo

My father and mother had moved to Port Charlotte and owned an ice cream store on Olean Blvd.

I first visited my parents in 1974 after they moved from Seaford, Long Island, NY. We drove down with our young son and stayed at the Sandpiper Hotel on Tamiami Trail our first night in Port Charlotte. My wife Ginger was up early the next morning ready to ride and was disappointed to learn this was it.

We stayed only a few months. Five years later Dad says Port Charlotte is booming, he and my brother are installing new roofs for Pete Taylor at ERB (and my sister is his secretary) they can use help and Dad will help me build a new house. The company was Cristina Roofing. Wanting a change, I moved my family here.

We went from installing new shingle roofs to tar and gravel roofs and eventually reroofing. I left to start All-Right Roofing when I found peace in working alone. I expanded into building homes and additions and enjoyed a good life of kayaking and fishing until I fell off a roof. Things changed and I no longer felt the need to continue in the direction I was heading.

In 1994 I went back to college in Tampa and got an associate degree in graphic design. In 1995 I worked for Buffalo Graphics for a short time. Then we opened up Marble Works making cultured marble vanity tops and tubs. We sold that to a gentleman who automated it and moved the company to North Port.

We started Granite Planet in Murdock after falling in love with solid surfaces and continued running All-Right Roofing. I had always been an artist; when I was a kid I came up with my own malleable substance, sort of like papier mache, a variant of which I still use today. I take ideas and try to take them to my kind of place, my kind of vision. But I don't consider that appropriation art. It's transformative art

because it tells a whole new story when it's put together this way. It becomes something different. In writing, as in art, they say the best writers are thieves. They steal but they make it their own, they transform it. That's what I do.

Rod Becklund

At age 16 I began sign painting and at 21 I got married and moved to Florida. I got a job sign painting I worked at for one year and then I got into sandsculpting and from sandsculpting I met my friend John Davis, the owner of Davis Cypress gallery. He was a chainsaw sculptor and he taught me chainsaw carving. In 1995 I was commissioned to create a 10-foot-tall carved monument of Thomas Edison it is currently at the Edison home in Fort Myers on McGregor.

While selling my work at Davis Cypress my sculptures were gaining popularity. I soon had to hire help to fill my orders. The '90s were hopping, I was expanding my business. I was selling in 30 shops across the states and then I built my website *www.rodbecklund.com* and picked up more shops in five states. I couldn't keep up with the orders even with help so I started limited edition reproductions of my birds in resin. That was the ticket for success for me.

We've had a couple setbacks over the years with 9/11, and in the recession of 2008 my list of gallery closings were coming fast and hard. In the past few years the sales are finally coming back. In 2016 I became a painting instructor and did that for two years. I taught roughly 5,000 people to pain in that time. In all the years the best shop I sold to was called Sanybels Finest. The owner, Jack Elias, has become a great friend and mentor to me. I have been selling art in his gallery since 1995. They sell both my paintings and sculptures at the gallery. One of my bestsellers are my paintings on reclaimed wood. I find old barn doors or wood pallets and make a wooden canvas that I paint birds and fish in my style. Another hit at Sanybel's Finest have been my driftwood emerging bird sculptures. I am currently working on a 4.5-foot-tall driftwood pelican in flight.

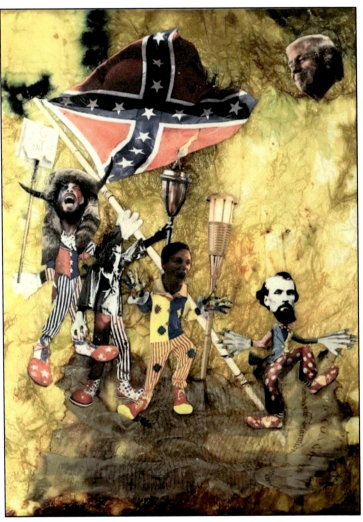

Patricia Turner

Patricia Anderson Turner addresses social and political issues with her mixed media and textile art as created in her Punta Gorda, Florida, studio. Issues Turner addresses are as varied as the history of white supremacy and of racial division, gun violence, and the environment, among other issues of our time. Turner's career highlights include a First Place at the Verona Museum of Modern Art, Italy, in 2011 as well as top honors in museums, art galleries, and art centers throughout the United States.

"Treasonous Clowns," above, which illustrates her disdain for white supremacists, was awarded First Place in the "Promise of Spring" exhibit may 4-28 at Art Center Manatee in Bradenton. It is 80" H x 60" wide with hand-cut paper collage printed on fleece and embellished with 3D elements.

Turner's social commentary work has been published in scholarly reference books about human rights and health and featured in the PBS film "Crossroads" as well as purchased for permanent public collections in museums, universities, and the travelling Human Rights Art Exhibition.

Turner's website is *www.patriciaturnerart.com*

PEACE OUT! THE FOURTH BRIDGE TO SPAN THE RIVER OPENS

AASHTO

On January 12, 1983, a new mile (1.6-kilometer)-long bridge across the Peace River in Charlotte County made its formal debut. More than six decades earlier, the first bridge spanning that section of the river had been opened. This original structure, located just east of the current bridge, connected Live Oak Point on the river's north bank with Nesbit Street in the city of Punta Gorda on the south bank. This structure was called the Charlotte Harbor Bridge after the Charlotte Harbor estuary that borders Punta Gorda and into which the Peace River flows.

The Charlotte Harbor Bridge was opened in that region of Florida in 1921 to accommodate the vehicular traffic that was expected to travel on the highway known as the Tamiami Trail starting later in the decade. The Tamiami Trail, which encompasses the southernmost 275 miles (443 kilometers) of U.S. Route 41, was opened in 1928. The Charlotte Harbor Bridge was a part of that highway, but It quickly became evident that the bridge could not adequately meet the needs of motorists driving across the Peace River. Among other things, the lanes on the bridge turned out to be too narrow for a large number of vehicles; motorists often needed to swerve over and stop to allow those coming from the other direction to safely make their way across.

Construction on a nearby replacement bridge to carry the Tamiami Trail across the river, and link Punta Gorda with the community of Port Charlotte, began in 1929. This replacement bridge was opened to a great deal of fanfare on Independence Day in 1931, and it featured a drawbridge span to allow for the passage of large vessels sailing on the Peace River. A huge proponent of building this new bridge was the high-energy businessman Barron Collier (1873-1939), one of the era's leading landowners and developers in Florida. Collier's vast array of enterprises in the Sunshine State included the Hotel Charlotte Harbor. The new bridge was named the Barron Collier Bridge in honor of him.

With the opening of the Barron Collier Bridge, the Charlotte Harbor Bridge was closed to traffic. In 1976, the Albert W. Gilchrist Bridge (named in memory of a one-time Florida governor and Punta Gorda resident) was opened near the Barron Collier Bridge. Southbound traffic was rerouted to the two-lane Gilchrist Bridge, and both lanes of the Barron Collier Bridge started carrying only northbound traffic. Within just about four years, however, a new and more elevated version of the Barron Collier Bridge was built to match the 45-foot (13.7-meter)-tall Gilchrist Bridge in height and therefore eliminate any further need for a drawbridge.

The opening ceremony for the current Barron Collier Bridge on January 12, 1983, started out on the south end of the structure in Punta Gorda. Those taking part in the festivities included Thomas Lewis, deputy secretary of the Florida Department of Transportation, and various other public officials. After a ribbon was cut for the bridge, these officials traveled in a motorcade across the new structure. Others on hand for this Wednesday ceremony included 62-year-old Port Charlotte resident Jay C. Alverez, who had also attended the 1931 inaugural event for the original Barron Collier Bridge.

"I never thought I would outlast the two-lane drawbridge," he said in an interview with the *Sarasota Herald-Tribune*.

American Association of State Highway and Transportation Officials

KING FISHER FLEET

Capt. Ralph Allen

King Fisher Fleet is a family-run business In Punta Gorda that marked its 40th Anniversary in 2020. The fleet was originally founded as a one-boat fishing guide service by Capt. Bob Allen and his wife Helen in 1980. Capt. Bob had retired and transplanted his family from Kansas City to a home in Punta Gorda Isles in 1975, joining his father Robert Allen who had done the very same thing in 1971.

All photos Kingfisher Fleet

After a few years of fishing for fun he earned his captain's license so he could run a few guided fishing trips. Bookings for guided fishing trips soon began to flood in and a thriving business was launched.

Fishing in Charlotte Harbor was good for snook, redfish, trout, tarpon and other fish while Gulf trips produced plenty of grouper, snapper, king mackerel, sharks and others so it wasn't long before another larger boat was added to allow fishing further offshore in the Gulf, and another guide boat for even more trips in Charlotte Harbor. The growing fleet was now too large to work from Capt. Bob's home in Punta Gorda Isles so he decided to secure a location at the then newly-opened Fishermen's Village in Punta

Gorda. That decision proved to be a wise one because King Fisher Fleet has since enjoyed a solid 35-year relationship with Fishermen's Village where the facility with its marina, shops, restaurants and resort has been the perfect base of operations. During this time King Fisher Fleet has grown to include multiple fishing boats and it now also includes large sightseeing excursion boats. King Fisher Fleet currently employs approximately 30 staff including boat captains, fishing guides, tour boat mates and booking agents.

Capt. Bob found himself becoming so busy with managing a successful and steadily growing operation that his fishing time began to suffer and he realized that he was not living out the retirement dream he'd envisioned when he moved to Florida. The solution: he brought his son, Capt. Ralph Allen, into the operation in 1985 and after a few years of training, Capt. Bob was able to pass the reins to his son.

Capt. Bob has since retired and moved to the mountains of North Carolina, but Helen continues to work in the business which has been run by her son Capt. Ralph for the last 35 years. Capt. Ralph's two daughters both grew up in the business. At a young age they scrubbed boats, then as they got older they both worked as crew members, and his daughter Elissa is now the General Manager of King Fisher Fleet. This means that if you take a trip with King Fisher Fleet you might encounter three generations of the Allen family working side-by-side!

While the business began as strictly a fishing operation, the tour boat side of the business has been successful too and thousands of people have ridden on King Fisher Fleet's family-friendly excursions on Charlotte Harbor. The boats make day trips to island destinations such as Cabbage Key, Cayo Costa State Park and Boca Grande. There are eco-tours which explore the Peace River upstream from Punta Gorda in partnership with the Charlotte Harbor Environmental Center, an arrangement which has been ongoing for more than 20 years. Harbor cruises and sunset cruises allow people to tour the waterfront and learn some of the area's history.

A People's History of Charlotte County

Malcolm Brenner

Easy Street, at the epicenter of GDC's Port Charlotte development.

1990s

LEFT HOLDING THE BAG

In early 1990 a small item appeared in the business section of the *New York Times*. The 4 by 5-inch news item may have been small, but its message, that the mighty General Development Corp. had declared bankruptcy, would be felt thousands of miles away and would cost millions of dollars to resolve.

Sometimes the best way to tell a story is to begin with the ending. General Development Corporation rode the second Florida land boom until it fell victim to its own formula for success. One of the best

1991
Oldest residential and business area of Punta Gorda declared a National Historic District by the U.S. Department of the Interior and listed on the national register.

Permanent campus of Edison Community College approved for Charlotte County.

1992
Hurricane Andrew struck South Florida on 24 August, with the town of Homestead suffering the worst damages. At the time, it was the costliest disaster in U.S. history

accounts of what happened to GDC was a quatrain-form derisory poem written by Chief Justice A. Jay Cristol of the Bankruptcy Court for the Southern District of Florida: Cristol and Greg Martin both offer compelling narratives of what went wrong with GDC later in this chapter.

From pride of place to being laughed out of court to a four-beat stanza,. GDC, was through.

For local governments that had once hailed GDC as a savior, the dissolution was a crisis. From inheriting or acquiring utilities once run by GDC to assuming responsibility for streets and roads to the loss of tax revenues, the death of the giant left a vaccum. Charlotte County, once more, had said yes and was left holding the bag.

The problem, of course, was larger than Charlotte County and reflected the detritus of the postwar housing boom's ebb tide. Now came time to pay the piper for the explosive growth in housing. As one author writes:

> *Vast American suburbs of the post-World War II era were shaped by legislative processes reflecting the power of the real estate, banking, and construction sectors, and the relative weakness of the planning and design professions. Despite the fact that FHA programs were effectively a developer subsidy, they were presented as assistance to the American consumer. Sprawl became the national housing policy. What's ironic is that as these suburbs were built, developers left future costs, such as transportation, schools, and other amenities to local governments, many of which were not equipped to handle the strain.*[67]

As General Development began its slow descent, the quality of work appeared to deteriorate. That led, in some instances, to homeowner lawsuits, part of the groundswell of resentment and reaction that led to the land giant's ultimate collapse.

> *The 360-acre development featured 80 by 125-foot lots. An official with GDC said that 40 lots had been sold prior to the opening. But the bright future*

---

[67] Colianni, Bill; *Democracy or Dictatorship.*

envisioned at the grand opening has never materialized. By 1980, sales projections had fallen far short of the original goal. General Development subcontracted with an intermediary outfit that began offering homes that existing residents complained were of lower quality. Led by members of the [homeowners'] Association, residents began picketing the building site of what was proposed as Independence Village. Association members pointed to an agreement with General Development which gave the organization the power to approve any construction that took place within the Gardens. Eventually the Association forced the builders to agree to stop building wood-frame homes and agree to construct cinder block houses.

Eventually General Development Corporation wound up in receivership, and the Gardens have been plagued with problems, both natural and man-made, ever since.[68]

1993

County Commission designates Town of Charlotte Harbor as an historic district.

American Forestry Association declares the live oak trees at Charlotte Harbor the "Historic DeSoto Grove" and offers seedlings for planting. Many scholars believe the Spanish explorer Hernando DeSoto landed there in 1539.

1994

In December 1994, Charlotte Regional Medical Center assumes new name and mission.

Bill Colianni

The author of the two passages above, William Colianni, is an Italian immigrant who grew up under Mussolini.

His book, *Democracy or Dictatorship*, describes his own battle with his local HOA in the Gardens of Gulf Cove, a development off Coliseum Boulevard and El Jobean Road (SR776) in east Englewood, and offers a compelling argument for reform of the enabling legislation governing such agencies.

One of the consequences of Florida's history of developers who either leave town or go out of business is the growth of homeowners' associations. With 47,900 such groups serving more than 9,664,000 people, based on 2016 statistics, Florida leads the nation both in the number of HOAs and the amount of people whose communities are governed by them.[69]

Some praise property owners' associations as the only local government of recourse for pothole-level problems, while others condemn what they call the high-handed tactics of such groups.[70]

---

[68] Colianni, Bill, *Democracy or Dictatorship*
[69] https://www.caionline.org/AboutCommunityAssociations/Statistical%20Information/2016StatsReviewFBWeb.pdf
[70] https://www.insurancequotes.com/home/honest-about-hoas

CENTURY

1995
The 104th United States Congress, the first controlled by Republicans in both houses since 1953 to 1955, convenes.

Oklahoma City bombing: 168 people, including eight Federal Marshals and 19 children, are killed at the Alfred P. Murrah Federal Building. Timothy McVeigh and one of his accomplices, Terry Nichols, set off the bomb.

1996
Punta Gorda named as one of the top 10 "Best Small Cities to Live In" by Money Magazine

As if the collapse of General Development was not enough, fortune dealt more blows to Charlotte County's growing mono-economy of building and its associated industries and commercial, from home sales to selling hammers. The savings and loan crisis, which resulted in the failure of nearly a third of the 3,234 savings and loan associations in the United States between

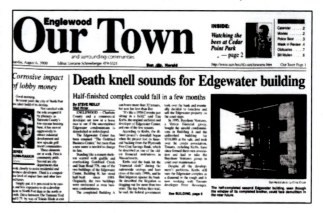

Charlotte Sun-Herald; 8-6-2000

The "Beirut Building," a casualty of the savings and loan crisis, haunted Englewood for years.

One of the last aerials of the Punta Gorda Municipal Trailer Park, which made way for progress in the name of Laishley Park, Laishley Marina, a law firm, and condos.

1986 and 1995,[71] brought construction projects to a near standstill.

Before the effects of the economic crisis took root in Punta Gorda, a group of Charlotte County residents began meeting to address the city's deterioration. In 1990 the committee released a report whose blunt, accurate assessment became a clarion call for change:

---

[71] https://www.investopedia.com/terms/s/sl-crisis.asp

A People's History of Charlotte County

Since its incorporation on December 7, 1887, Punta Gorda has served as the commercial, cultural, governmental, and residential hub of Charlotte County. However, during the most recent Florida development "boom" of the past 30 years, Punta Gorda's dominance as the County's focal point has diminished greatly as new residential, commercial, and governmental growth has occurred in the Port Charlotte/Englewood areas. The result has been a slow but steady deterioration in the physical appearance, residential living conditions, and economic vitality of the community that was platted and begun by Colonel Isaac Trabue back in the late 1800s.[72]

Many people today look to the actions of Team Punta Gorda, a citizens' group formed in the aftermath of Hurricane Charley, or the work of post-Charley Punta Gorda managers and councilmen, as responsible for the tourist-friendly town the city is today. They did more than their share.

But the genesis of this transformation, from a played out fishing and port town to one of the nation's best places to retire, took place in the 1990s, even as the politics of the city grew more fractious. Years later, Punta Gorda has reason to thank an unsung brigade of public servants who, as the politicians bloviated, worked to fulfill the vision so carefully elucidated in the 1990 report.

Phyllis Smith

The task force was led by Phyllis Smith, a councilwoman who, in a better world, would and should have become Punta Gorda's first female mayor. She was the first female member of the city council and also served as vice-mayor. Chauvinism kept her in the background, serving coffee even as she navigated the wars of changing times.

Years later, when Marilyn Smith-Mooney was sworn in as the first female mayor, one of the most heartfelt gifts was a floral display from Smith along with words that let Smith-Mooney know she had fulfilled a dream shared by the women for a place at the place of power.[73]

Smith's committee led the groundwork for the Punta Gorda enjoyed by people at the turn of the most recent century. From the walkways that take a perambulator from Fishermen's Village across town to the east side to the downtown parking garage and pocket parks, the Revitalization Committee delivered more than just a shelf document. But the most controversial aspect of the report was to urge Punta Gorda to evict residents of the Municipal Trailer Park, once welcomed so fervently, reclaim the land, and create a modern, aesthetic, and revenue-generating waterfront.

---

[72] City of Punta Gorda Community Redevelopment Agency, January 1990
[73] Marilyn Smith-Mooney interview, ----2020

1997

Edison Community College opens its Charlotte campus on a 204-acre site on Airport Road in Punta Gorda. Dr. Richard Yarger is provost.

U.S. President Bill Clinton issues a formal apology to the surviving victims of the Tuskegee Study of Untreated Syphilis in the Negro Male and their families.

1998

Former U.S. Senator and governor Lawton Chiles died in office; replaced by Buddy McKay

Son of U.S. President George H.W. Bush, Jeb Bush, elected governor

1997

Edison Community College opens its Charlotte campus on a 204-acre site on Airport Road in Punta Gorda. Dr. Richard Yarger is provost.

U.S. President Bill Clinton issues a formal apology to the surviving victims of the Tuskegee Study of Untreated Syphilis in the Negro Male and their families.

1998

Former U.S. Senator and governor Lawton Chiles died in office; replaced by Buddy McKay

Son of U.S. President George H.W. Bush, Jeb Bush, elected governor

Groundbreaking for the new waterfront development in Punta Gorda, 1990. Below, Joyce Hindman during his last term of office. Both photos Charlotte County History Services.

Marilyn Smith-Mooney, who entered office during those heady days, remembers the palpable need for change.

"I came down here to retire with then husband who was an airline captain," she recalled. "We built a house. Once I built the house I was bored because I had retired from a job up north. So I started going to city council meetings and the more I attended the more I got kind of concerned. I found a lot of stuff going on that was part of the good-old-boys system."

One instance galvanized her to get off the bench and run for office.

"There was a male council member at the time, Joyce Hindman. And he was actually in the hospital but they would bring him out from hospital by wheelchair to attend the meeting," she recalled. "And he was sitting next to the clerk who records the meetings and he would very often fall asleep during the meeting. Lindsay Harrington was the mayor at the time. Anyway, this meeting is being conducted, some item comes up for discussion and then for a vote. As they go to take the vote somebody points out to Lindsay that Joyce never voted. Lindsay asked why and they said because he was asleep. So he said. 'wake him up and get him to vote.' So they woke him up and told him he had to vote. He said, 'What, what? What do you want?' Lindsay said, 'Just say 'yes.' So he said 'Yes,' and that was the end of it."

A People's History of Charlotte County

Diana Harris

The Fishery, once an economic hub of Englewood, failed after the net ban became law. It survived as a restaurant and putative artists' colony, but eventually was sold to a developer.

Englewood during the '80s suffered a blow from which it never recovered. As more sports sailors and boaters moved to Florida, many became part of a push to limit the large nets used for decades by local fishermen. Fishing was still such a big part of the community that a local bank featured an electronic sign alerting fishermen to the tides.

But all that changed with the enactment of the ban, which instantly destroyed businesses such as The Fishery, a Grove City mainstay and economic hub of the maritime industry.

Smart fishermen became guides and joined the growing ecotourism movement. Consider the Futches, longtime watermen. Mark Futch became a pilot and was soon the premier air guide along the Southwest coast. Another Futch became a tour guide.

1999

New courthouse and justice center at Punta Gorda Harbor waterfront development opens in June. Construction of private condominiums and office building begin at Punta Gorda Harbor. Construction begins on new jail on Airport Road.

2000

County population is 141,627, a 27.6 percent increase over 1990.

Hurricane Gordon causes flooding in the Manasota Key area and along the Peace River shoreline.

CENTURY

Malcolm Brenner

A original Port Charlotte home on Easy and Key streets still standing after all these years.

THE FINAL DECREE OF GDC
Chief Justice A. Jay Cristol

(with apologies to Robert Service and Sam McGee)

There are strange things done in the Florida sun
by the men who moil for gold.
G.D.C. sales had their secret tales
that would make your blood run cold.

Bankruptcy fans have seen big plans but one of the biggest they ever did see,
was at the end of the second year, when hope did appear, and we reorganized G.D.C.
G.D.C. had its roots in nineteen twenty, in Detroit, Michigan.
Chemical Research Syndicate was formed, oil refining was the plan.

The Mackle Company started in Miami, in about the year 1948.
The Mackle Brothers built a bunch of homes that people said were great.
As the land boom grew, they knew what to do, they developed planned communities.
They gained fame far and wide, it was justified, and they never missed opportunities.

By 1954 Chemical wanted more and with partner, Yellowknife Bear,
they formed Florida West Coast Land which bought its Florida share.
Over eighty thousand acres in Charlotte County and Sarasota,
joined with three other subsidiaries and began to sell their quota.

A People's History of Charlotte County

At Port Charlotte, as of the end of 1957, 153 homes had been constructed and sold. Sales contracts for an additional 157 homes had been executed and 98 parcels of business property had been sold. But 13,782 home sites had been sold there, a problem that would plague county government for decades.

A deal was made with Mackle Company for fifty-fifty ownership.
A new name was picked, GENERAL DEVELOPMENT, it really was a pip.
In 1955 another subsidiary, Port Charlotte, Inc. came to be.
In 1956 the Chemical — Mackle subsidiaries merged into G.D.C.

By year 58 things were going great, they still built houses quite well.
In a proper way they built roads and canals that everyone thought were swell.
Things were going so good, they thought they should, and no one thought it strange,
that in that same year they were listed on the American Stock Exchange.

Later that year, the price was not dear, so they made a deal quite juicy.
For stock they got 6,000 acres that soon became Port St. Lucie.
The Mackle brothers did all the building, they had a deal exclusive.
But the joy they knew, of the right thing to do, eventually became elusive.

In 1962 the Mackle boys were through, they resigned and left the board.
Why they left I don't know, but they really did go, perhaps they just got bored.
Along came a crew, entirely new, smart and from the big city.
Straight shooting, no need, the new goal was greed, and what happened next was a pity.

"If it ain't broke don't fix it," they didn't know, no matter that things were fine.
They began a new game, that's known by the name, of "what's on the bottom line."
In '66 G.D.C. put in the fix, and moved to the New York Stock Exchange.
No more building good houses, and no more selling fine lots, the smart folks saw need for a change.

Soon all their attention was away from production, their eyes could only lock,
On the Dow Jones Average, the latest trade and the closing price of the stock.
By the year 79, things still seemed fine, they had sold over 148,000 acres.
More than three times Manhattan, take your pipe and put that in, they were really movers and shakers.

But the chase for the buck, caused a change in their luck, and a Federal investigation.
When the Feds dug in deep, to that moldering heap, it boggled their imagination.
The indictment was filed, the public was riled, the company copped a plea.
They agreed to restitute, but it didn't mean a hoot, it was the end for G.D.C.

They had no money to pay, there was no other way, they filed for Bankruptcy.
And that's how the trail, of this incredible tale, ultimately came to me.
And what a case, in no other place, was there filed a case more vast.
330,000 creditors needed to receive notice, and fast.

They had to explain, in language quite plain, that the pie that was left was too small.
They tried to do right, with all of their might, but everyone could not have it all.
So they did what was fair, with what they had there, and put a plan on the table.
They said, "it's the best we can do, we are telling you true, Judge, please confirm it, if you're able."

Almost everyone agreed, that the plan did exceed, what at first we thought we could do.
No one ignored it, almost everyone voted for it, and so the reorganization went through.
Almost no one got all, almost no one got none, and most folks think it was fair.
The concern is going today, in a much better way, I know because I was there.

There are strange things done in the Florida sun by the men who moil for gold.
G.D.C. sales had their secret tales that would make your blood run cold.
Bankruptcy fans have seen big plans but one of the biggest they ever did see,
was at the end of the second year, when hope did appear, and we reorganized G.D.C.[74]

$10 DOWN AND $10 A MONTH!: HOW GDC SOLD SOUTHWEST FLORIDA

Greg Martin

Some 35 years ago, when most of southern Sarasota and northern Charlotte counties was cow pastures and woods dotted with ponds, the founders of General Development Corporation (GDC) had a dream.

It was a simple dream in the beginning. Buy the pastures from the local farmers at $50 per acre. Then divide the land into quarter-acre lots and sell them at prices that would put them within the reach of countless thousands of blue-collar Northerners.

The dream came true, with sales soon outstripping the founders' wildest hopes. Eventually, sales grew to $100 million per year. But the GDC dream crumbled under the weight of thousands of lawsuits, criminal fraud charges and, finally, bankruptcy pleadings.

How could such success lead to such a failure? Much of the answer seems to lie in the techniques the company and its sales force used to sell its dream, techniques that started as early as 1957, when the

---

[74] https://casetext.com/case/in-re-general-development-corp-8

A People's History of Charlotte County

All photos Mackle family

Mackle mail order department

Miami developers known as the Mackle brothers bought large acreages from farmers and land holders in Charlotte County.

The Mackle brothers divided the land into smaller parcels and began marketing it to Northerners dreaming of eventually retiring to a sunny piece of ground in Florida.

At prices as low as "$10 down and $10 per month for 10 years," those Northerners bought the dream in droves, remembers Monroe G. "Randy" Randol of Port Charlotte.

"Ten-dollar bills came flowing into Miami by the bushel full," says Randol, who became one of the Mackle brother's first 10 Port Charlotte lot salesmen in 1957. The response, Randol says, convinced the founders to start similar projects in eight other areas of Florida, and General Development Corporation (GDC) was formed.

In order to keep profits expanding, the strategy grew ever more ambitious. More and more sections of land were subdivided into residential lots, and prices were increased every year.

To justify the annual price increases, GDC told buyers their properties would soon be part of "planned communities," with state-of-the-art roads and utilities and sites for public parks and schools.

Pointing to the annual price increases that the company itself had arbitrarily imposed, salesmen told prospects they were buying not only a retirement home but a fast-accelerating investment opportunity.

If any hapless buyer tried to put his property back on the market, however, he was likely to discover that instead of appreciating, his property would actually fetch less than he had paid -- in recent years, often as much as a third or even 50 percent less. GDC's sales people knew their prices were inflated; while many figured it was all just part of the real estate game, other salesmen felt uneasy and guilty.

"It bothered me," says one saleswoman who worked for GDC between 1985 and 1987. "It's actually the reason I quit."

The woman, although among those who have testified before a Miami grand jury that investigated GDC, consented to an interview only on the condition she would not be identified.

"I liked all the people I helped buy houses," she said. "You spend a lot of time with these people. It bothered me to turn around and burn them."

And apparently, a lot of people felt they were burned.

In January, the corporation agreed to settle out of court more than 100 suits filed in a Miami circuit court. The suits were filed by home buyers, including some from Port Charlotte and North Port, who alleged they had been defrauded into trading their lots for down payments on houses priced in some cases $20,000 higher than the fair market value.

The corporation also faces pending lawsuits filed by some 3,500 property owners with similar complaints. That suit, filed in a New Jersey federal court, includes some 500 owners from North Port and Port Charlotte who joined it after attending seminars in February, said seminar organizer Mark Binstein.

More than 30,000 lot owners have also sued in a class action alleging GDC failed to fulfill promises that lots would be developed by certain dates in installment-purchase contracts in other GDC communities.

Along with the civil litigation has come criminal investigation—by the federal grand jury in Miami. On March 16, U.S. attorneys indicted the corporation on 16 counts of fraud, alleging corporate sales staff concealed the true value of properties from buyers and misrepresented the values in mortgages granted the buyers through a GDC subsidiary, GDV Financial.

According to the federal indictment, the home buyers were given mortgages that reflected fraudulent appraisals. The appraisals were based solely on the price of similar GDC properties, not on the general market value.

In late March, the corporation, its former president, Robert F. Ehrling and its former chairman, David F. Brown, pleaded guilty to one count of conspiracy to commit fraud regarding its sales program aimed at out-of-state buyers. The pleas came in an agreement in which GDC pledges to pay $100 million in restitution to some 11,000 people who bought overpriced houses between 1983 and 1990.

But that pledge may be in jeopardy. On April 6, GDC, facing cash shortages, filed for protection from creditors under chapter 11 of federal bankruptcy laws.

Besides those in line for restitution, the bankruptcy also leaves local governments in its nine Florida communities short some $10 million in unpaid property taxes.

A People's History of Charlotte County

"There was never an intent to build a city here," says Randol, now the 74-year-old owner of Randol Realty, Inc. in Port Charlotte.

He says the Mackle brothers bought an estimated 100,000 acres in Charlotte County, then sold it to GDC, a company in which they were major shareholders. The company then hired the brothers to turn it into "Port Charlotte," Randol recalls. But he remembers the brothers saying they didn't expect many people to ever move there.

At first, lots were sold surrounding the center of what was to be "the community." When sales slowed down, as was anticipated, the outlying parcels were to be combined and sold as rural estates, Randol says.

But that slowdown never came, thanks to a key marketing decision. "They borrowed money, at 15 percent interest if my memory serves me, to run a full-page ad in Life magazine," says Randol, who was then a 42-year-old GDC lot broker. "The ad said $10 down, $10 a month or $795 to purchase a lot in Florida.

"When they ran this ad, it brought in so many buyers the original plan [to develop only around the community center] disappeared."

Sensing the enormous opportunities, GDC hired brokers in Northeast and Midwest cities to market the lots there. The brokers invited prospects to free dinners and meetings where they would paint a glorious picture of their sunny, affordable Florida communities. Soon thousands of new buyers had signed on, flooding the mails with their deposits and monthly payments.

Mackle Family

A 1957 Life magazine ad

And prices, of course, kept rising -- generally by $100 per lot per year, said Randol. It helped "to keep last year's buyer happy," he says.

In the first few years, very few promises were made -- only that buyers in 10 years would "own a lot in Florida," Randol says. But as promises of community development and increasing property prices became part of the sales pitch, Randol began to have doubts.

"It got to a point I couldn't sell it anymore. They were making promises I didn't see how they could keep." In the early 1960s, he quit the corporation.

During the 1970s, the corporation stepped up a program to allow lot buyers to trade their lots in as down payments for houses. Now a real estate broker for another Port Charlotte firm, Ron Struthers was involved in that program for GDC from 1978 until the mid-1980s. He started in Toronto as a GDC sales manager and later moved to Port Charlotte. In both places, he worked with prospective buyers who were flown to Florida on three-day sales trips.

"We were selling the trips -- not the houses," he says. "We were selling them on seeing what their options were. But the key ingredient was to go down and look at it for yourself."

The company would whip up interest with Northern lot owners by devices such as a newsletter that featured stories about rising land prices in Florida. Struthers also remembers sending telegrams about Myakka Estates. "One said the price for a lot went from $4,500 to $18,000 in 18 months on land that was not developed."

Struthers admits he knew the out-of-state buyers were paying much more for GDC properties than they would bring on the local market. "When brokers' commissions were 20 to 22 percent, it didn't take an Einstein to figure that out," he says.

By 1982, however, Struthers says prices really "jumped up." The increases coincided with changes in leadership at corporate headquarters. "They were interested in profit, profit, profit," he says. "There was pressure to produce a greater number [of sales] on a daily, weekly and monthly basis."

In Port Charlotte, it was part of Struther's job to keep prospects away from other agents. "An agent's job was to put them up and show them the community to represent the corporation," he says. "It's no different than the guy in a car dealership who doesn't want his client to see the dealer next door."

And Struthers insists that despite the inflated prices, no fraud was taking place.

"These people who bought houses were all 21 or older. Nobody glued them down so they couldn't check with other agents. They weren't handcuffed and locked in our cars," he said.

The old Ramada Inn, now an executive office park

That is not, however, the opinion of the Miami grand jury that indicted GDC this spring, nor is it the opinion of the saleswoman who requested not to be identified. She says the sales techniques and corporate policies did amount to fraud.

Like Struthers, her job was to sell houses to out-of-state prospects while they were on three-day visits to Port Charlotte. "You had to keep them busy as long as you could," she says. She would pick them up at the airport when they would arrive in the evening. Then she would drive them to the Ramada Inn in Port Charlotte.

"I'd tell them I'd wait in the lobby while they freshened up. Then I'd take them out to dinner," she says.

Beginning at eight the next morning, she would drive them to see GDC models and local sights such as the Port Charlotte beach complex and Fisherman's Village shopping plaza in Punta Gorda.

Mackle Family

The Mackles pulled out before it was too late

"You'd keep them out late and never say anything derogatory about the location," she explained. "You'd tell them how GDC created the community and how without GDC it would not be here."

If she passed by model houses with prices on signs in front or by real estate offices, she'd point in the opposite direction and say, "Oh, look over there," she says. "That worked a lot of the time."

Other corporate policies seemed more devious, she says. These included what was referred to in the criminal indictment as the alleged "monitoring" of phone calls to GDC clients' rooms by hotel staff. At GDC's request, if someone other than a GDC staff member called the client, hotel staff would take messages and pass them on to GDC sales staff, she says.

"I've seen the messages," she says. She also remembers that one new GDC employee could not reach his client at his hotel room because the hotel didn't have the new employee on its GDC employee list yet.

Ramada Inn staff were occasionally honored guests at GDC sales meetings, she says, where they were often given $200 bonds for their "fine service."

What bothered her most, though, were the inflated prices. She cites one waterfront lot, which sold for more than $65,000, although it would have brought only $10,000 on the open market. "They think that's a fabulous deal because you couldn't touch a waterfront lot in New York or New Jersey for that," she says. "But you had to lead them to GDV Financial [the GDC subsidiary that would deliver an inflated appraisal] so they wouldn't find out."

DAYS OF RECKONING

Many of the out-of-state buyers didn't find out the true value of their homes until they tried to sell or refinance them. That's what happened to Port Charlotte's Charles Grizzaffi, who traded a North Port lot in for a house priced at $74,000. After spending another $15,000 on improvements, he decided to sell it.

"When I told the broker what I wanted out of it [about $85,000], he just looked at me. He said, `You have to be realistic.'" Grizzaffi was told the current market price, including improvements, was $58,000. "I felt pretty devastated," he says.

Grizzaffi and his wife Innes have written half a dozen letters to state agencies. Although one agency, the Division of Consumer Affairs, sent a request for resolution to GDC, other agencies told the Grizzaffis their complaints fell outside their jurisdiction.

In fact, GDC's problems have raised questions about the integrity of at least one state agency. Over the past five years, about 500 complaints against the company were filed with the state's division of land sales in Tallahassee. The division placed no administrative sanctions against the company.

By March, however, both the director of the division, James Kearney, and the chief of the bureau where complaints are filed, Samuel Griffis, resigned.

In an interview this spring before he left office, Kearney said he failed to understand how GDC had kept potential customers from evaluating the deals they were signing. "It's hard for me to envision someone being so incarcerated," he said. The property buyers would have thoroughly investigated purchases in their home states, he said. "All of a sudden they come to Florida and they don't call a realtor, they don't call an appraiser, they don't call an attorney. It's frightening."

The divison's new director, Matthew Carter, has launched a review of the hundreds of complaints filed against GDC.

"We must restore the integrity of the division," he says. "We must reassure the home buyers that what they're getting has value. It's not going to be like the old days in Florida -- a pig in a poke. There are going to be safeguards."

Yet GDC has it supporters, including some former salesmen who like to emphasize the accomplishments of the company. Without GDC's contributions there wouldn't be a Ranger Stadium, a Port Charlotte beach complex or a cultural center, several say.

Many people of moderate incomes who bought lots years ago were able to trade them for homes in Florida they probably would not have otherwise been able to afford, notes Struthers.

But Randol, the former salesman who now owns his own real estate company, sees another side of the story. Clients come to him expecting to sell their properties at a profit and he has to tell them that instead they will probably lose money. "Have you ever seen an old person cry?" he asks. He believes GDC may weather its current crisis. But about some of the buyers, he's not so sure: "Those who have been hurt, I don't think can be unhurt."

COPYRIGHT 1990 Clubhouse Publishing, Inc.

HOAS: LIKE GOVERNMENT, A NECESSARY EVIL

Gerri Townsend

Most new homes are being built in associations. In Florida, almost 50% of the population live in 48,500 associations.[75] There are several reasons for this. A uniform-looking community with amenities such as pools, community centers, activities, and security are attractive to home buyers. Builders can maximize their profits through increased density while making the community attractive with common amenities and common areas. Finally, local governments are freed from the responsibility and expense of maintaining large developments, while reaping the benefits of increased tax revenues.

Most new communities are created and built by developers. The developer is responsible for creating the community through the articles of incorporation, the development of a master plan, the establishment of deed restrictions and the initial governance of the community. The developer may establish an association, a community development district or a combination of both.

During construction, the developer has full control of the association. The developer's goal is to get the community built and the homes sold. However, the developer is required to use reasonableness when amending the governing documents and cannot make amendments that are arbitrary, capricious, or in bad faith. He cannot destroy the plan of development or shift economic burdens to the members. However, the developer can make changes to the plan of the community and the amenity buildings while in control.

> Gerry Townsend is a licensed Florida CPA, a licensed community association manager and has an MBA from Monmouth College in NJ. She has worked both in private industry and government in various accounting positions.
>
> She is the co-author of the "Guides to Homeowners' Associations and Condo Associations."
>
> She remains active in her homeowners' association and community development district, serving on various committees.

---

[75] www.floridarealtors.org. Record Number of Homeowners live in HOA Communities. September 2020.

In accordance with the statutes and governing documents, the developer is required to turn the association over to the members. Turnover occurs when the members elect a majority of the board. The developer is required to turn over deeds, deed restrictions, finances, and all other official records to the association. Upon turnover, the elected association board becomes responsible for the operation of the association and the control of the deed restrictions.

A community development district (CDD) is a local unit of special purpose government. It is created by the state or the county to finance, build and maintain infrastructure. Some HOA's exist in community development districts but many do not. The design of the community is established by the developer.

Board members are responsible for management of the association, which may be complex. The association is a corporation, and the board members have all the legal responsibilities associated with a corporate board. They are responsible for overseeing the operations, enforcing the deed restrictions, maintaining the common areas, maintaining the values of homes, budgeting and collecting assessments.

Board members have a fiduciary duty to the members. This means board members are required to act in the best interest of the members and to exercise a high standard of due care in carrying out their responsibilities. Board members are legally required to enforce the governing documents and have broad enforcement powers.

The association manager is the hub of the organization, and a good manager is crucial to a successfully managed association. Their role is to keep the association running on a day-to-day basis, carry out the directives of the board, maintain the facilities, work with outside vendors, and provide service to the residents. The manager needs to be a jack of all trades because they are normally responsible for a wide variety of tasks such as preparing budgets and monthly financial information, managing the buildings, community amenities, common areas and other assets, supervising office staff, ensuring that the association has adequate insurance, enforcing deed restrictions, and working with the residents.

A paid manager must be licensed by the state for associations with more than 10 units and budgets over $100,000. Managers must also take continuing education credits to maintain their license.

A good manager will possess good customer service skills and an overall knowledge of the association. The board is ultimately responsible for the association and the manager derives their authority from the board.

A board may contract with a management company rather than hiring their own manager.

With a manager hired through a management company, the board loses some control since the manager is responsible to the management company and may not be able to respond to board requests quickly or easily. Board member requests outside of the scope of the contract will result in additional charges.

However, a management company can relieve board members of the time required to be more involved with the operations.

Owners give up some rights in exchange for living in a ready-made community with various amenities. The association governing documents are the rules and regulations which govern the association and homeowners. They are also called restrictive covenants, because they are the documents which outline the restrictions of the association. They are filed with the county office in which the association is located.

Beware of Construction Liens

Florida has a mechanics lien law. This law is great for subcontractors but not so great for owners. The owner has a liability for payment to a subcontractor if the developer/general contractor fails to pay the subcontractor. If the owner pays the developer/general contractor but the developer/general contractor fails to pay the subcontractors, a subcontractor can place a lien on a residence for non-payment of their services. What this means is that owners may have to make double payments for work performed on their homes. If the lien is not satisfied, your home can be sold against your will.

Association Members Right and Obligations

Association members have certain obligations to the association as well as rights.

Members are obligated to comply with the deed restrictions. Renters and guests of members must also comply. If members, renters, or guests violate the deed restrictions, the member will be charged with the deed restriction violation and may be subject to a fine. The member, guests, and renters may also be prohibited from using the common areas. In extreme cases, the association may file a lien on the member's home or parcel and foreclose.

Members are obligated to pay assessments and fines, or the board can take action.

One of the most important rights of the members is to vote for the board of directors. The board represents your interests and makes decisions on your behalf. Generally, only about 10 to 15% of the members vote in the annual election. Without active participation in a board election, a small group of people can control the direction of the association.

Members have the right to run for the board.

Members have the right to attend board and committee meetings. They have the right to record the meetings and to speak at meetings. The board can establish reasonable rules regarding meeting protocol.

Members have the right to review or obtain copies of official association records.

Members have the right to peaceably assemble.

There are many advantages to living in an association. Amenities, standards, a certain "look," consistent rules, security, and maintenance of home values are some of the advantages. However, associations are not a good fit for everyone. That is why almost half of Florida's population live in associations and half don't.

PUNTA GORDA, 1990s
Bill Curnow

My first experiences in Charlotte County came after being a lifelong resident of St. Petersburg. I had been hired by the Florida Marine Research Institute as part of a team that tracked fluctuations in fish populations around the state. In July of 1990 I was transferred from St. Petersburg to the lab in Port Charlotte.

Arriving in Punta Gorda to look for a place to live, I was pleasantly surprised driving thorough the historic district. Traffic was light compared to St. Pete and I was struck by the old time feel of the community. There was actually a horse in a yard on West Marion.. Eventually I found an apartment in Punta Gorda. It was cheap rent - five hundred dollars a month including utilities. This was hundreds of dollars less than I would have paid in the Tampa Bay area.

The first week after moving here provided me with more pleasant experiences. I went to the library in Punta Gorda to obtain a library card. I had my identification ready to hand to the lady. She said to me, 'Honey, I don't need to see your ID. Just fill out the form and I'll give you a card." That trusting nature

A People's History of Charlotte County

Charlotte County History Services

Street scene in a slow town—Vernon Peeples' boyhood home and most recently Cubby's Ice Cream, this building on the corner of Marion and US41 south, was a sign of the somnolent times in the early 1980s in Punta Gorda, before redevelopment took off.

continued the following day when I was renting a portable bed. The man at the rental business stated in a southern drawl, "I don't want to see your driver's license, just fill out the form."

Prior to being employed at Florida Marine Research Institute I had been a commercial fisherman for twelve years. The majority of that period I was a gill net fisherman targeting mostly mullet. I had also worked on offshore grouper boats and was involved in shrimping and crabbing. In that era, St. Petersburg had been totally urbanized, but working on Tampa Bay gave me a sense of freedom. There was still a feeling of wilderness being on the water. Eventually as the population of an area expands and shoreline development "maxes out," there is an explosion of pleasure and sport fishing boats. This causes a volatile situation basically between the rich and the poor.

The poor being commercial gill net fisherman. A movement had started by the sport fishing industry to rid the waters of commercial fishermen. This culminated in the 1994 constitutional referendum to ban gill nets in inshore Florida waters. The referendum passed and was implemented on July 1 of 1995. The referendum was not based on scientific data. Mullet populations were robust in near shore waters. What drove the propaganda against fisherman was that the majority of waterfront home owners and sport fishermen simply did not like seeing gill netters and their activities. Before this explosion in human population fishermen were respected. Luckily, I had the opportunity to experience that respect. However, as the population rose, fisherman were starting to be demonized by certain publications and citizens.

In our research with the Institute we used various nets to sample fish. Seines, trawls, and gill nets were used in a random sampling design to track fish in all parts of Charlotte Harbor which also included the lower Peace and Myakka Rivers. We basically identified and recorded the numbers and lengths of fish, shrimp and crabs that were captured in the nets. The goal was to have a data base to track fish populations over the years.

We trailered our research vessels (modified mullet skiffs) to different ramps around the harbor. Launching from Laishley Park I was delighted to see several commercial shrimp boats docked in the boat slips. On the harbor you would see an occasional commercial mullet boat plying the waters. Unfortunately, most of the commercial fishing in the harbor would cease to exist with the net ban restrictions implemented in 1995. Eventually the rural nature of Punta Gorda gave way to development and urbanization. Politicians would refer to development as an "improvement" and "expanding the tax base." Those are words they used to justify ruining a beautiful and natural area. Now a shrimp boat cannot be found in Laishley Marina but you will see an array of yachts owned by the rich.

REBUILDING HISTORY

Lynn Harrell

Throughout the years there have been many attempts to save Charlotte County's landmark structures; most have failed. One significant effort occurred in 1993. I call it the "Dewey-Denham Disaster." Three historic buildings on a very prominent site were slated for demolition – the Charles Denham house, the Albert F. Dewey house, and a cottage that had been Isaac Trabue's office. All three had been cited for violations of the City's "Outward Appearance" codes (in other words, they were shabby). The owners of these contiguous properties, Bob and Norma Henry, would have gladly spruced them up themselves, but were prohibited from doing so. The buildings were zoned for commercial use. Any repairs had to be done by state licensed commercial contractors, which the Henrys couldn't afford. In preservation parlance, this situation is called "demolition by forced neglect."

Public interest soared, and a new non-profit group, the Peace River Preservation League, Inc., was formed specifically to raise funds to save the buildings. I was elected president. We raised over $15,000 in pledges and cash in just the first two weeks, but it wasn't enough. We managed to save only one building – the tiny Trabue Office. The Henrys donated it to Old Punta Gorda, Inc. (now the Punta Gorda Historical Society), and it was trucked off to the corner of East Marion and Nesbit Street, next to the Post Office, to await rehab. The Dewey and Denham houses were bulldozed shortly thereafter.

But the outrage didn't fade away. The people had been woke, as they say nowadays. Within a year, the City Council approved the concept of a history park. The following year, a 50-year lease was signed by Old Punta Gorda, Inc., for a small parcel of acreage on Shreve Street. Thus began the Punta Gorda History Park, the city's official receiving site for endangered historic structures.

There is plenty of information available about the buildings there, but not a lot about the first dedicated volunteers that built the park, restored the buildings, and

TIME-LINE OF EVENTS

1983 Historical Society organized.

1987 The concept of a history park can be traced back to September 2 when the Punta Gorda City Council moves to establish a Historic Register Nomination Packet. This would include 3 individual historic sites and 2 historic districts.

1989 July 5 the "Punta Gorda Historic Preservation Ordinance" is adopted and a Preservation Advisory Board established.

1990 January - A Downtown Development Plan is adopted, part of which calls for the establishment of a permanent museum of Punta Gorda history.

1993 November - Three historically significant structures were lost due to the cost of maintenance and appearance code enforcement. This loss prompted the city council to provide a receiving site to which historic buildings can be relocated. The site on Shreve Street is chosen.

1994 August 3 - City council officially approves the offering of 4.1 acres of city owned land for the development of a museum and historic building relocation site.

1995 May 17 - A lease is signed for a term of 50 years at $1 a year, "provided that construction of a; permanent facility commences within 5 years."

1997 Railroad Depot deeded to Old Punta Gorda Inc.

1997 Don Atwell, a prominent realtor in the Punta Gorda area, on behalf of Mike Nickelson, offers free of charge, a cigar cottage to Old Punta Gorda Inc. It is also agreed at this meeting that Atwell will prepare a construction plan for the Shreve Street site.

1998 April 20 - Herston Engineering Services agrees to cut its price in half for engineering services for the park.

1998 June 17 - City council waives non-impact development fees for the park area. 1999 January 22 - A ground breaking ceremony is held at History Park.

1999 August 12 - A $4,500 check is presented to Old Punta Gorda Inc. by Steve Shafer Tire & Auto Center. The money was raised from a golf tournament and will be used for History Park expenses.

1999 September 27 - The Tourist Development Council votes to fund the restoration of the cigar cottage to a total of $12,000.
1999 October 7-8 - Twenty-three loads of bricks are donated by Bruce Laishley and Rick Treworgy to be used for a parking lot and walkways throughout the park.
1999 October 12 - Cigar cottage is moved to History Park.
1999 November 19 - A permit is issued for the removal of wood siding from the Church of Christ after a fire, leaving the church to be eventually demolished. Much of this siding and flooring will be used to refurbish the interior of the cigar cottage.
2000 January 14 - The old calaboose is found on Jim & Patsy Parker's Washington Loop property. Plans to move the jail to the history park are discussed at a February 22 meeting.
2000 October 18 - A Punta Gorda Herald newspaper includes an article entitled "History Park inches closer to reality". This article lists "key dates for a historic idea."
2000 November 16 - Trabue House moved to Park.
2001 & 2004 - Calaboose delivered to the Park.
2001 April 25 - Duffy's Way dedication at the Railroad Depot. 2002 The railroad depot is pretty much completed.
2004 March 7 - Railroad ticket office dedicated to Gerry Neils.
2004 March 24 - Neils Circle dedication at the Park.
2004 August 8- Hurricane Charley hits Punta Gorda.
2005 February 19 - Gilchrist B & B or Price House moved to Park. 2006 The original fountain from the old hotel is delivered to the Park. 2011 October - The 1925 Quednau-Hindman house is moved to the Park.
From this time line, the reader gets a further idea of the complexity and speed that many events were taking place and how OPG Inc. board members accepted that responsibility.

landscaped the site, which is still maintained by volunteers. Luckily, those stories were captured in a book written in 2012 by Carl Kimberly, one of those early volunteers. It's titled "The Restoration Team of Old Punta Gorda, Inc." and it's full of photos, anecdotes and details about the team members and how they labored to preserve the ACL Train Depot, the Punta Gorda Woman's Club, the Trabue Office and other buildings now in the Park.

Carl died in 2016, he was 81 and still an active handyman.

Restoration Team members (and supporting spouses) deserving special thanks: Omar "Duffy" Duff and Shirley Duff, Lloyd and Evelyn Stokes, George and Helen Gale, Gerry and Pat Neils, Richard and Judy Yando, Harold and Alice Allchin, and Roger and Maureen Sigler. Also, Don Atwell, the first History Park manager who created the site plan, and landscape artisan, Richard Polk, who purchased and planted most of the now-mature seedlings that grace the grounds.

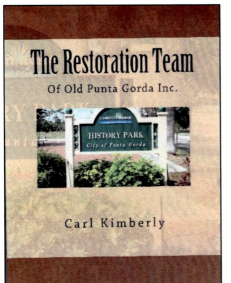

Epilogue: For those who weren't here during the Dewey-Denham Disaster – The Charles Denham house was on the southwest corner of W. Retta Esplanade and Cross Street (now SB US41), facing Retta. The original site of the Trabue Office was directly behind the Denham house, facing Cross Street. On the south side of the Trabue Office, also facing Cross Street, was the Dewey house. The City acquired the property after the houses were gone.

What's there now? Ironically, the former site of the sprawling Denham house is occupied by the relocated "Indian Statue" Calostimucu, and the relocated Queen Anne-style A.C. Freeman House. The former sites of the Trabue Office and the Dewey house were paved over for additional City Hall parking.

Dr. Robert Andrews, center right with white shirt and striped tie, helps dedicate the society's first mural.

THE PUNTA GORDA HISTORIC MURAL SOCIETY – PAINTING THE TOWN WITH HISTORY

Kelly Gaylord, President, Punta Gorda Historic Mural Society

The Punta Gorda Historic Mural Society started with a local doctor's dream to feature historic and educational murals around the city of Punta Gorda. The idea for the Society came from a trip Dr. Robert J. Andrews and his wife made in 1988 to Chemainus, a small town located outside of Victoria, British Columbia. The town's economy tanked after the lumber mill closed. By painting murals of local significance on downtown buildings, they helped foster pride and made the town a major tourist destination spot.

Dr. Andrews was immediately inspired, thinking that a series of historical murals might have the same effect on Punta Gorda's depressed downtown. After he came home, he talked with local leaders about the idea of doing a similar program in town. The idea finally caught on in 1993 when he made a presentation to the Revitalization Committee. He followed up with the Punta Gorda Business Alliance (forerunner of the Punta Gorda Chamber of Commerce) for help in promoting the idea. The proposal was an instant hit and a committee was formed.

After endorsement by the City Council, the group began collecting money for the first mural. Through a lot of effort and support, the Society was organized in late 1994 and approved to operate as a non-profit organization in January 1995.

The large wall on the south end of the Eckerd Drug Store building at what was once the Punta Gorda Mall, was identified as the site for the first mural. With support from the mall owner, local artist Tom Graham began painting the Hotel Charlotte Harbor mural in January 1995. It was finished nine months later, and the dedication took place on October 11, 1995. With the first mural completed, the program was off and running.

The mission of the Society's mural program was and continues to be to encourage and foster pride in and awareness of our local history, inspire community participation in the arts, and increase tourism. As of 2020, thirty Society murals grace the exterior walls of our city, each capturing a slice of our rich history.

The Society's success is attributed to the amazing support of the community and to its board members. Over sixty-five people have volunteered their time and talents as Society board members over the past 25 years, working tirelessly to build our city's successful mural program.

Throughout the years, the Society has remained committed to the "historic" in its name with the primary parameter of any mural to be that it is historically and environmentally accurate. The Society is looking forward to 'Painting the Town' for many years to come.

LLI – A PART OF OUR CULTURAL HISTORY

Bonnie Leroy

In 1996, long before Hurricane Charley and long after Donna, a nucleus of recent retirees were putting together the beginning of LLI (Lifelong Learning Institute). Carol Eliason, Mary and Marvin Johnson, Craig & Dotty Anderson were recruiting other retirees to attend and to lead classes and day trips, all based on expanding learning and enhancing their leisure hours.

Their efforts were then supported by the Executive Director of the Charlotte County Foundation, Jack Price, and his assistant, Caryl Sprague. At that time, the Foundation was a part of the hospital in Punta Gorda, and it had given a sizeable grant to the Charlotte County Healthy Aging Study that was being conducted at the University of South Florida in Tampa.

Dr. James Mortimer, director of that study, invited Jack and others from Charlotte County to meet with Lee Levengood about a program she had started at USF called "Learning in Retirement." The folks from Charlotte County were impressed with what they learned and all agreed to initiate an LIR chapter here.

Early class leaders included local residents Lindsay Williams, Vernon Peeples, James Abraham, Hasan Hammami, Sharon Whitehill, James Mallonnee, Ray Chapman, Charles Peck, Samar Jarrah, Martha Bireda, David & Victoria Klaussen, Jennifer Howell, Mike Wilson – to nme just a few. And many of them continued to contribute throughout the years.

Judy Berger began her tenure as chairperson of the Curriculum Committee in 2013 and continued her service through 2018. Through her love for learning, her personal curiosity, travels and explorations, she introduced class participants to many well-credentialed presenters on a wide range of subjects. Dr. Gene Laber, a seasonal local resident, Professor Emeritus at the University of Vermont, and an expert witness in regulatory proceedings and court cases in various states, continued his lifelong teaching experience with LLI classes on economics. Dr. Arthur Wenk, a seasonal resident from Canada, introduced and shared his wide knowledge and love of Western Civilization. A very popular class, led by Hasan Hammami for many years, was based on the "Great Decisions" booklet published annually by the Foreign Policy Association in New York City; Mr. Hammami's personal life experiences and travels abroad added an in-depth perspective on many world events and became a seasonal favorite. Joanne Ryder, who deserves credit for filing all the documents in 2005 for LLI's 501(c)(3) status and State Incorporation documents, led several classes on Genealogy. Samar Jarrah, former CNN contributor, author and professor of Foreign Studies at the University of South Florida, enlightened her classes on Islam and the Middle East. E. Alan Stewart, a Florida native, shared his boyhood memories of growing up in SW Florida and his perspective on the history of population expansion and environmental manipulation in our area. Bob Luther, another of Judy's "discoveries", was a direct descendent of Martin Luther and shared his perspective and personal research on this historical icon.

Early classes were held in the Freeman House in Punta Gorda before it was moved to its current location, the IMPAC University when it was still operating as an international educational institution, and the Sunnydell Plaza in Port Charlotte. Space for this growing program was quickly becoming an issue so when Edison College began construction for a new campus on Airport Road in Punta Gorda, Carol Eliason and Jack Price met with Dr. Richard Yarger, Provost of the Charlotte campus, to explore the possibility of moving the program to this new campus.

When Jack Price retired from the Foundation and Dr. Carolyn Freeland assumed leadership, changes were being made at the Foundation to focus on the management and enlargement of its endowment resources and distribution of those funds to qualified community projects. The Foundation gifted LIR $5,000 as a grant to help in the transition and in 2005 LIR President Craig Anderson and officers began the task of filing documentation to form itself as a stand-alone 501 (c)(3) not-for-profit organization.

The LIR Board then made two more decisions: to change the name from "Learning in Retirement" to the "Lifelong Learning Institute" and to enter into an even closer relationship with Edison College. The name change was advised by the Elderhostel Institute Network (EIN – now known as Road Scholar):

As the years rolled on and the LLI program gained in popularity, the Board of Directors and the programming committee chairpersons devoted many, many hours of research, investigation, planning and coordination with members of the community and other organizations. New programming ideas and changes in operations continued the goal of the founders. Bylaw changes and committee reorganization brought change as it was needed. Office operations required expanded space and more on-campus presence so the part-time Office Manager position was expanded in 2008. I became the Office Manager then and continued on and off until 2017.

During this period of growth, LLI adopted the slogan "Learning – just for the fun of it!" Under the presidencies of Charles Brox, Hasan Hammami, Phyllis Walker, and Larry Smith, the LLI mission remained throughout: to offer non-credit quality adult educational opportunities at a reasonable cost to the residents and visitors of Charlotte County

When local attorney Phyllis Walker joined the LLI Board, she and office manager, Bonnie Leroy, built a profile page on the Giving Partner website that qualified LLI to participate in three Giving Partner Challenges, a four-county fundraiser. She also supported and spearheaded a "Health Fair" in 2013, 2014, and 2015.

LLI's rich history is about so many people, many more than those who have been named -- all volunteers who filled committees, officer positions, Board of Directors memberships, led classes and shared their expertise and experiences, and participants with an interest in continued learning to enrich their lives and introduce new thoughts. June 30, 2020, diminished all that. But a lovely magnolia tree now grows on the FSW Charlotte campus to commemorate LLI's presence and a Presidential Plaque hangs in the auditorium as a reminder of the contributions made by the Lifelong Learning Institute of Charlotte County, the original PREMIERE LIFELONG LEARNING program in Charlotte County!

VIRGINIA B. ANDES CLINIC: A MORAL IMPERATIVE

Mark Asperilla MD FACP
Thomas Ferrara PhD.
David M. Klein MD FACS

It is a moral imperative that all people deserve quality healthcare; especially in a country that is as blessed as ours. To that end, the healthcare practitioners and the local citizens of our community have personified those words over the last forty years.

We have, in our county, a volunteer clinic that serves the needs of our medically indigent population who have no health insurance. These hard-working people might cut your lawn, or care for your children, or serve you in so many diverse roles.

Right, Virginia B. Andes; above, staff and doctors.

Although the local hospitals very often exceed the regulatory statutes that govern indigent care, and the local physicians always step forward to perform episodic emergency care, something else was needed.

That something is the Andes Clinic. This building and its mission is the namesake of the dear, sweet, and very generous Virginia B. Andes. The underpinnings of this clinic started with the "Care a Van" which was a healthcare outreach of St. Joseph Hospital, in order to bring medical care to the migrant laborers who help to feed us.

In the early '90s, two of the same founding physicians started the HIV-AIDS and Hepatitis-C clinics at the Charlotte County Public Health Department. Finally, after a cataclysmic tropical cyclone that devastated Charlotte County, a group of volunteers opened a FEMA Clinic in a 1,000-unit emergency village on Airport Road.

David M. Klein MD FACS, one of the founders of the clinic, examines a patient. Right above, Linda Thurston of Project Detect, Janice Chupka, clinic Director Suzanne Roberts, and Noreen Chervinski.

All of this was a rehearsal for what would become a world class volunteer clinic. It started in the year 2000 with a community pharmacy that would provide life-saving but prohibitively expensive medicines to needy and deserving citizens. Then, in 2007, one of the physician founders of the pharmacy called the other physician/doctor founders at 2 a.m. in the morning and said that we needed to put together a free clinic. Over the next three months, the physicians met for three hours every Friday in order to discuss the structure of this life-saving endeavor. The corporate and medical planning had to include the necessary governance and quality control. Above all, it was emphasized that the quality of care needed to be superb, and that the delivery of that care needed to be flawless.

The first patient on opening night turned out to have Hodgkin's Disease. That patient, who is a mother, sister, and grandmother, is still alive and well. That set the stage for this institution to become a mainstay of life in Charlotte County. Even if you don't need the medical services of this beautiful creation, it is a place where you can spend your time, treasure and talent.

Because of the mighty leadership of the board, the expert guidance of the executive team, and the solid partnership of the healthcare providers of Southwest Florida, the Andes Clinic has flourished. With the support of the community and the blessings of God Almighty, the dedicated and tireless work of the clinic has saved lives and has elevated the humanity of our wonderful community. This is a treasure of which we can all be proud.

2000s

WHEN CHARLEY MET CHARLOTTE

Where were you on Sept. 11, 2001?

For people who remember the twin towers falling and the horror of the attacks, the experience is as equivalent a touchstone as Nov. 23, 1963 was to an older generation of Americans. In one day innocence was shattered, America was vulnerable, and thoughts turned to consolation—and revenge.

Closer to home, the rage sparked by the attacks led to sporadic instance of vandalism at the Islamic Community Center on Harborview Road. In response, the author and the *Sarasota Herald-Tribune* partnered with the Islamic community to host a six-week series of discussions.

Hedging their bets, the Muslims rented extra seats to fill their meeting hall yet were apprehensive. Would there be violence? Would the event be shunned? But half an hour later, a line snaked out of the hall and down the lane to Harborview Road. Hundreds of Charlotte County residents came together to learn more about Islam. The tolerance shown by the larger community led Muslims to build a new meeting hall and engage in cultural exchanges with ecumenical and community organizations.

CENTURY

Sarasota Herald-Tribune

2001
The World Trade Center, Pentagon attacked during 9/11 attacks

Tropical Storm Gabrielle caused widespread flooding along Shoreview Drive and Gulf Blvd. Significant flooding also took place in the City of Punta Gorda. Over 300 homes were affected Estimated damages to infrastructure, residences, and businesses are between $4-6 million.

2002
Peace River Center for Writers established in Punta Gorda.

George W. Bush establishes the Department of Homeland Security; it commences operations the following year

---

How to avoid mistakes of the past: Meet at the mosque

JAMES M. ABRAHAM

"You may not be interested in war, but war is interested in you."
— Leon Trotsky, June 1919

Americans may not be much interested in the world, but the world is intensely interested in us. That fact came home with sad clarity Sept. 11. Now, as we in this nation work through the grief of the attack and prepare a response, it's incumbent that, in fighting the good fight, we do not lose sight of ourselves.

There's a hidden history in America, a record of shame and ignorance that always manages to poke up its head in times of national crisis.

During the 19th century a group, fittingly called the Know-Nothings, terrorized Irish and Catholic immigrants. The nation was going through a series of economic convulsions, and many long-time Americans feared they would lose their jobs to the immigrants.

In the following century, in the midst of the Great Depression, Father Coughlin preached from his Shrine of the Little Flower Church in Michigan, filling the airwaves with hate and invective against Jews, Communists, and eventually President Roosevelt.

And, during the McCarthy era, many lost their jobs and their reputations as so-called Commie hunters disgraced individuals, and the country, chasing ghosts.

Now we're faced with a great crisis, the likes of which we have never seen before. Odds are good that more than 6,000 people may have died in the Sept. 11 attacks. There's a strong mood for vengeance and, as days go by without retaliation, that sentiment may grow ugly.

Here in Charlotte County, the local Islamic Community of Southwest Florida's mosque has been attacked twice. The incidents were relatively minor, and may have been the work of some drunken knuckleheads.

But, if the war on terrorism gets worse, and the hate-mongers among us slink out from their holes, what will happen to us? Will we begin attacking one another, going after Arab-Americans, Muslims, and anyone else who looks like the enemy?

It's happened before. One of the most shameful examples of national paranoia was the forced removal of Japanese from the West Coast during World War II. That shame was magnified by the magnificent record of Japanese-Americans who volunteered to serve in our armed forces.

Let's not repeat history.

On Monday at 6:30, all are welcome to attend the first in a series of discussion groups on the national crisis, which will be held at the Islamic Community of Southwest Florida Mosque, 25148 Harborview Rd. For more information give me a call at 627-7521.

When we look at the Arabs and Muslims among us, it's understandable that we may worry that they could be sleepers, adders in our midst waiting for the moment to strike. But we surrender our American dignity and compassion when we accept this view. And, if we allow thugs to terrorize those people, eventually those same thugs may come for us.

I think of the words of Martin Niemöller, the German cleric who, during the Nazi terror, came to his senses a little too late.

"When Hitler attacked the Jews I was not a Jew, therefore I was not concerned. And when Hitler attacked the Catholics, I was not a Catholic, and therefore, I was not concerned. And when Hitler attacked the unions and the industrialists, I was not a member of the unions and I was not concerned. Then Hitler attacked me and the Protestant church — and there was nobody left to be concerned."

Years ago, after the assassination of Martin Luther King, Baltimore and other cities erupted in riots.

My wife's family then lived in a community which had recently become black. One white family remained, a mother and her blind daughter. Through the riots, as black thugs looted, burned and attacked whites unfortunate enough to be seen, my wife's family sheltered their white neighbors.

In Port Charlotte, after the attacks on the mosque, religious groups and individuals came forward to offer help and support.

Those examples embody America, and that's why I wave my flag, despite the large and petty insults people who look like me endure daily.

Join us patriots Monday at the mosque, as we celebrate the tolerance and diversity our enemies — at home and abroad — have long derided.

James M. Abraham is an editorial writer and columnist based in Charlotte County.

The event did not put an end to ugly instances of intolerance as America went to war in Iraq. But the coming together spoke to a groundswell of support for the idea of a more diverse Charlotte County even as demographics indicated that the cultural mix was changing.

One droll example of the change took place during a meeting between several Muslim representatives and editors from the *Charlotte Sun*. At issue was the paper's perceived negative bias toward the Islamic community.

At one point, one of the Muslim guests showed *Sun* editor Jim Gouvellis a collection of small ads from Islamic doctors and other Islamic professionals attached to a full-page ad featuring the restaurant in which the meeting took place.

"Um, why is this big ad attached?" asked the editor..

"The owner is Muslim," was the answer.

That afternoon the editor wrote a column extolling diversity and began exercising a tighter rein on potentially offensive or ill-informed material. The restaurant owner was a Muslim from New York who did very well selling homes for PGI—particularly to Muslims.

September 11 was a national tragedy with local reactions. But for many Charlotte County residents, one event outweighed all in its effect on their lives. And that event took place August 13, 2004, when Charley met Charlotte.

Zora Neale Hurston, a native Floridian, offers a most compelling description of our state's natural fury in her "Their Eyes Were Watching God." She describes how a party of carousing workers first saw groups of Indians walking slowly toward the east. Next, small animals and birds joined the migration. All the while, the roustabouts drank, partied, and gambled, oblivious to the glassy surface of the water or the dead calm of the air. But then they got the news, special delivery.

Hurston's novel draws from one of South Florida's great tragedies. Lake Okeechobee, driven to fury by the high winds of the San Felipe Segundo hurricane of 1928, smashed its dikes and overflowed. The death toll from the disaster is still debated but is listed as between 1,600 and 2,500 people. The hurricane, an ominous coda for the excesses of the Roaring Twenties and a fierce harbinger of the Great Depression, led to the first wide-scale building codes in South Florida.

Similarly, Hurricane Charley led to major changes in the lives of Charlotte County residents. Some are obvious in new buildings, others less so manifest, as new leadership, and, for at least a few years, a healthy respect for the weather. As Charley, then Frances, with Ivan and Jeanne, scourged the county, the despair and fear was palpable. The year 2004, with its concentration of four hurricanes that shook the county as if it were a mop, left strains and stains that may take years to go away. Researchers at the University of Florida found that the death rate went up after the summer of storms.

> Results suggest that there was an elevated mortality for up to 2 months following each storm, resulting in a total of 624 direct and indirect deaths attributable to the storm. Trauma-related deaths that can be associated directly with the storm account for only 4% of the total storm-related mortality, while indirect mortality accounts for most storm-related deaths. Specifically, a large percentage of the elevated mortality was associated with heart (34%) and cancer-related deaths (19%), while diabetes (5%) and accident-related deaths (9%) account for a smaller but still significant percentage of the elevated mortality... The results further suggest that the elevated mortality was the result of additional deaths that would not have otherwise occurred within that 5-month period, and not simply a clustering of deaths that were inevitable between 1 August and 31 December 2004.[76]

2003

Peachland Branch of Charlotte State Bank opens

Punta Gorda named one of the top 10 "Best Small Cities to Live In" by Money Magazine a second time

Two killed in failed prison escape at Charlotte Correctional Institute on Oil Well Road

New Sallie Jones Elementary School built

Beneath such giant storms, one may be driven, like poor Job, to turn one's eyes to the sky and ask why such tragedies would be visited upon humanity. But why not? Hurricanes are part of a cleansing cycle that nature has employed since before we knew there was a nature. To paraphrase Mark Twain, Florida owes us nothing, it was here first.

The storm is credited with the most invasive urban renewal ever practiced in the county. The high winds and rain also swept away a

Charlotte led a consortium of communities along the Peace River watershed in fighting Mosaic, a major phosphate miner, from damaging the area.

---

[76] Direct and indirect mortality in Florida during the 2004 hurricane season, Nathan McKinney, Chris Houser, Klaus Meyer-Arendt, Department of Environmental Studies, University of West Florida

2004
Tsunami from the Indian Ocean earthquake kills over 230,000

Hurricane Charley destroys six CCPS schools on August 13, including Baker Center, Peace River Elementary, Neil Armstrong Elementary, East Elementary, Punta Gorda Middle, and Charlotte High.

2005
Hurricane Wilma Heavy rains of 4 to 8 inches caused urban street flooding and filled ditches to capacity.

2006
The Richard D. Yarger Science Hall is dedicated at Florida Southwestern State College

The event center that replaced the auditorium in Punta Gorda destroyed by Hurricane Charley. TEAM Punta Gorda spearheaded the design; it was one of the last major projects built by Peter Taylor.

Punta Gorda governing team that many felt had failed to meet the challenge of both storm preparation and the clean-up.

"People thought we weren't living up to what they needed at the time," said Marilyn Smith-Mooney.

Dissatisfaction with a city council that had become more of a sideshow and hindrance than a public good led to meetings between a new breed. Men and women such as Nancy Prafke, an Ohio professional who relocated to Florida and John Wright, an energetic ambassador from the British Isles and former liquor salesmen, began filling the vacuum left by a government overwhelmed with what to do next.

They helped participate in a series of charrettes, commissioning nationally known planners to help create a place that would reflect urban infill and the growth of a city center. TEAM Punta Gorda was adopted as the formal name of this ad hoc group. And as they gained power, a new type of politics grew in Punta Gorda. Professionalism and competence replaced party loyalty or the good-ole-boy network. It's important to note, for example, that Pittsburgh transplants Steve and Nancy Johnson, are both TEAM members and active Democrats in a sea of red. But make no mistake about it, TEAM in itself is the latest permutation of politics in a city known for shedding political leadership the way snakes shed skins, urban planning became the new cachet.

Their plan was to create a touristy variant of old Punta Gorda— a downtown populated with folks, but not necessarily loud kids or raucous bars. Their goal was different. The peninsular city, shorn of its importance as a sea or rail link, would become a hinterland of the new western communities such as Burnt Store Isles, Punta Gorda Isles. The result? The growth of outdoor dining, the construction of a huge, free parking garage in the heart of downtown, and a continuation of the 1990 redevelopment plans for open spaces, long, winding walkways, and increased urban mobility. In short, the goal was to keep downtown humming. Now Punta Gorda is a walking and dining town and, in keeping with the city's century-old dependence on the tourist trade, many of those walkers and diners are visitors.

TEAM represents the ultimate expression of a movement to reclaim communities that began in the 1980s when business organizations, government, and private individuals formed partnerships to promote local culture and lure tourists. TEAM is not only well-represented in local government, but also sponsors paint parties, community beautification events, and a variety of civic endeavors—including a free bike sharing program.

As the 2000s showed us nature's fury, the decade also saw unprecedented efforts on the part of private and governmental groups to become stewards rather than exploiters of Charlotte County. The most dramatic example of this concern for the environment was a decision by Charlotte County Commissioners in 2002 to sue Mosaic, the phosphate giant, to stop them from building a mine that would endanger the Peace River watershed.

Charlotte County spent about $12 million as it took the lead role in a regional lawsuit, joined by Lee and Sarasota counties.[77] Eventually the legal bill got too be too high, particularly as the county and nation endured the Great Recession of 2008. During the past decade, Charlotte County's taxpayers led the region's legal battle by chipping in $12 million trying to keep phosphate companies from chipping away at the watershed. The action was eventually dropped after the Great Recession because it was too expensive to maintain in a fraught economy.[78]

"The county commissioners stopped challenging Mosaic's permit applications in 2008," wrote a *Sarasota Herald-Tribune* columnist. "But it's not because they suddenly believed it was OK to strip-mine forests, decimate wetlands, disrupt natural hydrology and threaten one of the most productive fisheries in the country. They quit fighting because the economy went south, and it cost too much trying to do the job that state regulators should be doing."[79]

Charlotte County's fight for environmental integrity was thwarted, in part. by another big decision—one that went horribly wrong.

In 2006 county commissioners, spurred by planners from the Urban Land Institute, embarked on an ambitious program to clean up General Development's mess and revitalize the central population area of Charlotte. The result was Murdock Village, a project by which county officials paid more than $100 million to purchase 1,200 acres of lots sold by GDC to owners who, for whatever reason, never built on the sites.[80]

The goal was to turn around and sell parcels of the land to developers. But government learned an expensive lesson—shield, never expose, taxpayers to the vagaries of the open market. A series of economic downturns culminating in the Great Recession of 2008 made committed investors such as Syd Kitson, who would later successfully develop Babcock Ranch, walk away.[81] Soon Murdock Village became a money pit, eating up interest and fees rather than being a powerhouse of economic development. Once more, Charlotte couldn't say no and was left holding the bag. Only in the 2020s would the investment begin to pay.

2008
Summer Olympics commencing in Beijing

Stocks fall sharply: Lehman Brothers' bankruptcy filing; Merrill Lynch's acquisition by Bank of America; and AIG's unprecedented request for short-term financing from the Federal Reserve heralds U.S. Great Recession, fueled by the 2007 subprime mortgage crisis

Barack Obama is elected the 44th President of the United States, making him the first African-American president.

---

[77] New York Times, 8-4-2007
[78] https://www.heraldtribune.com/news/20100205/ernst-mosaics-baseball-deal-is-more-foul-than-fair
[79] ibid
[80] https://www.businessobserverfl.com/article/murdock-village-westport-kolter-group-jim-harvey-private-equity-group-charlotte-county-brett-low
[81] https://www.heraldtribune.com/article/LK/20080311/News/605207612/SH

CENTURY

2009

US Airways Flight 1549 ditches in the Hudson River in an accident that becomes known as the "Miracle on the Hudson", as all 155 people on board are rescued.

Flu pandemic begins in Mexico, soon spreading to the U.S. and then around the world.

2010

County population 159,978, a 12.96 percent increase over 2000

Every financial disaster is made up of pieces as discrete as human beings. And one personal story of how the Great Recession ended dreams is that of Charlotte County's premier builder, Peter Taylor.

We had a good business, but one day Wells Fargo said they're not going to loan money, have credit lines with any developer or general contractor. So they called up one day and said, "You don't have a line of credit." And that was $400,000. And we survived with $2 million worth of business the year before. Now I had contracts for $4 million dollars, two contracts, but I didn't have a line of credit. And we negotiated the contracts and they were due to start in just a couple of months but you needed to survive for those couple of months. That's what a line of credit is for. It's not capital. It's in the interim until you have the cash flow again. So they pulled it, and then I think I told you, all the other banks were frightened. "If they pulled it, why should we give you a line?" That's one thought I had in my head. The other is the feds may have said, "Don't loan money unless you're 100% confident" or something, whatever they said. So there was no credit. So I cashed a life insurance policy. I had a $200,000 life insurance policy and I sold it for $65,000 and put it in the business and I just sucked it up. I paid all my people and all with benefits, vacation time, all they had coming to them and nothing is happening. I said, "I'm going to close it up," and that's what I did. If I had time I could have sold it as an ongoing business.

And so in the blink on an eye a 35-year-old business was brought to an end. Taylor had spearheaded efforts to build the community's first moto-cross facility and had put his prestige and money into renovating the venerable H.W. Smith Arcade in downtown Punta Gorda. Now the Great Recession had reduced him to scrambling for cash. Like so many others, Taylor's bright, shining, decade had morphed into the stuff of nightmares.

The Great Recession would, in part, fuel an ominous political development, particularly in homogeneous Englewood and parts of Port Charlotte. Barack Obama's election stoked racial divisions and old animosities were reawakened. In the decades to come, the vitriol of grievance, race-based politics would come home to Charlotte County to occupy a place as solid and unshakeable as its position in state, national and even international affairs.

A People's History of Charlotte County

Wikipedia

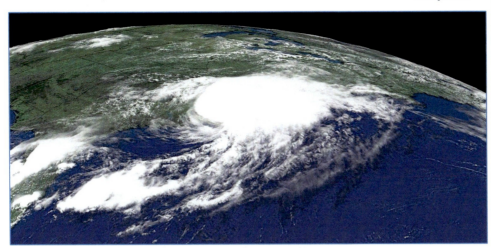

HURRICANE CHARLEY

Karen Clark

Florida Weekly

Robert Van Winkle and Jim Reif cover Hurricane Charley in 2004 in the NBC2 studio.

My husband Terry and I moved to Punta Gorda in 2000 for retirement and had been exposed to a number of storms before Charley. So we weren't very concerned since Hurricane Charley was supposed to go up to Tampa as a Category 2 storm. We were watching TV all day that day, however, following the storm's progress. About 1 PM that afternoon, Jim Reif, the weatherman for ABC-7 News in Ft. Myers, made a very disturbing announcement. He told us that Charley's path had changed, that it had taken a turn to the northeast and was going to go right up Charlotte Harbor. They were also saying that we could have a significant storm surge. We knew we could handle the wind and rain from a Category 2 which was what Charley was supposed to have been, but the change in the path, increased storm strength, and the possibility of storm surge made us quickly change our plans.

It was too late for us to head over to the East Coast. We knew that the only hurricane shelter near us was the Port Charlotte Cultural Center. We had to decide quickly what to take with us. We ended up loading all of our family photo albums into laundry baskets and lugging them out to the car; they were the only things we felt we couldn't replace. We packed a small bag with a change of clothes, some food and water, and sleeping bags. We got to the Cultural Center about 2:30 p.m. and checked in. We were routed to a large room that was pretty full with other families. We staked out an area and sat down to wait. A couple next to us had a small battery-powered TV, and many folks were gathered around watching the progress of the storm. The room had no windows, but we could hear the rain and wind howling. At one point, we joined some people who had gathered at a door with a window in a hall, and we watched the rain flying by sideways. The eye of the storm passed over Punta Gorda shortly after 4 p.m. and about that time some of the roof lifted and flew off the Cultural Center. The power had gone out, and it was fairly dark inside. The biggest problem was that the bathrooms needed water to flush the toilets, so they began to back up and became unusable.

At 6 p.m., we were told that we could leave if we wanted to, but that if we left, we couldn't return. We wanted to get home and out of the unpleasant shelter.

It was still raining when we left. Our car's bumper cover had a hole punched in it, but luckily, the windows were intact, so everything inside was safe.

We saw a lot of damage on our way out to Tamiami Trail. Limbs blocked the roads, roofs were ripped off houses, and windows were blown out. The more damage we saw, the more determined we were to get home and check our house. We first tried to go over the bridge to Punta Gorda but were turned away by the police who said that it was too dangerous for us to return to our home because so many power lines were down. We turned around and went out Kings Highway to I-75 and were able to get across the river but getting back to Punta Gorda Isles wasn't easy. We would turn down a street only to find it blocked by huge trees and impassable. Damage was even worse than what we had seen in Port Charlotte. I will never forget seeing a mobile home at the intersection at Taylor Road and Cooper Street. There was a man standing in the doorframe of his home, but there were no windows or roof. He looked absolutely stunned. There were wires down everywhere, and we didn't want to drive over any of them because we didn't know which might be live, so it took us over an hour to wind our way back to our home. I remember finally turning onto our street and seeing our house with the roof intact and thanking God that we still had a house.

When we examined the house, we found that everything inside was safe. We had lost roof tiles and our pool cage had collapsed, but we had a roof, walls, and no broken windows, which is much more than many others had. The yard was full of debris, limbs, and roof tiles. Our sailboat, which we had secured with 8 lines in the middle of the canal, was hanging on by one single dock line and had bent stanchions and a few cosmetic dings from flying debris.

Of course, there was no electricity. The first night we spent in our hot house with windows and doors open in hopes of getting a breeze, but it was August in Florida, so no luck. It was a miserable night. The main thing I remember from that first night was the total silence. There was NO noise – no birds, insects, voices, quietly-humming appliances, generators. Just dead silence! The next day we began cleaning up the yard and were amazed to find that our palm trees had survived, but the native plants which we had been required to plant had not fared well. They had been destroyed by the wind. One weeping hibiscus tree was simply gone – ripped out of the ground; we never did find that plant.

We had moved into our new house in 2000. Since it was fairly recently, the next day my husband called our builder and the subcontractors who had built our house, and we got on their lists for pool and roof repair. That turned out to be a smart move because builders quickly filled their lists of people needing repairs. We were able to drive to Sarasota and get a small generator which we used to run the refrigerator for a few hours a day. We moved onto our sailboat behind the house and kept it fairly cool with that small generator for the 10 days we lived on it before power was restored.

We didn't have any electricity, cell phone service, or running water. We had filled the bath tubs with water before we left for the Cultural Center, but they had leaked and were then empty. So we took buckets of water from the swimming pool to flush the toilets in the house and to use for showers up until the pool water turned green since we couldn't run the pump with the generator.

Our cellphone had no Sprint service; we had to drive out to I-75 where the Sprint tower was located to have any reception. However, one of our friends had an account with Verizon and did have service. He allowed many of us to call our families and let them know that we were OK. Over those first few days we would ride our bikes to friends' houses to see how they had faired. We had filled up both cars with gas a few days before the storm, but we didn't want to use up that gas because gas stations were closed since they couldn't pump gas without electricity, so we rode our bikes most places.

Friends had varying degrees of damage. Everyone had roof damage and pool cages gone, but many had much more severe problems – windows blown out, doors blown in and indoor furniture carried right out into the pool. Some had lost everything inside. Some had boats that had blown away or were lying upside down in the canal. Most conversations centered around getting someone to do repairs. Roofs were covered with blue tarps.

Within a day or do, members of our PGIslanders Cruising Club set up a convenient way for all of us to keep in touch. At 7 p.m. every evening, we would all get on a special channel on our marine radios

and have some time to check on each other and for anyone who needed help to ask for it. Someone might ask members for help cleaning up their yard the next day, and the next day, that help was there!

Stock Development was just getting ready to begin construction on Vivante Condominiums out Marion Avenue, and they set up a huge, air-conditioned tent and prepared 3 free meals a day. We ate there and met friends there for meals for over a week. It was great to go to the tent at the end of the day and have a hot meal. We had plenty of food at home but heating food on the grill got old after a few days.

Pike Electric sent trucks and crews to help get the power restored. When we would see a truck near our street, we would go ask how long it would be before they got to us. We got sympathetic looks, but they had to repair the lines according to the plan. Some people tried to pay them, but that didn't work either.

I remember thinking a few weeks after the storm that things would begin to get back to normal in a few months. How utterly naive I was! It took years!

The mangroves along the canal on the way out to Ponce Inlet took about 10 years to look fully recovered. The town took less time, but there were many places that to this day have never come back. Many were small local businesses that couldn't afford to rebuild. Many stores and restaurants were able to rebuild, and as that happened, downtown began to look better; many of the old, dilapidated buildings were gone and replaced by newer ones. We called that "urban renewal by hurricane."

PUNTA GORDA RENAISSANCE

Nancy Prafke

When I was asked to tell a story of Punta Gorda's history from the perspective of someone who went from private citizen to volunteer leader of a local nonprofit to an elected official, my first reaction was what could I possibly say that hasn't already be told many times over. How could I pen something compelling and worth your time to read? However, there is a message that I feel is important to tell. It is one of leadership.

Spending a career in the Fortune 100 corporate world, I experienced a variety of leadership styles firsthand. When leadership was patriarchal and autocratic, bosses gave orders. Employees were an expendable resource. When leadership subscribed to stewardship, bosses became coaches who encouraged and inspired the team to achieve. Empowerment and collaboration were essential in attaining corporate goals. The human resource was the most valuable resource.

What does this have to do with Punta Gorda? I submit that leadership styles played a significant role in our city's history. We are a community rich with involvement to make this a better place. What catalyst would energize the actions that transpired? When Isaac Trabue refused to pay Kelly B. Harvey for surveying the land of the town of Trabue, it angered Harvey who spearheaded an effort to rename our city to Punta Gorda, for the fat area of land that juts out into Charlotte Harbor. The spirit of resident engagement was born. Like today, when Punta Gorda was incorporated in 1887, new residents would come to town and bring their ideas with them that would influence our development.

The damage from Hurricane Charley on Aug. 13, 2004, became another catalyst that spurred significant change. While local government was concerned with provision of basic services, businesses, organizations, and residents were looking ahead. They wanted to know what our community would look like when we "put Humpty Dumpty back together again." They wanted the recovery to be more than mere replacement. Their hope was to make the community better than they had it before.

Who were these people who wanted to make an impact on Punta Gorda's future? Some were "old timers" whose families were steeped in Punta Gorda's past. They wanted to protect the historic character of Punta Gorda and her ambiance. Some were retirees from all over the world who brought with them well-honed skills from successful careers. As one person described it, they knew how to push buttons and pull levers to get things done. How could the collective talent be harnessed for the better good?

These eager citizens formed a nonprofit organization, TEAM Punta Gorda, and raised over $250,000 in approximately eight weeks to hire renowned urban planner from the University of Miami, Jaime Correa. His firm engaged the community through charrettes and guided the development of the Citizens' Master Plan 2005. TEAM gifted the Master Plan to both the City and County and then the real work began. The Master Plan became the foundation for a revision to the City's Land Development Regulations, adding new urbanism principles and tightening up codes.

Howard Kunik

Interestingly, the Punta Gorda Chamber of Commerce also formed about the same time as TEAM Punta Gorda in November 2004. The Downtown Merchants Association, also founded at the same time, was another very active and influential group. Both would become partners with TEAM Punta Gorda in shaping Punta Gorda's future along with many other organizations.

In 2005, the relationship between the city and TEAM Punta Gorda was a contentious one. Was government ready for this level of community involvement? Did TEAM have a realistic expectation of what their role should be going forward? Was TEAM ready to run out of the gate? The leadership styles of those in charge varied with the backgrounds they brought with them. It was an interesting meld of talent.

In 2005, new Punta Gorda City Manager Howard Kunik arrived on the scene. How could he help improve working relationships? Did you know Howard believes that we manage projects and we lead people? His support for collaboration — the power of partnerships — would prove to be a critical component to our future.

How could TEAM Punta Gorda improve their acceptance in the community and improve the working relationship with local government? One way was through community projects from beautification to enhancing the design of the Charlotte Harbor Event & Conference Center. In 2006, community leaders who had been involved in the formation of TEAM Punta Gorda won seats on the Punta Gorda City Council, helping open lines of communication.

After volunteering for TEAM Punta Gorda in early 2006, I became the volunteer CEO at the end of 2007. City staff members were invited to participate in TEAM's committees. We were amazed to find the empowered city staff taking community ideas back to the city to implement when possible. It was also an honor when we received calls from the city asking us if we could take on a project. The partnership had become a very productive one.

Five years after Hurricane Charley left his mark on this community, the City, businesses, organizations, and residents held an Xtreme Makeover celebration to showcase how difficult it was to tell that anything had happened here before Charley other than some vacant lots where buildings once stood. The community was so very proud and rightfully so! The Federal Emergency Management Agency (FEMA) said our miraculous recovery should not have been possible in 20 years, let alone healed in five years. FEMA's lesson learned from our story was that the empowerment of the community increased the speed of recovery. It was the will of the people to recover and rehabilitate that made it happen. Collaboration is truly a force multiplier!

City Manager Howard Kunik documented our recovery in a presentation titled "Results through Collaboration: The Power of Partnerships." It shows the variety of teams that came together to get things done, all in the name of recovery and revitalization. This presentation won an award from the International City/County Management Association. It is on the city's website.

In 2013, I resigned my position in TEAM Punta Gorda to run for the Punta Gorda City Council. It has been my pleasure to be an advocate for collaboration with not only TEAM but the myriad of businesses and organizations that enrich this special place we call home. An empowering stewardship leadership style has proven to be so successful in Punta Gorda that City Council made this a requirement in hiring a new City Manager.

Howard Kunik retired from his City Manager duties effective Oct. 2, 2020. In his final column in *The Sun* on Sept. 18, 2020, he wrote, "And confident you will give new City Manager Greg Murray the support you gave me in making the power of partnerships a reality." Ours is a story of the right leadership style at the right time in the right place to manage change.

NEW KID ON THE BLOCK

John Wright

Imagine going from above to below in just 15 years.

The Punta Gorda Chamber of Commerce used to be the "new kid on the block" as it was only officially formed in November of 2004. Our Mission – "To promote our member businesses in Punta Gorda."

The City of Punta Gorda, nestled away in a quiet corner of SW Florida, was all but destroyed by Hurricane Charley back in August 2004. Over 85% of our downtown commercial district was destroyed. Our infrastructure was gripped by crisis. Previously reliant on tourism, our hotels were gone and we were handed a situation that no community could possibly envy. Either Punta Gorda could simply pack up and go home, or as a community we could band together and create a new city for ourselves.

A People's History of Charlotte County

Connie Kantor, above. Below, the trolley was one of the many ways we introduced people to Punta Gorda.

The board of the Punta Gorda Downtown Business Alliance gathered together within three weeks of the storm's destruction and decided to make a bold decision—dissolve and become a Chamber of Commerce.

"At no other time has our business community needed the direction, assistance and guidance of a Chamber as it does now," said the then Board Chair Connie Kantor. As the only incorporated city in Charlotte County, Punta Gorda's business community needed assurances, assistance, and guidance.

It needed representation with our local government, the city of Punta Gorda as well as representation at county level with the County Commission of Charlotte County. A decision was made and on November 19, 2004, the Punta Gorda Downtown Business Alliance officially became the Punta Gorda Chamber of Commerce Inc.

With its office in the downtown Bank of America complex destroyed, refuge was offered by one of local tourist attractions, Fishermen's Village (www.fishville.com). Itself destroyed by the winds of Charley, Fishermen's Village, a mixed-use wharf, made up of restaurants, retail and service providers, was up and running within three months of the storm, following a multi-million-dollar renovation and restoration. The newly formed Chamber of Commerce for Punta Gorda was offered space at a very affordable rate, which was to allow the Chamber to get off to a flourishing start. With the usual resilient spirit of the business and residential community that Punta Gorda is famous for, the PG Chamber was formed and started its life with approximately 100 members. Under the direction of then-Executive Director, Donna Heidenreich, the Chamber got off to a flying start and managed to double in size within one year of operation.

Tragedy was to strike again. Donna was diagnosed with cancer and having fulfilled her dream of leading the Business Alliance to Chamber status, she died prematurely at too young an age. The Chamber found itself once again in transition. A temporary president took over, until a permanent replacement could be selected.

In June 2006, the Chamber Board recruited me. I'm an ex-British diplomat who had come to Punta Gorda as a direct response to the international disaster efforts of Charley. The Chamber has made a remarkable leap forward, tripling its membership of 2006 to a level just short of 1,200 in 2020.

I made a strategic move to relocate the Chamber offices to a central downtown location, near the construction of new hotels, an event and conference center, new retail shopping locations and professional office space, all within yards of the new Chamber location.

The Punta Gorda Chamber is now the true center for business connectivity in this city. Out of season more than 200 people per week drop by the office for information and in season that figure easily doubles. We have revamped our website to draw visitor traffic. Daily requests are made through this site for visitor information, guides, maps, reservations, airport information, as well as B2B referrals, and much more.

The Punta Gorda Chamber is an entity that has taken on, sanctioned by Punta Gorda and its council,

Mindi Abair has long been a headliner of our successful Wine & Jazz Festival

the role of business development for the area. Working in conjunction with the county economic development office, the Punta Gorda Chamber works to recruit, locate, and site assess new entrepreneurs to the City. New construction has brought great and affordable opportunities for small business in the city. Following a consumer survey undertaken by the Chamber, we have created a target list of business types that would fit the mix of already diverse businesses in our core downtown and access corridor areas.

The Punta Gorda Chamber has a long list of successful events that are designed to meet our mission statement. For fifteen years, we have created, promoted and executed the Punta Gorda Wine & Jazz Festival. The economic impact of this event has now reached over $545,000 to local businesses, as each year we bring in top-of-the-line jazz performers that attract visitors for all over the United States. This year over 60 percent of all ticket sales were made to ticket holders outside the state of Florida!

All of them needed hotel rooms, meals, shopping, and services from our members. The success of this event was recognized this year by the Southeast Tourism Society, as being one of the Top 20 events in the whole of the Southeast USA, from the Carolinas to Florida!

The Wine & Jazz Festival is just one of our events. There are quarterly street craft fairs, farmers' market and so much more, all sponsored and presented by the "we-can-do" Punta Gorda Chamber.

We also conducted a new international consular mission, bringing foreign embassy officials to our city to show them just how well Punta Gorda has recovered from Hurricane Charley and how we are open for business.

As a direct result, we are now talking with German, Mexican and Icelandic businesses, with a view to attracting them to this area for both regional and international trade opportunities.

Sitting shoulder to shoulder with our local Airport Authority, we have helped encourage airlines to fly non-stop into our local airport from close to 50 locations around the USA. To complement the arrival of these flights, we now have formed a sister-chamber network of all chambers of commerce connected through Punta Gorda airport (PGD) and regularly exchange information about events that can be cross-promoted to encourage airline traffic through our airport. Events such as the Wine & Jazz Festival are a classic example, as hotels and airlines work out packages through our local CVB to attend.

The most lasting accomplishment is the fact that we are now the "go-to" Chamber, as reflected in our membership numbers. Our regular staple monthly events (BOB – Business over Breakfasts, BAH – Business after Hours and Networking Luncheons) are all considered must events for networking. Our weekly e-newsletter goes out to all members and now to over 15,000 local and regional subscribers who all see the PG Chamber as their informational source. For a city as small as Punta Gorda, we have a major event going on practically every single week. Added to the growing list of Chamber programs, we conducted Trolley Tours, allowing newcomers and visitors to see for themselves what a great place Punta Gorda is to visit, reside and do business in.

ENGLEWOOD STREET BEATS, SUMMER 2010

Signs are as necessary as they are ubiquitous. Before the first human stop sign was erected, churning waters warned of shoals and enchanting bays signaled peace.

At the Mango Bistro, 301 West Dearborn Street near the intersection of the eponymous Mango Street, no one needs a newspaper or a menu—*comentario de texto* and signs advertising specials plaster the windows. "Coffee," scrawled on the Mango Bistro's window, spells redemption and revival every morning.

The Bistro's revolving library is a heartening sign that folks still read. And at the intersection, signs tell us how fast to go, when to stop, where we are, and why this part of town is so important. But probably the most eloquent sign is the one in the lower forefront,

a wedge of an ad board at the Mango Bistro that offers a simple injunction we all can obey with joy.

"That's All Right, Momma" if one gets "All Shook Up" every first Saturday of the month on Dearborn Street. That's when the King and the Earl hold court. The King, of course, is Elvis Presley, whose rollicking rock and roll spirit resonates on Dearborn Street when the classic cars come out every month. The Earl is Harley Earl, the Detroit

CENTURY

The Village Voices perform at a fundraiser held at Village Gifts and Gallery. The owner, Shelley Smith below, was a key mover in bringing culture to Dearborn Street during the first decade of the 21st century.

designer whose tail fins and chrome inspired by high-performance fighter aircraft defined American automobiles through the Age of Elvis.

"Are You Lonesome Tonight?" for one of the classic cars, each parked like a gleaming "Hunk of Burning Love" along Dearborn Street? "One Can't Help Falling In Love" with the well-kept vehicles, whose sparkling bumpers and glossy paint jobs whisper "Love Me Tender."

* * *

If you get lost on the road to Englewood, just look for a handmade sign advertising a benefit event; it will lead you here. The summer opened with a benefit at The Mango Bistro for Pat Newtown and October ended with an Artists' Breakfast for Gene McCall; both Newton and McCall are respected, longtime members of the Dearborn Street community. And in between, neighbors from a girls' softball team to a woman battling life-threatening disease were beneficiaries of homegrown benefit events.

Before they learn the rhythm of our place, newcomers often complain that there are no seasons here. We who live here know of the seasons; we know the time of year when the fish come in close to get warm, or when it rains every day at 4 p.m., or when it's time to get some hurricane insurance. So yes, we do have seasons. But when it comes to giving, the season never changes. The signs of the season—or the next bake sale—never disappear in Englewood.

For I was in hunger and you gave me meat: I was thirsty, and you gave me drink: I was a stranger, and you took me in: Naked, and you clothed me: I was sick, and you visited me: I was in prison, and you came to me.

Matthew 25, American King James Version

A People's History of Charlotte County

Charlotte Harbor park off US41 NB; below, airport development area.

2010s

CLEARED FOR TAKEOFF

In 2010, Charlotte County economic development officials and those with the best interest of the county at heart paid allegiance to Allegiant, the giant budget airline that has revolutionized local air travel.

To mangle metaphors, the county hitched itself to a star on a wing and a prayer.

The Punta Gorda Airport was a gift to the county, a piece of wartime surplus whose barracks provided lumber for Punta Gorda homes and whose airfields offered excellent driving training.

But by the turn of the century, county officials, particularly the resurgent economic development office, began ramping up efforts to market a relic that spawned a renaissance, the Punta Gorda Airport. They plumbed an old source, the ever faithful gold mine of tourism.

CENTURY

Businesses in the Airport Area
Allegiant Air
Air Ambulance by AirTrek, Inc.
TGH Aeromed
AirTrek, Inc.
Classic Air Ventures
Aeronautical Services, Inc.
Arcadia Aerospace
Aviation Partners Group, Inc.
Sarasota Avionics and Maintenance
APG Aviation – Cirrus Service Center
PSC Warbird Aviation
Charlotte Technical College
AeroGuard Flight Training Center
Air Tours LLC
Harborside Aviation
Flight Fast Track
LPC Aviation
APG Avionics
Worldwide Flight Services
Gulf Contours
Civil Air Patrol
Experimental Aircraft Association Chapter 565
Asphalt Developers
Halfacre Construction
FAA Pilot Examinations
Dick Solar
Sport Pilot and CFI-Sport Practical Tests
CFI Renewals and Reinstatements
Charlotte County Sheriff's Office
Gulf Coast Car Service
New World Trade
AmeriGas Storage Facility
Pulsafeeder
4-17 Southern Speedway and Events, LLC
The Junction Restraraunt
Aviation Security Management
Federal Express
SuperTrak
Gulf Machine Works, LLC
Mike's Auto Glass

Charlotte County Airport Authority

And the decision to promote the airport also harkened back to the region's importance as a passenger and transshipment point to New Orleans, the Midwest, Miami, Cuba, and points beyond. Now air traffic would accomplish what rails and sails no longer made possible.

After World War II concluded, the airport complex was turned over to Charlotte County by the War Assets Administration and was managed by the Charlotte County Board of County Commissioners. For years it was almost a hobby airfield, used by the Civil Air Patrol and private pilots.

Starting in 1949, the Punta Gorda Squadron of CAP{managed some of the airport's facilities and assisted in ground search and rescue missions. Scratch teams of cadets and community volunteers often gave time and money to keep the airport in shape. In 1965, government stepped in, As part of a state revision of its fiscal structure, the Charlotte County Airport and surrounding commerce park became an independent special district with taxing authority.

2011

Legislation re-codified for the Airport Authority to change the name of the airport to the Punta Gorda Airport. Effective on June 21, 2011, the Authority amended Chapter 98-508, Laws of Florida by expanding the purpose of the Authority to include any airports within the boundaries of Charlotte County and all facilities, real estate, and commerce parks within the Authority's boundaries.

New rebuilt Meadow Park Elementary School opens

New rebuilt Lemon Bay High School Gymnasium opens

A People's History of Charlotte County

Charlotte County Airport Authority

2012
Hurricane Sandy, the largest Atlantic hurricane on record (as measured by diameter, with tropical-storm-force winds spanning 900 miles (1,400 km)), wreaks havoc, resulting in 233 total deaths and $68.7 billion (2012 USD) damage..

Barack Obama is reelected President of the United States.

2013
The first Charlotte County sheriff's deputy to be shot and killed in the line of duty, Michael Wilson, honored

That authority was codified in 1998 under the auspices of the Charlotte County Airport Authority. With the rise of budget air travel through the decade, the airport was well-positioned to greet Midwesterners feeling the cold or to embark residents returning to their hometowns for a visit. In 2007 commercial airline service was restored.

The Bailey Terminal, named after the Bailey brothers who were all from Punta Gorda and served in the military during WWII and the Korean War, was expanded in 2015 to accommodate the growing number of passengers traveling in and out of the airport. [82]

But with growth has come new problems. As the airport and the surrounding business park has become an economic engine, moves are afoot to privatize or otherwise change the operating structure that has worked for decades.[83] In some ways, such efforts reflect the growing value of what was once a surplus relic of World War II.

One indication of the growing emphasis on development in the area was a recent news story on an innovative business attractor service. Punta Gorda Airport is streamlining its commercial and aviation development on the airport's property in south Punta Gorda:

The Charlotte County Airport Authority has launched an interactive map for the Aviation Expansion Area (PGD AviEx) on the north side of the property, to make it easier for businesses to develop on the airport land, 28000 Airport Road, Punta Gorda. All of the parcels available for lease are in the Interstate Airport Park and fall within business-friendly Enterprise Charlotte Airport Park zoning guidelines. "Businesses looking for a new site can be at a desktop anywhere in the world using the interactive map, and it will help them get a better understanding of PGD and what the area has to offer," wrote PGD spokesperson Kaley Miller in an email to The Daily Sun. "It's meant to improve internal efficiencies as well, so staff can more quickly respond to requests for information.[84]

---

[82] https://www.flypgd.com/airport-authority/airport-history/
[83] Charlotte Sun, 2-23-21
[84] Charlotte Sun, 4-8-21

CENTURY

Babcock Ranch

An aerial view of Babcock Ranch, above, and model homes displayed on the development's Web home page.

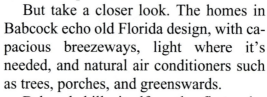

If one continued somewhat south from the airport toward the former Babcock preserves, the next stop would be a new city rising in what was once forgotten land at the least-populated areas of Charlotte and Lee County.

In Babcock Ranch, the city beautiful idea has come full circle—and picked up sustainability along the way. Babcock Ranch is a return to the ambitions of finely-crafted urban settlements reminiscent of those on display at the 1893 Columbian Exposition.

But take a closer look. The homes in Babcock echo old Florida design, with capacious breezeways, light where it's needed, and natural air conditioners such as trees, porches, and greenswards.

Babcock bills itself as the first solar city. In the Sunshine State, that's a natural first step toward sustainability. As one writer noted:

"While new residents are drawn by sustainability and community, they are also attracted to the wholistic nature of the development and its comprehensive live-thrive paradigm incorporating completeness in residential, recreation, retail and dining and professional opportunity, all within walkable spaces, with automated transport on the way."[85]

In many ways, Babcock represents lessons learned in the ten decades of Charlotte County residents building their way around Charlotte Harbor and beyond.

2014

Numerous provisions of the Patient Protection and Affordable Care Act, better known as Obamacare, go into effect.

New rebuilt Lemon Bay High School Administration & Media Center opens

2014 BCS National Championship Game: The number-one-ranked Florida State Seminoles beats the number-two-ranked Auburn Tigers at the Rose Bowl in Pasadena, California by a score of 34–31.

---

[85] https://www.charlotteedp.com/shining-a-light-on-charlotte-county/

2015

Charlotte County last hosted a USA BMX Sunshine State Nationals event in February 2015. That competition generated an estimated $750,000 in direct expenditures, with participants and spectators contributing to more than 1,500 hotel room nights.

Punta Gorda Isles and much of Port Charlotte was created by gouging trenches with draglines and using the dirt to build berms for homes, a process so injurious that Florida curtailed it in 1995.[86] Tamiami Trail was dynamited through the Everglades.[87]

But Babcock was built with an eye toward preserving what was already there. And there's one new wrinkle: Punta Gorda Isles was initially advertised as a place away from the city. Babcock Ranch trumpets its centrality, its position athwart transportation links to three counties, the fact that it's convenient to both Ft. Myers and Charlotte county, along SR36. The major thoroughfare also connects Babcock Village with Arcadia, thus creating another potential linkage.

That geography is important because the metropolitan centers of Lee and Charlotte counties are about 40 miles apart. The demise of the railroads and the diminution of coastal commerce has exacerbated that cultural and commercial distance. Babcock Ranch has the potential to serve as both an attracter and a connector, bringing a new regionality to intercounty culture and commerce.

Consider that Syd Kitson, the CEO and Chairman of Kitson and Partners, de-

velopers of Babcock Ranch, had to work his way through duplicative layers of county government as he gained permitting for the project. That practical experience alone speaks to the potential for Babcock Ranch to be a strong first step in forging a new regional nexus.

According to the company, things are going great:

Even in the midst of the pandemic, the development's robust home sales continue to rise, up 50% this year alone, for a total of 900 homes since startup less than three years ago. It's a 73% year-over-year increase, Pears notes. Earlier this summer, the development ranked 39th on RCLCO Real Estate Advisors' list of the nation's top-selling master planned communities. That's in addition to accolades in publications such as ideal-LIVING, which named the development the nation's "Best Eco-Friendly Community."

---

[86] https://floridadep.gov/sites/default/files/62-312_eff_080795_0_0.pdf
[87] https://www.youtube.com/watch?v=teKUN9ENXzw&ab_channel=NaplesParks

2016
Donald Trump elected President

Ron DeSantis elected governor

2017
Hurricane Irma passes just 18 miles to the east while moving north with 100 mph winds.

The average employee salary for Charlotte County, Florida was $54,694. This is 11.3 percent lower than the national average for government employees and 8.4 percent lower than other counties.

All photos from Allegiant

The national debate on race reached Charlotte County during April, after the killing of a black man in Minneapolis at the hands of police. Local college students organized a March for Justice that prompted an angry counterdemonstration of older white veterans clustered around the Vietnam Wall replica. They gathered based on unfounded fears that the march would turn violent. It didn't, but the clash of cultures mirrored the national mood entering an pivotal election year. The 2010s, then, were the years of big ideals, a time when the fear and uncertainty of the Great Recession subsided and optimism took wing. And perhaps nowhere in Charlotte County, the county that couldn't say no, was that optimism more evident than on a vacant stretch of property at the southernmost point of Charlotte Harbor, near the spot where the first bridge crossed the Peace River to Punta Gorda.

There, the airline that had catapulted the Punta Gorda Airport to stardom held a groundbreaking to launch their latest venture, a luxury complex of condos, shops, and apartments labeled "Sunseeker." In a potentially beneficial coordination with county officials, Sunseeker managers began surveying and site preparation on the west side of the twin bridges that span the Peace River even as the county developed parks and a walkway that girdled the area.

Once the county work was done, Sunseeker's work commenced. In short order cranes, six of them, soared toward the sky. Daily passersby and drivers heard the sounds of power and progress as teams of workmen secured rebar, poured concrete, and erected a long wall around the development.

Sunseeker officials aimed for a regional impact and began buying up golf courses and similar amenities in anticipation of restive tourists and guests.

Not since the Hotel Punta Gorda was built as a destination hub a century earlier was the potential for generational transformation of the county so close.

But there were already concerns. For example, the plans kept changing:

2018
A survey of 42 responding businesses throughout Charlotte County determined the county sustained a loss of more than $500,000 by August due to red tide. A follow-up, more expansive survey of 89 respondents in September that suggested the losses exceeded $2.1 million in Charlotte.

2019
Sun Country Airlines is launching air service at Punta Gorda Airport

A major outstanding issue with the site plan remains the public easement for a 2,150-foot harbor walk. Cullinan said Friday that he is not aware that the issues have been resolved. Calls Friday to Allegiant for comment were not immediately returned, but company officials have previously said they are working out legal technicalities with the county. The 90-foot towers are an apparent hallmark of the resort architecture. They require public access to the harborwalk, according to the rules of the Charlotte Harbor Redevelopment Authority. Without that easement, Allegiant could build up to 35 feet above the flood level, Cullinan said. Allegiant told its investors in a presentation Thursday morning that the company will build roughly 680 units, which is less than half of the 1,495 sought in their unapproved site plan. Among other changes, Sunseeker will now be completed in phases — the first with two condo towers. Originally, plans stated there would be a total of nine towers, but now the website states "any additional condo towers would be built in subsequent phases."

Cullinan said he was not aware of any issues with Sunseeker's scaled-back plan. "We're trying to digest it all ourselves," he said. The construction completion date has also been pushed back to fall 2020. Previous reports stated the resort planned to open in Feb. 2020....John Redmond, Allegiant's president, described the resort as a catalyst in Allegiant's evolution as a travel company.

"Sunseeker Resorts Charlotte Harbor will be nothing short of extraordinary – an incredible integrated resort experience that builds on the natural beauty of the area and brings tremendous value to guests and local residents," said Redmond. "And it marks the launch of an unprecedented pairing - a world class hospitality brand with an airline at its heart – which will bring synergies to our customers and spark innovation in truly transformative ways."[88]

Worse, the county was sinking a lot of eggs in one basket. Sunseeker was owned by Allegiant, the same low-budget airline that fuels economic development at the airport. But Charlotte County couldn't say no, the prospects looked to bright and shiny.

And then the pandemic came.

---

[88] PRNewswire, 4-20-9

CENTURY

Military Heritage Museum/ David Sussman

FREEDOM ISN'T FREE: HISTORY OF THE MILITARY HERITAGE MUSEUM

Gary Butler

  The Military Heritage Museum first opened its doors to the public in Fishermen's Village in Punta Gorda, Fla., on Pearl Harbor Day 2001. The goal of the Museum — then as now — was to honor veterans from all branches and eras of U.S. military service and to help the general public better understand the contributions and various experiences of American servicemen and women through authentic artifacts and individual stories.
  From the start, individual veterans and numerous veteran groups enthusiastically supported the Museum. They generously donated their own personal artifacts and funding; helped build display cases,

paint walls and lay carpet; and volunteered as docents. Retired Air Force Brig. Gen. Paul Warfield Tibbets, Jr., the famed pilot of the "Enola Gay," the plane that dropped the first atomic bomb on Japan, agreed to serve as the Museum's initial honorary chairman, a position he held until his death in 2007. At that point, Sean O'Keefe, a former Secretary of the Navy and former NASA Administrator, took over the role and continues to serve to this day.

Within six years of its grand opening, the Museum had grown significantly in artifacts, financial support, popularity within the community and annual number of visitors, who now hailed from all 50 states and other countries. This led to a move in 2007 to a larger space within Fishermen's Village that could accommodate the growth. This marked the Museum's first significant transformation into a more professionally managed museum. In 2013, the Museum expanded again, this time adding space on the second floor above the exhibit area to provide a conference center (available for rent), a military research library, administrative offices, and storage. As the Military Heritage Museum continued to grow in popularity, it gained a reputation among tourists and the local community as Southwest Florida's most treasured museum, in large part because of its personal touch. Veteran volunteers led all tours and offered visitors a unique perspective and understanding of key moments in history that cannot be obtained from a textbook.

By 2017, the Museum had once again outgrown its space, limiting the variety of services and experiences the Museum was able to provide. It also was unable to display many of its artifacts. In November 2018, the Museum obtained a lease to a much larger prominent, professionally designed and hurricane- and flood-resistant building located on the former IMPAC campus two blocks east of Fishermen's village. After significant renovations, the Museum opened in April 2019 in its new facility. This move allowed the Museum to better tell the stories and impact of the men and women who have served in all five U.S. military service branches across nearly four centuries and to better display and protect its priceless collections of artifacts, books, and photographs. Among the upgrades are more exhibit space, a 247-seat theater, library, flight and ship simulators, virtual reality experiences, and the latest in video displays, interactive capabilities, touchscreen technologies and educational youth programs. Today the Military Heritage Museum is one of the largest history museums located on the gulf coast south of the Florida panhandle and has become a family-friendly popular destination attraction for both residents and tourists.

LGBTQIA+ HISTORY OF CHARLOTTE COUNTY

Michelle Bone Williams

The LGBTQIA community in Charlotte County has been in every job field; we are your friends, and neighbors. In 2017, Statistics from Statista state that 1 in 100 people identify as LGBTQIA+. Historic LGBT people have been part of the community. Ollie Brackett, also known as "Big 6", was a transwoman who owned and ran a brothel in the area of Fisherman's Village during the beginning of the 1890s. According to local lore, her identity was determined upon her death in 1894.[89]

In the early 1920s a political official of Punta Gorda, owned a bar called "Mothers" where LGBTQIA people from all over the area would come to enjoy music and libations. The official himself was a gay man who liked to dress in women's attire. Allegedly, the bar was burned to the ground.

---

[89] https://pocketsights.com/tours/place/Ollie-Bracket-aka-Big-Six%5BPotters-Field%5D-29929

Malcolm Brenner

Several modern versions have sprung up. There have been four LGBTQIA establishments in Charlotte County—Charlotte's Web, The Forum, Pulse, and Masquerades.

In January of 1999, Glenn Ligneu and his partner, James, opened a small LGBT beer and wine dive bar called Charlotte's Web. The first openly LGBTQIA venue was located in the industrial area of Port Charlotte located off of SR 776 and US41. Shortly after opening, James died. Glenn and his beloved Charlotte's Web encouraged young and old to live their lives freely.

Unfortunately, times got hard for Glenn, and he closed Charlotte's Web in June of 2015. In 2016, Glenn died. He left a legacy of "come out, out, wherever you are and have a gay old time." What became Charlotte County Pride, an annual festival, was dedicated to him in 2016.

The Forum and Pulse Bar were opened by Jason Gotfried and a silent partner at different times. The Forum was only in place for a short time. The Pulse Bar was in business for over nine years and was sold in 2011. When my wife, Susan, and I purchased it, we decided to open the first LGBTQIA restaurant and cabaret bar called Masquerades. It became a destination for good food, libations, and exceptional drag shows. Entertainers came from all over the country to work there. Unfortunately, Masquerades only lasted until 2014. There has been no revival of LGBTQIA establishments since.

Charlotte County Pride was manifested in the Pulse Bar one day just by discussing the needs of the community. In 2012, Charlotte County Florida had their first LGBT Pride festival held at the Fairgrounds located on SR 776. In 2019, ARAY (All Rainbow and Allied Youth), a nonprofit that successfully has

> **LGBTQIA+ GROUPS of Charlotte County**
> **Equality Punta Gorda:** A gay centric organization that celebrates diversity and is all inclusive.
> www.equalitypuntagorda.org
> **SAGA/LGBT of Charlotte County:** Sexuality and gender acceptance group of Charlotte County. An inclusive group from LGBTQIA+ to allies. Community events, fundraising efforts, and helping our community. Facebook group only at this time.
> **ARAY:** LGBTQ+ youth organization

been meeting the needs of the LGBTQIA youth community with inclusion and advocacy, took over being the pride organization of Charlotte County. They held their first PEACE RIVER PRIDE January 18, 2020 at Laishley Park in Punta Gorda. It was a successful transition, and a welcomed change for this community.

In 2005/2006 a young gay male named Asher Levine (now a fashion designer) started a group called Gay Straight Alliance (GSA) at Port Charlotte High School. Over 75 students attended the first meeting. There was push ack not only from some parents, but also from students. Some students organized a countergroup called TAG "Together Against Gays" and generated a petition that attracted more than 100 signees asking the district to ban the group. A challenge from Westboro Baptist Church bigots caused it to weaken, but the group still remains at the high school.

On April 2nd of 2014, Punta Gorda City Council approved an ordinance that creates a Domestic Partnership registry for Punta Gorda. People from all walks of life, and orientations came in solidarity together wearing red shirts as a symbol of unification and asking the council to approve the domestic partnership registry. This was a huge moment for Punta Gorda as it was the first city in southwest Florida to act for decency.

A year later, on June 26, 2015, the U.S. Supreme Court struck down all state bans on same-sex marriage, therefore legalizing it in all 50 states.

CHARLOTTE COMMUNITY FOUNDATION

Ashley Maher
Executive Director

There is no doubt that Charlotte County is a vibrant community with caring residents; there may be no better example of that than by visiting our philanthropic side.

In 1995, after the sale of the Adventist Hospital in Punta Gorda, the Adventist Foundation, that had existed to support the hospital and health and education in Charlotte County, became a separate organization and transitioned into the Charlotte County Foundation.

Two of the founders, Leo Wotitzky, first Chairman of the Board and Vernon Peeples, a former Chairman and President, both of whose families can be traced back to the 1800's in Charlotte County, had a shared vision for the progress of the Foundation. Post Hurricane Charley, after a strategic planning workshop with leadership, the Board of Directors, and invited members of the community, a plan emerged with a stronger focus and attention to a broader area of the philanthropic needs of Charlotte County.

Charlotte Community Foundation

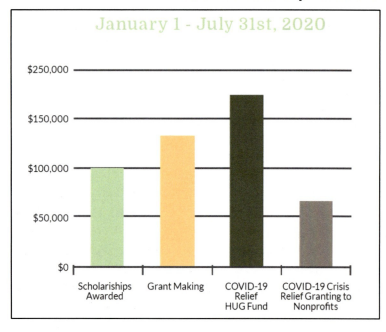

With the new clarity came a new name, Charlotte Community Foundation, that was more indicative of an organization serving the whole community. The Foundation has its roots in serving others but with a new vision, mission statement and broader direction it would expand its outreach. One of Vernon Peeples' goals for it was, "to make a greater impact on more people's lives."

Charlotte Community Foundation now serves a range of philanthropic passions driven by community need by partnering with many local nonprofits. Some areas of focus include Community Development, Human and Social Services, Arts and Culture, Youth Development, Natural Environment and Animal Welfare, while still serving Health and Wellness and Education as well as our veterans.

Our mission statement is "connecting people who care with causes that matter." Thanks to our generous donors and volunteers during our 25 years of serving Charlotte County we have bestowed a total of $9.2 million in funds to nonprofit organizations. Included were 68 Community Investment Grants that have helped local nonprofits to assist those most in need.

From the inception of our first scholarship, the Leo Wotitzky Scholarship Fund on November 15, 2006, to date we have awarded 152 scholarships with a total amount of $405,000 to deserving students that paved the way for those recipients to create a more positive future. We have also funded studies, such as our eight-year endeavor, Charlotte County Healthy Aging Study, that among other findings identified markers for Alzheimer's disease. These combined efforts have been making an impact on many people's lives.

With the challenges that faced our residents due to the unwelcome arrival of COVID-19, through our leadership role in forming the COAD (Community Organizations Active in a Disaster) partnership with Charlotte County Human Services, United Way of Charlotte County, and Gulf Coast Partnership, that resulted in the HUG (Hand Up Grant) Fund receiving $200,000, including match donations from Cheryl Berlon and the James and Marian Pennoyer Fund, that were distributed to those most affected, we were able to continue fulfilling our mission.

2020 is our 25th anniversary year and during all these years we have had the privilege of working with many caring and hardworking nonprofit organizations. We have our ears to the pulse of life in Charlotte County. By continually convening and collaborating we stay abreast of changing issues and needs.

It has allowed us to act quickly to address them. Our combined efforts have helped in each of our target areas of philanthropy, our goal being to enhance the quality of life for all residents.

In 2019 we saw a partnership form between Charlotte County Homeless Coalition and Charlotte County Habitat for Humanity that provides a program to address homelessness more adequately to homeownership, thanks to one of our generous donors, Millie Hill.

A People's History of Charlotte County

Charlotte Community Foundation

We were able to organize and convene the Community Roundtable in June 2020 hosted by Charlotte County Sheriff's Office and Punta Gorda Police Department, that brought together concerned members of several organizations, representatives from government and our schools, to address equality in law enforcement.

Throughout our 25 years we have been involved many positive actions and programs, all of which were a result of the vision of Vernon Peeples and Leo Wotitzky, to "make a greater impact on more people's lives." Our leadership, present Board of Directors and staff have continuing goals such as providing the means for a Community Assessment Study and convening another round table that will address equality in education and expanding our family of donors to be able to do more. Each of these remain true to this vision. Our enduring history, as it weaves its story of assisting those most in need, is one that will continue to honor their ideals. When Charlotte County's 200th anniversary is celebrated we are sure that Charlotte Community Foundation will still be here. Perhaps due to our continuing efforts the needs will be different. We hopefully will have helped to break the cycle of poverty and the resulting enhanced equality in the lives of those living in 2121 will have created an even better place that future generations will be proud to call home.

SAY HER NAME

Naomi Pringle

"Say her name," a voice blasted the order. "Breonna Taylor," marchers responded firing off the dead woman's name.

Like infantry at the ready, troops of senior citizens, college students, high schoolers and young children holding fast to their parents' hands hoisted homemade signs with slogans printed in large block letters. They unfurled Black Lives Matter banners which spanned four sometimes five abreast while others waved cardboard placards bearing photos of innocent black people put to death by police.

The 'March for Justice' launch was at Laishley Park in Punta Gorda. It was a late spring evening with rain in the forecast. Covid precautions were to be observed and most marchers wore facial masks and kept six feet apart.

"Say his name," a female voice called from the ranks of the boots on the ground.

"George Floyd," marchers answered, paying

homage to the slain man who bore the weight of a cop's knee on his neck for eight minutes and forty-six seconds.

In moments marchers stepped off the curb. The parade followed a route to the Justice Center on East Marion. Along the way, while onlookers who supported the cause jumped into the march adding their voices to the loud and clear shout out of victims' names-- a dozen, maybe more, white veterans and their supporters stood watching—arms crossed or akimbo. They'd heard about the rally. The meet-up was not far from The Wall, which listed the names of the dead from their own long battle. Vets dressed in present day fatigues—uniform service jackets and jeans. They sported ball caps memorializing their tours of

Betsy Williams

duty--some wore sunglasses in the cloudy light, but dark shades could not disguise disgust nor disdain for this parade when none had ever been feted for them or fallen comrades victims too, of injustice.

Later, as speaker after speaker called for change or prayed for peace—I thought of a former love, a black man—who was stopped repeatedly by police. He drove a BMW with New York Press plates. Cops thought he'd stolen the Bimmer. He'd show them his New York Times photographer I D, but they still told him to step out of the car. He also served in the Vietnam war. He'd been shot down while bailing from a helicopter flying over Cambodia, a place the U.S. Government claimed we were never involved. When he got back to the States—a victim of exposure to the U.S. defoliant Agent Orange—the veterans department made another claim—Agent Orange did not cause his liver disease therefore he did not qualify for disability benefits. When he suffered from what we now call PTSD—and he and I described the symptoms—the government denied that, also. Years later after my dear friend died at age 38—the powers that be decided there were a lot of diseases caused by Agent Orange and a lot of men and women did suffer from PTSD—oh gee, thank you America, I thought.

As the Black Lives Matter March ended that evening in June, participants offered a final shout-out:
"What do we want?"
"JUSTICE"
"When do we want it?"
"NOW"

THE BALLAD OF TIM BERINI

Sue Wade

Among the scrub pines along Florida's Myakka River, history is too quickly overgrown. Tim Berini knew that.

Over a century ago, in 1919, Boston-area real estate developer Joel Bean had purchased enough land there for a glittering waterfront "City of Destiny."

The first buildings at the city's Garden Road hub, meant to serve an anticipated flood of tourists and investors, were a utilitarian wood-frame post office/general store (also train station for the railroad connecting Arcadia and Boca Grande) and a hotel catering largely to fishermen. Originally called the Grand Hotel and Fishing Lodge, the inn had 24 guest rooms, a lobby, office, dining room, kitchen and two bathrooms. Bean intended both rough structures to be replaced with grander rebuilds in the Mediterranean Revival style.

The 1929 stock market crash toppled all of his dreams.

A People's History of Charlotte County

The overgrown entrance to the old hotel/ Sue Wade all photos

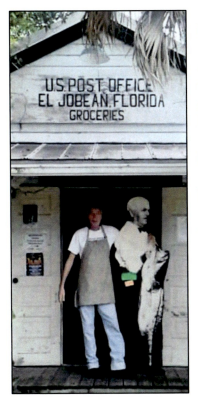

By 1931, the only inhabitants of El Jobean were Bean himself, tourists, and a scattering of early residents.

But the hotel continued to attract fishermen, carnies, and circus folk.

Among them were San Antonio daredevil Leopold "Suicide" Simon (aka "The Human Firecracker") and his wife, Donna, who'd crisscrossed the country with traveling carnivals and circuses throughout the 1930s, then settled down in El Jobean.

Almost totally blind and deaf toward the end, Leo insisted on continuing to drive, with Donna riding shotgun, hollering directions. Against all odds, he died of natural causes in 1972, leaving to his wife the estate that Tim Berini would carry on.

No one better understood how easily the past can slip through our fingers than Berini, who devoted himself to preserving it from the day he arrived in El Jobean.

He once claimed he didn't much care about history. But the Michigan native, who'd built custom motorcycles all his life, was hooked fast by El Jobean itself; by its founder, Joel Bean; and by colorful former resident Leopold "Suicide" Simon.

Berini himself would become El Jobean's most unforgettable character.

Tall and lanky, really nothing like the stocky Texas stuntman, Berini nevertheless channeled Simon's spirit in the town Christmas parade, riding an old Cub Cadet lawnmower and wearing an airman's helmet, goggles and a "Suicide Simon for President" T-shirt. He befriended Donna and got better acquainted with her late husband's story.

His son, Don, remembers riding, never in a car, but on a motorcycle, his diapers stuffed into his dad's back pocket.

"He'd hold me on the tank when I wasn't big enough to sit up. When he bought a Christmas tree, he'd have the guy selling them strap it to his back. Once, he got pulled over, his arms and legs sticking out of a Christmas tree.

"As a kid I'd hear stories like Suicide Simon conditioning himself for high dives by jumping, chest first, off a barstool."

In her eighties, Donna Simon would ask young Don, "You know the most important thing in life? Staying flexible!" Then she'd bend over, knees locked, and lay her forearms flat on the ground.

For Don, it was like growing up in a circus.

"I grew up thinking that's just the way people are. But get out in the real world and they start telling you, 'Wow, those are some crazy, neat people!'

"My dad was El Jobean's biggest fan. It's a special place, there's no denying it—everything from the vegetation to the unique people who gravitate there. Pop used to say, 'This place is special. It's Old Florida, and it's not always going to be like this.'"

Trying to keep the place the way it had always been, Tim and two partners acquired the last 3.5 acres of Joel Bean's century-old community after Donna died.

Tim at once set about preserving the modest center of Bean's planned metropolis. In 1998 he opened Bean Depot Café & Museum—a museum, café and bluegrass stomping grounds—in the old depot at the foot of the abandoned railroad bridge.

Printed on the back of its menu, alongside the beer and wine list, is Tim's vow "to preserve the site as an attraction to include a museum, time period luncheonette, bait and tackle, and a boutique to be operated out of the Post Office/Railroad Depot structure, and the fishing lodge as a time period bed and breakfast." Beside it he proudly reproduced the site's National Register of Historic Places certificate, which he'd worked tirelessly to obtain.

But El Jobe-An Hotel, last open to the public 60 years ago, is almost completely overwhelmed with palmettos. Suicide Simon's show trailers, left on the grounds, are rust-rotted down to the tires. Despite staying open most days since Tim opened it, the Bean Depot Café & Museum went shuttered and dark during the coronavirus pandemic.

Its facade is classic general store— "Live Bait" sign, front porch lined with chairs. But a faded flamingo peers quizzically down from the gutter, and a bicycle unaccountably dangles in a nearby tree.

After demolition started in 2019 at the equally historic 14-acre Fishery property in nearby Placida, Tim saved a rusty anchor and its hand-lettered plaque from the site, giving them a place of honor in the café's yard.

"Man, was he proud of that," said Don. "He wasn't in the best of health and didn't have the money to hire a crew to move it, but he got it done."

Two months later, before he could even consider restoring the El Jobe-An Hotel, Tim Berini, 65, guardian of history, died—half an hour after his son had arrived to say goodbye.

"He never once went to a doctor," said Don. "Didn't want fire engines and ambulances coming to the house, but he did agree to hospice. It's amazing how much he hung on, given his condition. The only thing that reminded me of him in the end was his eyes, and when you looked into his eyes, you could still see the good there. I got to give him a hug and joke with him, and I swear he gave me a jab though he could barely lift his arms."

On October 20, 2020, Don Berini reopened the Bean Depot Café & Museum. His dream, mirroring his father's, is: "Not change it, but make it a better version of what it already is."

He's installed a phone and takes credit cards, but won't change the menu much.

At the end of October, Charlotte County placed a historical marker directly across Garden Road from the depot, to honor the historic heart of El Jobean which Tim Berini had kept beating.

They've even discussed a future for the hotel.

THE SNOW BIRDS
David Abraham

Every year in the fall, when the leaves turn rainbow colors, the geese fly free and blacken the sky with their silhouettes on their way south. I too, with my wife of sixty years, pack the car and away we go following the geese as they go.

I start by traveling south from my home on Route 8, a back-country road, with many farmer sheds and cows to show. I stay the course until we get to Sidney, a small town we visit as a gas stop and watering hole.

After a cup of coffee we leave Sidney and that two-lane road and continue on to Binghamton on Route 88, a four-lane interstate. The drive is about a half-hour long and soon we are on Route 81 south through Pennsylvania with the Pocono Mountains all around. Pennsylvania is the worst section of road of our trip. But that interstate carries us to Route 64 where I turn east for Richmond, Virginia. More mountains are in my mirror. As the four-lane road we adore passes along the Blue Ridge divide, the valleys and mountains are too beautiful to hide. For two hours I hold the road until the car merges onto Route 288.

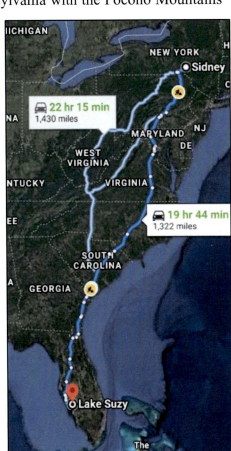

By now the sky is beginning to turn purple-gray and my Johanne pauses her knitting.

"We better start looking for a place to stay," she says. In Petersburg I glide onto I-95 and pass a sign for lodging up ahead. Johanne peruses the motel offerings and selects one she deems to be fit; she is sometimes wrong. The Hampton Inn is where we stayed until the long night darkness turns to light the next day and we change the clocks back as we start on our way. We didn't even stay for a breakfast because the coronavirus frightened us away. We did, however, stop for coffee a short way down the road as we continued on I-95. We were St. Augustine-bound. Three hours through North Carolina and another three through South Carolina brought us into peachy Georgia and its red clay scenery. The day again was closing in as we went from Savannah down into Florida. We only stopped for gas and convenience. When we reached St. Augustine, we found a place to stay; it was near the many outlets so Johanne had her way. Back on 95 south we headed for Ft. Pierce where I gassed up and took SR170 west through Lake Okeechobee, rich in history. A two-hour drive took us to Arcadia, where I intersected onto SR17 south then SR776 and on to Lake Suzy to my Florida home.

Betsy Williams

2020

DREAMS AND DISILLUSIONMENT

Dr. Sharon MacClaren

Nothing exhibited the death of dreams and the onset of disillusionment as the silent cranes of the abandoned Sunseeker development. All the hopes tied up in what had been billed as a transformational project are now dashed. But those losses pale beside the human losses in friendships, relationships, and the ultimate loss—of life itself.

For many in Charlotte County, the first sign that something very bad was unfolding came during the last year of the teens, in 2020.

News came of the tragic loss of academician Dr. Sharon MacLaren. She had been on a cruise ship with her partner when she died, an early victim of Covid. Dr. MacLaren, born in 1940, was a professor who came to Charlotte to lead the Cultural Center's educational component. She soon became a popular lecturer and raconteur. She died on April 4, 2020, age 79 from complications of the COVID-19 virus. Because the president had yet to figure out how to address what fast was becoming a crisis, the ship MacLaren sailed on was forced to anchor offshore for days as

A People's History of Charlotte County

2020
County population is 188,910, an 18.1 percent increase over 2010

March through July deaths attributable to covid

Date	Deaths
3.11.20	2
3.18.20	7
3.25.20	22
4.1.20	87
4.8.20	309
4.15.20	609
4.22.20	910
4.29.29	1240
5.6.20	1605
5.13.20	1898
5.20.20	2173
5.27.20	2400
6.3.20	2650
6.10.20	2889
6.17.20	3110
6.24.20	3489
7.1.20	3650
7.8.20	3991
7.15.20	4626
7.22.20	5183

friends and loved ones waited in anguish. In short order the death knell began to sound with grim regularity.

Isaac Thomas, a stalwart scion of Punta Gorda's black community with a local legacy that went back generations, left this world in Thomas had been a frontline soldier, one of the first generation of black students to integrate Charlotte High School. Thomas, the son of a leading spiritual leader, served in Vietnam and came home to eventually pastor St. Mary Primitive Baptist Church. He was also once the director of New Operation Cooper Street Center, built on the site of the former segregated black Baker Academy.

Those who knew him spoke of his strength and vision for the church that rebuilt from Hurricane Charley, when Thomas stepped up the way his father had to rebuild and expand the congregation.

Civil rights icons John Henry Allen, on porch, Gertha Haddock, and Isaac Thomas.

And the icons continued to leave us. Eunice Gault Albritton, a matriarch of Englewood's once-thriving fishing industry, also died in 2020. Eunice carried on for her father who had built The Fishery in Placida into a commercial fishing hub at the mouth of Coral Creek. Fish were shipped over all the world from Placida and the fishery was one of the largest producers of mullet in Florida.

The Albrittons carried on the business at the fish house until voters called for the state commercial gill-net ban in 1995 that crippled commercial mullet fishing.

But those are the public deaths, the ones that merit newspaper headlines and which leave gaps in the public fabric of our lives. But what of the thousands who died here in Florida, victims not only of a pandemic but also of politics gone bad?

Relationships frayed, institutions crumbled, and loved ones perished as a president turned what should have been a common cause against a pandemic into a political football. And as national politics grew more divisive, so did local affairs. Governing bodies seeking to do the right thing were bullied and shouted down by citizens who felt wearing masks or shutting down facilities were invasions of personal liberty.

Some relations flourished in the months of stay-at-home orders while others languished. Likewise, institutions withered and died while Zoom and other platforms brought a new way of doing things to those with the withal to learn.

Unsung heroes included health care professionals who faced the pandemic head on and school personnel, who honored an arbitrary back-to-the-classroom edict in such a way as to minimize Covid infection.

The Lifelong Learning Institute was the first institution to fall, a victim of diminishing attendance and a lack of capacity for distance learning. Florida Gulf Coast University's Herald Court Centre tried the

CENTURY

Zoom route, but never mastered it. They folded as well. Shuttered restaurants meant jobs lost, even as some vendors learned quickly how to master deliver and take-out techniques. Most of them survived.

Midway through the pandemic, during the worst wave, a look at the daily paper gave a succinct account of Charlotte county's new way of life. Like men and women around the country, county residents squared off over wearing masks, coped with the lax reopening policies of the governor, and saw a drastic cutback in elective surgeries because of surging Covid cases.

Amid the fear and desperation, however, some folks not only survived, but thrived in the new environment.

Banker Maryann Mize, for example, continued regular church services for her family via social medias, making a joyful noise every Sunday. Businesses such as The Yoga Sanctuary grew online, virtual audiences that may continue to swell even as stay-at-home orders cease.

But probably the grimmest symbol of what was lost in the pandemic is made up of six giant towers and skeletal members of the colossus that may never come to be, Sunseeker. In a terse statement released shortly after the pandemic struck full force, Allegiant CEO John Redmond gave the grim news:

> We at Sunseeker Resort Charlotte Harbor are entirely focused on the experience of our guests and team members. Our priority is always your health and safety. Because of the evolving COVID-19 (Coronavirus) pandemic, we are saddened to inform you we have halted all work on Sunseeker Resort Charlotte Harbor until further notice.
>
> This action is to ensure the wellbeing of all parties involved with Sunseeker Resorts, including team members, construction workers and future guests. At this time, we will be canceling all future reservations without penalty and issuing full refunds on any deposits or full payments collected. In addition, the ability to make new reservations will be placed on hold for now.
>
> This was not an easy decision, but we are adhering to the latest information and protocols from the world's leading health experts and government authorities. We will keep you informed on all future developments and cannot wait to welcome you to back for "your piece of the sun" at Sunseeker Resort Charlotte Harbor.

July through December

Date	Deaths
7.29.20	6457
8.5.20	7751
8.12.20	8898
8.19.20	10067
8.26.20	10872
9.2.20	11651
9.9.20	12269
9.16.20	13100
9.23.20	13782
9.30.20	14488
10.7.20	15372
10.14.20	15788
10.21.20	16308
10.28.20	16775
11.4.20	17131
11.11.20	17512
11.18.20	17949
11.25.20	18482
12.2.20	19012

A People's History of Charlotte County

December through March 2021

Date	Deaths
12.9.20	19716
12.16.20	20490
12.30.20	21857
1.6.21	22647
1.13.21	23759
1.20.21	24965
1.27.21	26249
2.3.21	27472

Late one day almost a year after the pandemic struck our county as the awful year of 2020 drew to a close, news came of the death of Mac Horton, an unselfish icon who steered his community of Englewood along with both Charlotte and Sarasota county, toward improving the lives of many. He died on Dec. 4 of Covid, a premature end to a life of service. His death punctuated a sad year full of untimely ends and uncertain beginnings. As the *Sarasota Herald-Tribune* described him:

Maryann Mize

Maryann Mize and family at Sunday Service

Horton served on the Englewood Water District board, was on the Charlotte County School Board for 12 years, was a county commissioner for eight years and ended his career in 2008 as Charlotte's supervisor of elections. The Mac Horton West County Annex opened last December on San Casa Drive in Englewood. The Winchester Boulevard extension, a 3-mile-long, four-lane road that connects Placida residents with River Road, was named in honor of Horton when it opened in 2015. He was the first to drive on the road, and news photos show him tooling down Winchester Boulevard as a passenger in a white Jeep.

The Charlotte Sun

Horton's legacy brings to mind one of Lincoln's best speeches, during which he referred to us the living. He meant that our job was to learn from past sacrifices in order to build both a better life for us and a greater world for posterity.

Charlotte County has faced a World War, too many hurricanes, devastating fires, a Great Depression and a Great Recession. Red tide and green algae, years flush in the black and years deep in the red, all are part and parcel of our story. Charlotte is indeed the county that couldn't say no. Now, as we emerge from the pandemic to a world very different from what once was normal, maybe county residents can embrace their shared past and say yes to a better future

EPILOGUE

The book began with a sweep around the crescent, from Englewood through Murdock and points south to Punta Gorda. One of the most comprehensive, human, and humane snapshots of the same area is the 2020 Community Health and Needs Assessment Report, compiled as a collaborative effort of the Florida Department of Health in Charlotte County, Charlotte County Human Services, Charlotte Behavioral Health Care, United Way of Charlotte County, and the Health Planning Council of Southwest Florida. Below is a reproduction of its community capsules, which neatly define the three major population areas of Charlotte County.

ENGLEWOOD has the lowest population size of the three major population centers at 14,863, of which 15 percent are veterans. Fifty-one percent of its population are 65 or over. Similar to Punta Gorda, 95.4 percent of the population are white, however, 4.3 percent are Hispanic or Latino, 2.2 percent are Asian, 1.5 percent are two or more races, and 0.2 percent are black or African American. Females make up 50.1 percent of the population and males, 49.9 percent. Of the number of persons 5 years and over, 8.7 percent speak a language other than English at home.

Twenty-four percent of the Englewood population have a bachelor's degree or higher and 93.3 percent have a high school diploma or higher with an area workforce participation rate of 34 percent.

A People's History of Charlotte County

Between 2014 and 2018, 79.9 percent of housing units were owner-occupied with a median value of $162,300 and a median monthly owner cost of $404. There were also 7,547 households with an average of 2.01 persons per household. The median household income and the median per capita income is significantly lower than Punta Gorda at $48,793 and $32,847, respectively. The area's poverty rate is, therefore, higher than Punta Gorda's at 11.1 percent.

PORT CHARLOTTE

has an estimated population of 54,392; 12 percent are veterans, the lowest percent proportionally of all three areas. As the most populous of the three regions within Charlotte County, Port Charlotte has a slightly more diverse population by race and ethnicity and the largest percentage of individuals in the county population who are foreign born at 13.5 percent. Racially, 84 percent are white, 10.1 percent are black or African American, 9.5 percent are Hispanic or Latino, 3.3 percent are two or more races, and 1.4 percent are Asian. Additionally, 12.1 percent of persons age 5 years and over speak a language other than English at home.

Of all the three areas, Port Charlotte was the least educated, with only 18.9 percent of persons age 25 years or over having a bachelor's degree or higher and 89.5 percent of persons 25 years or over having a high school diploma or higher.

Between 2014 and 2018, the percent of owner-occupied housing units was 75.6 percent with a median home value of $150,200, the lowest in the county. Median monthly owner costs were $402. Port Charlotte has the highest number of households and the highest number of persons per household at 24,578 and 2.47, respectively.

PUNTA GORDA

has a population of 20,057, representing roughly 12 percent of the overall county population; veterans represent 20 percent of the city's population at 3,408. The most recent U.S. Census Bureau estimates report that as of 2018, the city is 95.3 percent white, 2.4 percent black or African American, and 6.1 percent Hispanic or Latino. Well over half of the city's population (56.1 percent) are persons 65 years and over and females are the majority gender at 53.1 percent. Roughly 9 percent speak a language other than English at home and 8 percent of the population are foreign born.

The percent of persons with a bachelor's degree or higher is the highest of all three Charlotte County regions at 38.9 percent, while 94.5 percent have a high school diploma or higher. The city has a 30.9 percent workforce participation rate, which is the lowest in Charlotte County, FL.

2020 Community Health and Needs Assessment Report

In **Charlotte County**, the median rental price for a two-bedroom home is **$1,350 per month** as of July 2018. Conservatively estimating $100 per month in utilities costs, that totals **$17,400 annually in housing costs**. In order to afford this level of home – without paying more than 30% of income on housing – a household must earn **$4,833 monthly or $58,000 annually**. Assuming a 40-hour work week, 52 weeks per year, **this level of income translates into:**

an hourly Housing Wage of **$27.88** /per hour

Minimum Wage: **$8.25** per hour

Average Hourly Wage in Charlotte County: **$18.33** per hour

Average Monthly Social Security (SSI) Check: **$1,180**

Work Hours per week at Minimum Wage to afford the home: **135**

Number of Full Time Jobs at Minimum Wage to afford the home: **3.4**

A shortage of affordable housing, tied to a low wage base, is a problem facing county residents, particularly in Englewood and Port Charlotte where incomes are less.

CENTURY

Between 2014 and 2018, Punta Gorda had 9,825 households with an average size of 1.93. Eighty-one percent of housing units were owner-occupied with a median value of $313,200. Median monthly owner costs were $740 while the median gross rent was $998. Punta Gorda also has a higher median household income and a higher per capita income than Charlotte County and the nation at $61,598 and $45,839, respectively. As a result, the percent of persons in poverty is also the lowest in the region and below the national rate at 9.2 percent.

To understand and prepare for Charlotte County's future, go to the low-rent district. It's where the failed come to rest and the strivers set forth. Both parties have stories to tell about how they got there and how they're trying to get out. And in those stories you can see both the past and the future as clearly as a view through a storefront window.

https://www.sunnydellproperties.com/property/office-spaces-for-rent-in-port-charlotte/

Sunnydell Plaza looks like most older strip malls in Port Charlotte—-and the community has plenty. Its architecture speaks of a past when long, low, lean facades of glass were mall signatures. The cupolas and towers that mark the post-Tuscan style of mall architecture in the late 20th century has eclipsed the old-line strip malls like Sunnydell. And it is the low-rent district: 700 square feet of space for $700. Rents average twice as much up and down Tamiami Trail, from Murdock to Punta Gorda.

But Sunnydell Plaza is a place with a past and a place filled with promise. It's the original Charlotte County campus of Edison College, which is now SouthWestern College of Florida. John Davenport recalls taking classes in the strip mall and how what he learned propelled him from being a correctional officer to commanding the Charlotte County Sheriff's department.

The only predominantly Anglo entities in the mall are the Democratic Party and Democratic Club offices located at the point where the bank of shops make a right turn, what military men call refusing the line. Across from the Democrats is a Haitian church. Close by is a thinly stocked *carniceria*, a laundromat, and a shop that does business in things few Anglos buy. *Envios,* which are remittances home to relatives south of the border, passport and immigration information, are all sold in Sunnydell Plaza. That speaks to the growing influx of Hispanic-speaking families. Hispanic speakers make up the largest minority in the Charlotte County School District and their numbers are growing.

Most of that growth is taking place in Port Charlotte.

A People's History of Charlotte County

Charlotte County Community Development

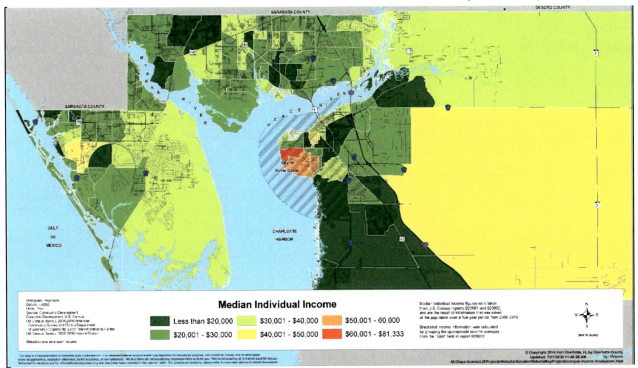

Perversely and inversely, green represents lack of wealth while red symbolizes the greatest wealth. Below, the school census reflects two immediate challenges; there's a large number of students ready to step into post-high school jobs or education and a growing number of minority students in the district.

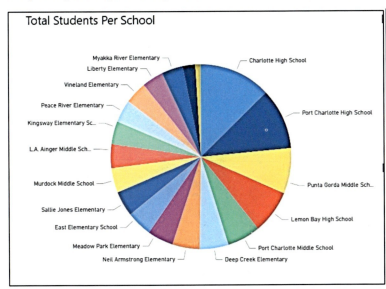

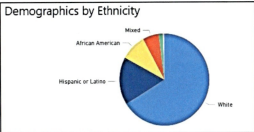

Charlotte County Public Schools

If Sunnydell Plaza continues its role as a social mobility launching platform, then many of the families who pray, shop, or use the services in the mall will soon become as much a part of the community as any snowbird from Michigan or upstate New York who knows the route down and back here like the back of a hand.

But is the community ready? CHAIR Cesar Ramirez, chairman of the Democratic Hispanic Caucus of Florida, said once that defining Hispanics is like describing east Asians—the diversity is too broad to categorize with one label. There are older Hispanics from South America who have little in common with immigrants from Central America or even Mexico. Because of the large hospital employee count in the county, many Filipino allied health workers are making our community their home. Their growing numbers speak to an emerging challenge, as Charlotte County is not a diverse community and has not been one for years. Actually, the proportion of minorities—particularly blacks—in the county dropped precipitously when gang labor industries such as timbering and turpentine tapping or large ranches such as that owned by A.C. Frizzell ceased operations.

The county school district, arguably the most democratic (definitely small "d") and ubiquitous institution in the county because of its census of students and staff, only ended segregation sixty years ago and, judging by news stories[90] and discussions with students and staff, still wrestles with issues of inclusion. Charlotte County has never come to grips with diversity and will face an even greater challenge as more people of color who speak a different first language come here seeking the same opportunities as those who came before. They're already here and are doing the best they can—just look to places like Sunnydell Plaza.

Or, again, look to the past, when people who shared their stories in the pages of this book also did the best they could. When Christine Goff Maerski's boy Steve had a school vacation, he'd travel from Brooklyn down to Charlotte County to spend time with his Uncle Woody. Woodrow Goff was a well-known builder who'd often pack up his crew and their wives for a combination build-out and week-long barbecue on Captiva Island. But for Steve, Uncle Woody was his tour guide to a place of wonder.

"Every morning I woke up with a fishing rod in one hand and a gun in the other," McDermit recalled.

He still lives near Charlotte County, farther down the coast in Bonita, a short drive from the assisted care facility where his mom lives. Christine Goff Maerski loves to talk about growing up in Charlotte County. After six decades of marriage and a life in New York, she returned to the area when her husband passed.

When Aratha Jones' husband retired from the military, she knew home was where she wanted to be. She now lives near Punta Gorda, close enough to be an active member of her church, All Souls Harbor, in the city. Her accomplishments of which she is most proud include her family.

Steve McDermit's summers in Charlotte County influenced his decisions to join the Navy and become a charter boat captain. Below, his mom, Christina Goff Maerski.

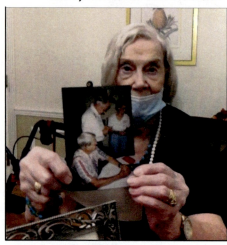

Aratha Jones and her husband gather with her two sons, three daughters, and their spouses./Aratha Jones

---

[90] Charlotte Sun-Herald, Mar 27, 2019

A People's History of Charlotte County

Ellison Haddock has found peace while Bob Roberts can't stop selling.

"You know, when you get to be my age most of those people you knew have gone on to glory," she says. "I have had a wonderful life; I have three children—two of them are engineers and one of them is a contractor. We have five grandchildren as well."

Aaron "Jim" Marshal lives in El Jobean, in a huge home he's trying to sell. Like Aratha Jones, He's proud of his church and, like Aratha Jones, was a big part of All Souls Harbor's recent commemoration.

Frank Desquin, Marilyn Smith-Mooney, Bob Roberts, and Lindsay Harrington are still active members of the community in 2021.

Bob shows up regularly at age 98 to man the Century-21 office in Port Charlotte.

Smith-Mooney helped rescue the Military Heritage Museum, was a key volunteer in the botanical gardens, and still serves as a consultant on community matters.

Frank continues his mom's legacy of running an attenuated Charlotte county Historical Society and Lindsay Harrington would love to show you some of the county's last frontier, east of I-75, as a lead salesman with the Punta Gorda Coldwell-Banker office.

Odie Futch looks to be at peace with the world. He has all the comforts of outdoor living, including a swing, under his oak tree. He's content to sit there and remember, baron of his piece of land in a corner of the empire once owned by A. C. Frizzell.

"We have to be, so we should be in harmony," said Ellison Haddock, now an associate pastor at First Macedonia Baptist Church.

It's our job to pass these stories on, to help young people and those who'll never meet us understand that we too lived, cried, laughed, and died. Some of the people who shared their words in this book are still with us. Others are gone. But their voices, living and dead, disparate and as alike as two peas in a pod, speak to us. It is to be hoped that they speak well and wisely to generations yet unborn.

CENTURY

Ginger Abraham

THANKS

I wish to thank the Charlotte County Libraries & History division of Community Services, specifically historian Jennifer Zoebelein and Community Services Director Tommy Scott, for their assistance and for maintaining an accessible and exhaustive collection of county history.

Charlotte County Historical Center Society, specifically Frank Desguin, for its fidelity to the original goals of that organization, to educate through hands-on exhibits and lectures.

The CCHC Society is a private, non-profit organization supporting Charlotte County History Services with fundraising, volunteers & membership.

For more information, call 941.613.3228 or email at ccmuseumsociety@gmail.com.

Maryann Mize, one of the county's most prolific bankers who was willing to help find a generation of men and women who deserved to have their stories told.

Steve McDerment, whose pride in his Goff heritage led him to contact me and introduce me to his mother, Christine Goff Maerski. Both of them are good people who shared freely with me.

Cheryl and Paul Frizzell, whose experiences growing up in Charlotte County enliven this book. Cheryl's book, "A.C. Frizzell, His Family, Life, and Times," is a valuable addition to Charlotte County history and a treasured resource in writing this book.

Charles Peck, whose photography made this book come alive.

Other resources that I found of value and that are gracious when it comes to community requests are included in this list of historical contacts published by the Charlotte County Libraries & History Services division.

A People's History of Charlotte County

Arts & Humanities Council of Charlotte County - www.charlottearts.org
Charlotte County Genealogical Society - webliaison@ccgsi.org | www.ccgsi.org
Charlotte Harbor Environmental Center - www.checflorida.org
Florida Public Archaeology Network, Southwest Regional Center - flpublicarchaeology.org/swrc

Englewood
Barrier Island Parks Society, Inc. - www.barrierislandparkssociety.org
Boca Grande Historical Society - www.bocagrandehistoricalsociety.com
El Jobean Community League - heraldhosting.net/otherwebsites/eljobeannews
Friends of Cayo Costa State Park - friendsofcayocosta.org
Lemon Bay Historical Society - www.lemonbayhistory.com

Punta Gorda
Babcock Wilderness Adventures - www.babcockranch.com
Blanchard House Museum of African American History & Culture - www.blanchardhousemuseum.org
City of Punta Gorda Historic Preservation Advisory Board - novuspublic.ci.punta-gorda.fl.us/Boards.aspx?BoardID=11&Filter=3
Military Heritage Museum - www.freedomisntfree.org
Ponce de Leon Conquistadors - www.conquistadors-florida.com
Punta Gorda Historical Society - www.puntagordahistory.com
Punta Gorda History Center - puntagordahistorycenter.blogspot.com
TEAM Punta Gorda - www.teampuntagorda.org
Punta Gorda Historic Mural Society - www.puntagordamurals.org

Port Charlotte
Sons of Confederate Veterans, 2nd Lt. Joel Knight Chapter - poniu1@aol.com

Other Local Groups
Collier County Museums - www.colliermuseums.com
DeSoto County Historical Society - www.historicdesoto.org
Sarasota County Historical Resources - www.scgov.net/History
SWFL Museum of History - www.museumofhistory.org
Warm Mineral Springs & Little Salt Spring Archaeological Society - fasweb.org/wmslssas

A special thank you is due the History Services division of county government.
The staff of History Services are committed to the preservation of and education about Charlotte County. Each bring their own professional abilities and personal passion for history (art history, history education, archival history) in order to better serve the Charlotte County community. Archivist Samuel Alexander joined History Services in November 2019, after graduating with a Master of Library and Information Science from the University of South Carolina in 2018. Samuel's work includes describing materials in the archives; updating the archival database; fulfilling patron research requests; preserving the historical collections; improving the archives and himself to meet the latest professional standards of the field, which includes taking an active part in the Society of American Archivists and striving for certificates to benefit the archives.
Program Coordinator Crystal Diff earned a B.A. in Art from Florida Gulf Coast University and has ten years of experience in archives, exhibits and art education. She has been the program coordinator for History Services for over 6 years and works to share vibrant local history with the public in meaningful and interactive ways. Although communicating virtually right now, Crystal is normally found out in community libraries, parks, schools, cemeteries, and meeting centers presenting programs, exhibits, and activities for all ages. Crystal has also spearheaded self-guided tours and programs including History Quest, which involves geocaching and questing at historic sites across Charlotte County.

CENTURY

Assistant Joe Guerzo joined History Services in 2016, having received his B.A. in U.S. History from SUNY Buffalo in 1995 and previously working for the University of Georgia and the Atlanta Braves Museum and Hall of Fame. In addition to assisting the other History Services staff, Joe started the Charlotte County Oral History Program in 2017. Since then, he has conducted around 50 interviews with long-time county residents and in the last year, Joe expanded the program to include a monthly oral history interview in front of a live audience and led an instructional program for the public called "How to Record a Family Oral History."

Historian Dr. Jennifer Zoebelein joined History Services in November 2019, following the completion of her Ph.D. in 2018 and work at the National WWI Museum and Memorial in Kansas City. A native of Long Island and very passionate about history, Jennifer is the supervisor for History Services, overseeing all programs, exhibits and archive collections while also assisting the public with research requests. Having participated in the 150th anniversary of the Civil War as a National Park Service ranger in 2011 and the 100th anniversary of World War I in 2017–2018,

A People's History of Charlotte County

PEOPLE, PLACES, AND THINGS

1944 Cuba–Florida hurricane, 77
Abraham, David, 245
Ace Hardware, 56, 93
Acline, 51, 102
Adams, Hugh, 132, 147
Adams, W.H., 44
Addison, Judi Duff, 124, 155
Addison. Judi Duff, 132
Ainger, 24, 64, 69
Ainger, L. A., 174
Airport Road, 39, 163, 210, 211
Albert W. Gilchrist Bridge, 185
Albrecht, Albert, 161
Albritton, Eunice M. Gault, 247
Alexander, Buddy C., 36
Alexander, Samuel, 257
Alford, G. Floyd, 114
Allapatchee Lodge, 51
Allchin, Harold and Alice, 207
Allegiant Airlines, 28
Allen, Bob, 185
Allen, John Henry, 132, 137
Allen, Ralph, 185, 186
Alligator Creek, 51, 140
Allison, Ruth, 120
Alwood, Bob, 161
Anderson, Craig, 210
Anderson, Craig & Dotty, 209
Anderson, Dr. Oscar, 71
Anderson, James, 165
Anderson, Norm, 170
Anderson, Stuart, 70, 71, 72
Andes, Virginia B., 211
Andrews, James, 48
Andrews. Dr., 208
ARAY, 238
Arcadia, 31, 40, 49, 67, 68, 69, 76, 89, 111, 134, 152, 173, 233, 245
Ashley, Teri, 42
Askew, Governor, 37
Asperilla, Mark, 211

Atlantic Coast Fish Co., 45
Atwell, Don, 207
B & B Grocery, 137
Babcock Village, 18, 233
Babcock, Fred, 158
Babcock-Webb Wildlife Management Area, 94
Baer, Max, 93
Bailey Sr., Berlin J., 97, 156
Bailey Sr., Harding C., 97
Bailey, Cpl. Arthur J., 96
Bailey, Lt. Carl A., 96
Bailey, Maurice, 96, 97
Bailey, Pfc. Paul, 96
Bailey, Sgt. Maurice M., 96
Bailey, Sr, Lt. Charles, 94
Baileys, 84, 92, 97
Baker Academy, 80, 131, 133, 138, 144, 160
Baker, Gussie, 90, 132
Bal Harbor, 167
Barnett-Harrell, Marcia, 170
Barron Collier, 31, 114, 141, 185
Barron Collier Bridge, 47, 185
Bartlett, James, vi
Bartow, 54, 69
Bayshore Road, 147
Bean Depot Café & Museum, 244
Becklund, Rod, 181, 182
Belk-Lindsey, 137
Benande, Bonnie, 180
Bent, John P. 'Jack', 39
Berini, Tim, 242, 243, 244
Bernd-Cohen, Max, 149
Bethune-Cookman College, 84, 95, 96
Bill Anger Fishing Pier)., 150
Birden, Louis, 133
Bireda, Martha, 48
Bittner, Dave, 173
Blanchard House Museum, 48, 117, 257
Blocksom, L. T., 44
Blount, R. Chester, 36
Boca Grande, 23, 48, 68, 169, 186, 257

259

Booth Street, 138
Brackett, Ollie, 237
Brancaccio-Dorotich. Danette, 170
Brawner, Helen, 36
Breezeway, 168
Brown, David F., 198
Brown, George, 28, 29, 48
Brownie, Gaye Johns, 123, 124, 155, 166
Brox, Charles, 210
Buchan, Pete, 20, 21, 22, 32
Burchers, Sam, 155
Burdett, Mr., 77
Burmeister, Marion, 180
Burnt Store, 50, 51, 52, 109, 110, 147
Burnt Store Isles, 52, 216
Burnt Store Lakes, 51, 52
Burnt Store Marina, 51, 52
Burnt Store Meadows, 51, 52
Burnt Store Road, 50, 51, 52, 109, 110, 147
Burnt Store Village, 52
Burnt Store Villas, 51
Butler, Gary, 236
Cain, Burdette, 97
Calder, Louis, 51
Caloosahatchee River, 49
Cameron, Bill, 41
Camp Cloverleaf, 65
Camp McRoy, 65
Camp Ocala, 65
Cape Coral, 50
Cape Haze, 18
Captain's Club, 74
Captiva, 55, 254
Carmalita Street, 93, 118
Carousel Realty, 43
Carr, Darol, 173
Carr, Reggie, 170
Carter, Matthew, 202
Casino Hotel, 33
Catts, Albert Sidney, 25, 26
CH &N Railroad, 68
Chadwick, 34, 35, 44, 73, 74
Chadwick Beach Subdivision, 34
Chadwicks, 22, 74
Chamber of Commerce, 33, 42, 43, 162, 209, 223, 224, 225

Charles P. Bailey Funeral Home, 95
Charlevoi Condominiums, 114, 115
Charlotte Community Foundation, 239, 240, 241
Charlotte County Airport Authority, 92
Charlotte County Democratic Women's Club, 88
Charlotte County Development Authority, 94
Charlotte County Foundation, 209, 239
Charlotte County Habitat for Humanity, 240
Charlotte County Healthy Aging Study, 209, 240
Charlotte County Historical Center, 147, 256
Charlotte County Historical Society, 115
Charlotte County Homeless Coalition, 240
Charlotte County Pride, 238
Charlotte County Public Schools, 160
Charlotte Harbor, vi, ix, 18, 23, 44, 45, 46, 47, 49, 51, 52, 57, 58, 79, 89, 111, 112, 113, 114, 117, 125, 141, 142, 157, 158, 165, 184, 185, 186, 205, 209, 219, 222, 223, 232, 257
Charlotte Harbor Environmental Center, 52, 117, 186, 257
Charlotte High, 37, 70, 78, 80, 87, 102, 112, 118, 138, 144, 161, 170, 239
Charlotte Hospital, 90
Charlotte Memorial Gardens, 55
Charlotte Park, 153
Charlotte Shopping Center, 137
Charlotte Street, 93
Charlotte's Web, 238
Chidori, 150
Chokoloskee, 44, 70
Church of the Living God, 156
Cincinnati College of Embalming, 95
City Hall, 33, 43
Clark, Karen, 219
Clement, Bill, 174
Clement, Dr. Walter B., 40, 89, 90
Clement, William E., 40
Clerk of Court, 35, 36
Cleveland, ix, 28, 29, 48, 56, 96, 97, 140, 145
Cleveland Marine Steamways Company, 28
Cochran, 80
Coleman A.B., 48
Colianni, William, 189

A People's History of Charlotte County

Collins, LeRoy, 91
Conquistadors, 156, 157, 257
Cooper Street, 78, 80, 81, 131, 220
Coronavirus, 43
Cortes, Josephine, 20
Cristol, Chief Justice A. Jay, 188, 194
Crosland, Thomas C., 36, 44, 45
Cross Street, 100, 137, 145
Cuba-Florida hurricane, 78
Cultural Center, 105, 219, 221, 246
Cummings, Jaha, 48
Curnow, Bill, 204
D'Andrea, Tom, 171, 172, 173
Daily Herald News, 31, 90
Danforth, Charles, 144
Daughtrey, Rufe, 112
Davenport, John, 41, 252
Davis, Earl, 112
Davis, John, 182
Davis, Robert, 137
Daytona Beach, 84, 95, 96
Dearborn Merchants Association, 175
Dearborn Street, vi, 20, 21, 22, 32, 33, 34, 35, 74, 227, 228
Dearborn Street Book Fair, vi
Dearborn Street Literary Magazine, vi
Dedo, 181, 182
Deegan, David, 39
Deep Creek, ix, 28
DeGaeta, Paul, 169
DeLand, Florida, 95
Democrats, 25, 252
Desguin, Frank, 49, 53, 69, 93, 256
Desguin, Louis Victor, 56
Desguin, Peggy, 147
Desguin, Vic, 54
Desoto, 23, 66
DeSoto, 36, 37, 49, 62, 257
Desquin, Frank, 147, 174, 255
Desquin, L. Victor, 37
Dewey, Albert F., 37
DeYoung, Craig, 163
Diff, Crystal, 257
Dixon, Col. V. B., 93
Dooley, Bruce, 170
Duff, Omar, 155

Duff, Shirley, 207
Duffy, Omar, 132
Dunbar High School, 131
Dunn-Rankin, Derek, 31
East Charlotte Avenue, 57
East Elementary School, 160
Easy Street, 119, 120, 164
Edison Junior College, 163
Edna Jane, 87, 88, 89
Ehrling, Robert F., 198
El Jobean, ix, 22, 23, 24, 26, 38, 60, 73, 75, 100, 101, 102, 108, 189, 257
Eliason, Carol, 209, 210
Eliott, Robert, 145
Elise Haymans Butterfly Garden, 117
Elkcam Boulevard, 106
Englewood Lives, vi, 20, 21, 24, 26, 79
Englewood Sun, vi
Escambia, 35
Everglades, 18, 233
Fair Rents Committee, 93
Farr, Earl, 93
Fehr, Jeff, 164
Felder, Legusta, 96
Ferrara, Thomas, 211
Fink, Rev. Ralph, 121
First Baptist Church of Punta Gorda, 45
First Federal of Charlotte County, 43
Fishermen's Village, 79, 82, 185, 225, 236, 237
Fishermen's Village, 46, 47, 179
Fitch, Bessie L., 95
Five Corners, 78
Flagler, Henry, 113
Fleischman, Martin, 114
Flores, Hector, viii
Florida A&M University, 91, 96
Florida Adventure Museum, 147
Florida Cattleman's Association,, 66
Florida Constitution, 36
Florida Fish and Produce Company, 44
Florida Frontier Days, 147
Florida Land Boom, 32
Florida Southern College, 70
Florida Southern Railway, 30, 113
Florida SouthWestern State College, 163
Florida State University, 89, 91

Fort Myers News-Press, 112
Freeland, Dr. Carolyn, 210
Freeman House, 43, 210
Friends of the Punta Gorda Charlotte Library, 145
Frizzell, Cheryl, vi, 26, 59, 60, 62, 85, 101, 103, 240, 256
Frizzell, Dorothy, 102, 121
Frizzell, Patti, 26, 59, 60, 102
Frizzell, Paul, 64, 256
Frizzell, Robert Preston, 103
Frizzell, Steve, 124
Frizzell. A. C., vi, 26, 55, 68, 101, 103, 108, 255
Ft. Myers, 29, 110, 131, 165, 169, 219, 233
Futch, Mark, 193
Futch, Odie, 100, 101, 102, 106, 109, 255
Futches, 22
Gale, George and Helen, 207
Gant, Don, 165
Gay Straight Alliance, 239
Geary, Florence White, 149
General Development Corporation, 83, 96, 105, 106, 119, 161-162, 187, 189, 196—202
Giles, Mrs., 48
Gilmore, Jeff, 169, 170
Glades, 36, 147
Goff, William, 20
Goff, Wayne, 179
Goff, Woodrow, 254
Goldsmith, Coach Fred, 169
Goodpaster, Floyd, 112
Gotfried, Jason, 238
Gouvellis, Jim, 214
Graham, Ben, 170
Graham, Tom, 209
Grand Hotel and Fishing Lodge, 242
Great Atlantic Hurricane, 77
Great Depression, ix, 54, 56, 58, 60, 64, 72, 78, 88, 89, 108, 215
Great Freeze of 1895, 35
Green Street Church, vi, 34
Green's Fuel Gas, 138
Griffis, Samuel, 201
Grizzaffi, Charles, 201
Grove City, ix, 22
Guerzo, Joe, 258

Gulf Cove, 189
Gulf of Mexico, 18, 94
Gunn, Barbara Thorp, 155, 156
Haddock, Ellison, 24, 109, 110, 131, 134, 156, 255
Haddock, Gertha, 109, 110, 133, 134
Haines City, 53
Hamilton, Julia, 137
Hammami, Hasan, 210
Hanes, Lt. Col. R. A., 94
Harbor Blvd, 161
Harborview Road, 161, 213
Harbour Heights, ix, 142, 143, 144, 168
Harbour Heights Clubhouse, 144, 202
Hardee, 36, 38
Harold Avenue, 165
Harrell, Chuck, 137
Harrell, Leila, 137, 143
Harrell, Lynn, 46, 125, 137, 206
Harrell, Marla, 137, 138, 139, 140, 141, 143, 144
Harrell, Toni, 137, 138, 141
Harrington, Lindsay, 172, 173, 174, 255
Harris, Diana, vi, 20, 21, 24, 26, 32, 67, 70, 79, 109, 115
Harris, Sam, vi
Hartwig, Scoop, 161
Harvey, Kelly, 28
Harvey, Kelly B., 222
Haymans, Kenton, 145
Haynes, Booker T., 132
Heidenreich, Donna, 225
Henry Street, 146
Heritage Landing Golf & Country Club, 51
Herlovich, John, 170
Hickory Bluff, ix
Highlands, 36
Hilenski, Ferdie, 161
Hilenski, Louisa, 161
Hill, Millie, 240
Hillsborough County, 19
History Park, 117, 118
Hoadley, Mr., 149
Hobbs & Cowan, 51
Hobbs, Harvey, 51
Holleyman, Dr. Alfred T., 140

Horton, Mac, 174
Horton, Robert, 170
Hotel Charlotte Harbor, 31
Hotel Punta Gorda, 31, 113
House of God Church, 68
Howard Academy, 95
Hurricane Charley, v, 41, 43, 115, 181, 209, 215, 219, 223, 224, 239
Hurricane Donna, 43, 125, 130, 142, 143, 170, 209, 225
Hutchinson, Liz, 178
Hygeia, 33, 35
IMPAC University, 41, 210
Indian Mound Park, 150
Indian Spring Cemetery, 70
Indiana Avenue, 35
Ingram Hotel, 48
J. C. Rigell and Company, 53
Jackson, Andrew, 35
Jacksonville, 44, 53, 114
James, David, 133
Joel Bean, 24, 26, 59, 60
John Henry Allen, 142
Johns, Al, 123
Johnson, Bob, 149, 151
Johnson, Felix, 133
Johnson, Margaret, 96
Johnson, Mary and Marvin, 209
Jones, Arantha,
Jones, Aratha, 78, 79, 153, 255
Jones, Jim, 79
Jones, Judy Lloyd, 133
Jones, Max, 51
Jones, Sallie, 69, 70, 88, 118, 132, 138, 140, 143, 144, 160
Jordan, Adrian Pettus, 30
Kantor, Connie, 225
Kearney, James, 201
Kimberly, Carl, 207
Kincaid, Arlene, 152, 160
King Fisher Fleet, 185, 186
King Street, 69
King, Fred, 146
Kings Highway, 175, 220
Kitson, Syd, 217, 233
Kiwanis Club, 55, 57

Klein, David M., 211
Knight, William and Mary Smith, 138
Kretzler, Kent, 157
Kunik, Howard, 223, 224
Kwik Chek, 161
Laishley Park, 49, 117, 205, 239, 241
Lake Garfield, 54
Lake Placid, 65
Lakeland, 70
Lampp, Sandy, 150
Lampps, 22
LaPlaya Shopping Center, 43
Lasbury, Leah, vi, 150
Lawhorne, John T., 36
Lawhorne's Grocery, 78
Lawless, Burton, 168, 169, 170
Lazzell, Rufus, 171, 174
LeBeau, Alan L., 39, 40
Lee County, 19, 39, 40, 41
Lees, Betty Jo, 112
Lemon Bay, vi, 21, 22, 33, 34, 37, 64, 72, 73, 74, 75, 115, 116, 160, 257
Lemon Bay Historical Society, 175, 257
Lennar, 52
Leroy, Bonnie, 209, 211
Levine, Asher, 239
Liberty Elementary School, 161
Lifelong Learning Institute, 209, 210, 211
Ligneu, Glenn, 238
Lipscomb, J. H., 38
Little League, 125, 165
Little School, 138
Live Oak Point, 47, 49, 184
Live Oak Point Park, 49
Liverpool, 28, 29
Lowe, Louise (Driggers), 51
Mack, Harold "Mackie", 169
Mackle brothers, 104, 108, 119, 120, 121, 194, 195, 197, 199
Mackle III, Frank E., 104
MacLaren, Dr. Sharon, 246
Maerski, Chris Goff, 58, 60, 83
Maerski, Christine Goff, 89, 254, 256
Maher, Ashley, 239
Manasota Key, 33, 149
Manatee, 78, 140

Mango Bistro, 227, 228
March for Justice, 241
Marion Avenue, 48, 56, 57, 78, 80, 93, 115, 141, 144, 147, 155, 222
Mark Avenue, 93
Marshal, Aaron "Jim", 255
Marshall, Aaron "Jim", 77, 122
Martin Drive, 106
Martin Luther King Jr. Blvd, 80
Martin, Greg, 188, 196
Masquerades, 238
Maud Street, 45
Maurice, Matt, 72, 73
Maurice. Al, 72
McCall, ix, 67, 68, 228
McCall,, ix
McDerment, Chester, 89
McDerment, Steve, 256
McDougall, John J., 40
McGregor Street, 143
McKenzie St., 78
McQueen, N. H. "Doc", 63, 65, 66, 121
Medical Center Hospital, 140
Melton, Howard, 152
Memorial University, 33
Merit Gas Station, 161
Miami, 49, 87, 88, 104, 164, 170, 194, 197, 198, 200, 223
Middleton, Ronald, 133
Midway Blvd., 43
Military Heritage Museum, 236, 237, 255, 257
Milus Street, 57
Miss Englewood, 35
Mize, Maryann, 163
Monson, Homer, 112
Moore, Derril E., 112
Moore, Don, 84, 94
Mr. B's Restaurant, 161
Munger, Maj. Forrest H., 93
Murdock, 18, 22, 23, 26, 58, 61, 75, 100, 101, 103, 250, 252
Murdock Village, 217
Murphy, John, 174
Museum of Charlotte County, 147
Myakka, vi, 24, 73, 100, 160, 171, 200, 205
National Register of Historic Places, 43

Neil Armstrong Elementary School, 160
Neils. Gerry and Pat, 207
Neisner's Department Store, 161
Nesbit Street, 49, 184
New Boston, 24
New Point Comfort, vi
New Theater, 144
New Theatre, 56
Nichols Brothers, 33
Nightingale, Abe, 67, 68, 69
Nightingale, Mary, 67
Nocatee, 53, 54
North Port, 108, 162, 169, 198, 201
O.B. Armstrong Grocery/Restaurant, 48
O'Keefe, Sean, 237
Ocala, 65, 95, 114
Ocala National Forest, 65
Ocooee, 25
Odom, Lee, 165
O'Dowd, Bill, 104
Oglesby, Charlotte, 57
Old Charlotte County Courthouse, 48
Old Englewood Road, 35, 75
Old Punta Gorda, Inc., 206, 207
Oliver, William T., 36
Olympia Avenue, 124
Orlando, 72
Page Apartments, 93
Parent-Teachers' Association of Charlotte County, 88
Parnell, Travis, 38
Patterson, Deanna, 145
Peace River, vi, ix, 28, 29, 31, 49, 79, 83, 112, 117, 118, 136, 140, 144, 156, 160, 161, 164, 184, 185, 186, 217
Peace River Lodge, 38, 140, 142, 165
Peace River Preservation League, Inc, 206
PEACE RIVER PRIDE, 239
Peachland Boulevard, 163
Peeples, Lois, 87
Peeples, Vasco, 87, 88, 153
Peeples, Vernon, v, vi, 28, 87, 88, 89, 90, 92, 113, 145, 172, 173, 239, 240, 241
Pepper, Claude, 93
Persons, Lou, 55

A People's History of Charlotte County

PGI, 52, 63, 123, 124, 128, 129, 130, 132, 153, 155, 156, 166, 168, 214
Pine Island, 50, 70
Pinellas Gladiolus Company, 109, 110, 147
Pioneer Days., 176
Pirate Harbor, 51
Placida, ix, 68, 75
Plant City, 67
Plant, Henry, 113
Plaza Theater, 144
Polk, Paul L., 44
Polk, Richard, 207
Ponce de Leon Park, 155, 167
Pond's Dodge, 161
Poppell, Sherra, 111
Port Charlotte Civic Association, 121
Port Charlotte Community Center, 120, 213
Port Charlotte Diner, 161
Porter, Doctor, 75
Poteet, 170
Potts, Vicki L., 37
Powell, Carl & Jerry, 51
Powell's Nursery and Landscaping, 146
Prafke, Nancy, 216, 222
Price, Jack, 209, 210
Pringle, Naomi, 241
Promenades Mall, 163
Prummell, Bill, 41
Pulse, 238
Punta Gorda Airport, 51, 77, 229, 231, 234
Punta Gorda Army Air Field, ix, 77, 93
Punta Gorda Herald, 30, 31, 34, 44, 45, 61, 90, 92, 113, 154, 155
Punta Gorda Historic Mural Society, 88, 208, 257
Punta Gorda History Park, 206
Punta Gorda Isles, v, ix, 52, 79, 83, 128, 143, 146, 154, 178, 185, 216, 220, 233
Punta Gorda Isles Yacht Club, v
Punta Gorda Mall, 141, 209
Punta Gorda Planning Commission, 97
Punta Gorda Rotary, 90
Punta Gorda State Bank, 45
Punta Gorda Wine & Jazz Festival, 226
Quality Self Storage, 54
Quast, Erich and Lydia, 51

Quednau, Arthur F., 38
Quiet Garden at the Woman's Club, 117
Quille, Gary, 92
Ramada Inn, 200, 201
Ramirez, Cesar, 253
Ranch, Babcock, 158, 217, 232, 233
Randol, Monroe G., 197, 199, 202
Reading, Bernie, 72
Reconstruction, 35
Redmond, John, 235
Reif, Jim, 219
Renshaw, James, 106
Retta Esplanade, 43, 45, 145, 147
Revitalization Committee, 176, 191, 208
Rigell Lumber and Supply, 54, 55
Rigell, Frank, 53, 93
Rigell, Freddie, 54, 55, 56, 57
Rigell, Peggy, 57
River Road, 35
Roberts, Bob, 171, 172, 174, 255
Roger D. Eaton, 35, 36
Rogers, John, 120
Ron Middleton, 133
Roosevelt, Eleanor, 84
Rosewood, 25
Rotonda, vi, ix
Royal Casino, 35
Runkle, Marlon, 170
Russell, Bernice Andrews, 48
Russell, Dale, 170
Ruth Richmond Homes, 165
Sacred Heart Church, 138
Sailors Way, 68
Samson, Roseann, 180
Sandy Point, 49
Sanibel, 55
Santa Gertrudis cattle, vi
Sapp, Glen E., 39, 40
Sarasota, v, 19, 21, 33, 39, 64, 93, 108, 137, 185, 194, 196, 213, 217, 221, 257
Sarasota Herald-Tribune, v, 185, 213, 217
Scott, Edward H., 36
Scott, Tommy, 256
Sea Grape Gallery, 180, 181
Second Seminole War, 35
Segger, Graham, 50

Seminole Drugstore, 144
Seward, Robert Kirby, 30
Shaefer, Ralph, 161
Shannon, John P., 39
Shively, Scott, 48
Shreve Street, 146, 163
Sigler, Roger and Maureen, 207
Simon, Leopold and Donna, 181, 243, 244
Sisk, Randy, 170
Smith, Dan, 48
Smith, Henry W., 29
Smith, Larry, 210
Smith, Pat, 148
Smith, Phyliss, 191
Smith's Arcade, 29
Smith-Mooney, Marilyn, 27, 191, 216, 255
Smokehouse Restaurant, 78
Solana, ix, 93
Souls Harbor Church of God, 78, 80
South Gulf Cove, ix, 100
Southland, 24, 25
Spanish Flu, 29
Sprague, Caryl, 209
Springman, Marie, 160
SR776, 68, 73, 101, 116, 131, 189, 245
St. Johns, 35
Starlight Barbershop, 48
Stepp, Ed, 170
Stickley, Richard A., 38
Stokes, Lloyd and Evelyn, 207
Stout, Oden and Ecil, 139
Struthers, Ron, 199, 200, 202
Stump Pass, 135
Sunny Dell Plaza, 163, 252, 253, 254
Sunseeker, 234, 235, 246
Swing, Dr. Fred P., 43
Tallahassee, 29, 35, 41, 54, 91, 92, 96, 103, 201
Tamiami Trail, 23, 30, 31, 35, 42, 43, 49, 50, 51, 152, 161, 163, 164, 184, 185, 220, 233, 252
Tampa, 25, 45, 49, 69, 74, 94, 114, 204, 205, 209, 219
Tate, Jack, 174
Tax Collector, 37
Taylor Contractors of Florida, 162
Taylor Road, 54, 147, 220
Taylor Street, 69, 70, 115

Taylor, Peter, 161, 218
TEAM, 117, 216, 223, 224, 257
Ten Thousand Islands, 44
The Florida Times-Union, 53
The Forum, 238
Thomas, Isaac, 133, 247
Thomas, Jolivet, 133
Thomas-Bryant, Bessie Mae Haynes, 132
Thrifty Drugs, 137
Tiffany Square, 24
Tin Can Tourists, 63, 64, 152
Town and Country Shopping Center, 57
Townsend, Gerri, 202
Trabue, ix, 22, 28, 191, 222
Tropical Gulf Acres, ix
Turner, Patricia, 181, 183
Turtle Club, 161
Turtle Crossing, 51
Tuskegee, 84, 85, 94, 95
Twin Isles Country Club, 51
University of Tampa, 114
US41, 30, 57, 69, 73, 106, 131, 147, 161, 164, 165, 238
Vanderbilt, Alfred and William, vi, 69, 141
Vanderbilt, William, 149
Venice, 23, 31, 34, 53, 93, 116, 122, 123, 164
Venice High School, 150
Vincent Road, 51
Virginia Ave, 137
Virginia Avenue, 81
Visual Arts Center, 178, 179, 180
Vivante Condominiums, 222
Wade, Sue, 242
Walker, Phyllis, 210
Walled Garden, 138, 139, 140, 143
War Tales, 84
Warren G. Harding, 17
Washington Loop, 45
Waste Management, Inc., 116
Weaver, Harold "Boo Boo", 170
West Charlotte Avenue, 69
West Coast Fish Company, 44, 45
West Coast Lumber and Supply, 54
Whidden, George, 69
Whisenant, Pete, 170
Whitten, Emily Adelia, 44

Whitten, William, 29, 31, 44, 49
Wilford, Robert, 145
Will J. Brown, 48
Williams, Lindsey, 156
Williams, Michelle Bone, 237
Witzke, Sandra, 106, 119, 146
Women's Club, 151, 174
Woodmere, 53, 116
Woods, Lou, 55, 74
Woolum, Wendell, 170
Worch, Richard H., 40
World War II, ix, 76, 82, 85, 87, 89, 92, 93, 94, 96, 97, 188
Wotitzky, Leo, vi, 36, 90, 91, 92, 239, 240, 241
Wotizky, 25
Wright, Sonja, 132, 133
Wright. John, 216, 224
Yando, Richard and Judy, 207
Yarger, Dr. Richard, 210
Yeager, Areta Alderman, 37
Yeager, Edward B., 37
Youth Museum of Charlotte County, 147
Zemel Road, 51
Zoebelein, Jennifer, 256, 258